Risky
BUSINESS

Also by Annabelle Slator

The Launch Date

Risky
BUSINESS

A Novel

ANNABELLE SLATOR

AVON

An Imprint of HarperCollinsPublishers

FIRST EDITION

Interior text design by Diahann Sturge-Campbell

Library of Congress Cataloging-in-Publication Data

Names: Slator, Annabelle, author
Title: Risky business : a novel / Annabelle Slator.
Description: First edition. | New York : Avon, 2026.
Identifiers: LCCN 2025023236 | ISBN 9780063383692 trade paperback | ISBN 9780063383685 ebook
Subjects: LCGFT: Romance fiction | Novels | Fiction
Classification: LCC PR6119.L374 R57 2026
LC record available at https://lccn.loc.gov/2025023236

ISBN 978-0-06-338369-2

25 26 27 28 29 LBC 5 4 3 2 1

For the people who take big swings and make big mistakes:
don't regret any step of the way.

Risky

BUSINESS

CHAPTER 1

Business Account (WYST) BALANCE: £13,366.57
Personal Account BALANCE: -£1,957.73

January 6, 2026

Dear Miss Cole,

Thank you for your application to Pioneer Lending's business grant scheme. While your proposal is impressive, investing in the FemTech space can be unpredictable compared to other ventures. Consequently, we have decided not to move forward with your application.

We wish you all the best in your future endeavors.

Pioneer Lending Ltd.

I blink rapidly at my phone screen. This is fine. Everything will be absolutely fine. The pit in my stomach screams otherwise, but I roll my shoulders and let the bitterly cold London air bring me back to the task at hand: meeting a potential new investor for my fledgling company, Wyst. At first, this process was a fun adventure, figuring out what kind of investment firms, angel investors, and venture capitalists could be interested in FemTech or a women-led business. Then one of life's greatest pleasures: adding all their minute details to a comprehensive spreadsheet to research who would be a good fit. Little did I know it would become the spreadsheet of desperation and doom. Finally, individually tailoring my introductory letters to each recipient. Adding personalized touches and flairs to my pitch deck. How investing in my company would expand their portfolios or grow their already vast investment streak even further, stroking their egos by promising to help make them a trailblazer of the FemTech industry. A hero to women everywhere for the low, low price of a few quarterly cash injections. So far, the process has been hit-and-miss. The intrusive thoughts tell me it's because they recognize me, my name a cautionary tale echoing down the halls of every investment company in London.

As I approach the Withering Vine, a wine bar chain the investor recommended for our meeting, my phone buzzes in my pocket.

"Hey, I'm about to go in. What's up?" I say to Cecily, Wyst's PR and marketing manager and my general partner in crime.

"Yeah, sorry, you just got another call from Greg Holmes? He asked if you are free this afternoon to go to the bank to . . ." She begins to read in a monotone voice, "Discuss the necessary steps to rectify your recent overdraft debt."

My cheeks blaze red-hot against the icy wind.

"Jess?" Cecily says. "Are you still there?"

After a pause, I clear my throat. "Yeah, it's fine. Just a mix-up. I'll call him when I get back to the office." I have zero intention of actually doing that, but I'm hoping my most recent excuse of having a very sick imaginary dog will hold for at least a few more weeks. Why is he chasing me this early in the year anyway? Surely there is a legal emotional buffer of at least a month after Christmas to start collecting on debts owed.

"Exactly, maybe this guy today will be a good lead," Cecily chirps, and I imagine her nonchalantly tossing her glossy black hair over her shoulder.

"He was enthusiastic to connect, so fingers crossed!" I say, swallowing the tiny tingle of doubt back down.

"Good luck! I just know you're going to smash it!"

Cecily has the instinctual ability to see the best in everyone and everything. Her sunshine attitude has been the definitive thing that has kept me going in between the emotional turmoil of rejections. She's my best friend, but sometimes, when the pessimism creeps in, I wonder how she would react to the truth. If I showed her under the hood and revealed that this business is a ticking time bomb. While, in a way, it would be nice to have someone wade through the mud with me, this is a mess I've made and need to deal with myself.

I step through the door, the frigid January air melting away under the heat of thirty bodies packed into a tiny wine bar.

Spotting a man matching the headshot, I hold out my hand, preparing for a firm handshake. "Hi, Will? I'm Jess, lovely to meet you."

He looks up from his phone with a blank stare.

"Jess Cole, from Wyst?" My megawatt smile starts to fizzle out, making room for the rising panic.

He blinks. "Right, hello," he says, finally putting me out of my social anxiety and taking my hand in his. The shake isn't hard, barely a squeeze as he stands up and kisses me on the cheek. Electricity singes my skin like a tiny Taser.

"What are you drinking?" he asks as I slide off my coat and sit in the uncomfortable wooden chair opposite him. The tables are so tightly packed my legs instantly press against his. I fold my body uncomfortably, contorting myself like a depressed accordion.

We're in a wine bar, but maybe this is a test. "Oh, well. It's lunchtime so—"

"We'll take a bottle of the Château Batailley 2005," Will says to the waitress before glancing at me. "That good with you?"

"Sure." I smile, smoothing down my one "fancy meeting" outfit, a black dress with room for a shirt and tights underneath and a blazer on top. It makes me feel like I'm playing dress-up.

Will leisurely scans the edges of my face before leaning back in his chair, the loud creak like a crack of lightning. "You look a lot older than your profile picture."

I should be shocked by the comment, but after business school and working at a finance company, I've had much, much worse said to me. The photo was taken last year, which feels like it's within the boundaries of acceptable LinkedIn photography. I've been in meetings with men who still use their university graduation photos, fresh-faced and taut jawed, when in reality, they arrive balding, bearded, and beer-bellied.

"It's been a very, *very* long day," I joke. He doesn't laugh. His downward-facing mouth only reaffirming his lack of amusement.

"Uh-huh," he replies, half listening, half watching the pretty blond waitress heading straight for us with a bottle and corkscrew. "I always find it's best to keep that sort of thing up to date, so as not to hinder expectations. You don't want to come across as a catfish."

I agree to an extent, but it's still a weird thing to say. I play it off. Like his choice in wine, maybe his humor is just a bit dry.

"I would have thought my experience would be more important than the image on my profile."

One eyebrow raises. "Depends what type of experience." He chortles and I follow suit, forcing a laugh despite a rising sense of discomfort like my future self is elbowing me in the stomach.

Between the sounds of clinking glasses, roaring laughter, and raucous conversation at the other tables, I watch him swirl the red wine he selected so it licks against the side of the glass, sniffing it, then taking a slow gurgling sip to let the flavor penetrate every taste bud. It's early in the week, I suppose, for serious drinking. But London, whether in the heat or the cold, makes everyone thirstier.

"How do you find it, sir?" the doe-eyed waitress inquires.

He unabashedly looks her up and down, still mid-slurp, then finally announces, "Delicious."

She shoots back a forced smile and fills my glass, then his. When she turns to leave, I raise my glass by the stem. "To the passage of time."

He hesitates, the wine sloshing up the side of his glass. "What?"

I falter. "What we were just talking about? My profile picture?"

His shoulders tense. "Oh, I'd prefer to cheers to something else."

"Sure, what do you want to cheers to?" I ask, pulling my glass back.

"My Christmas bonus just came through." His posture lifts like a proud kid who just won the egg and spoon race on sports day.

"*Congratulations*," I choke out, suddenly desperate to down my wine.

He offers his first genuine smile since we sat down, clinks his glass into mine, and takes a laborious sip. The wine isn't great, but now I know he's flush with cash and clearly getting commission on investments, I'll play ball to try to put some gas in this engine.

"Mmmm, good choice." I smile sweetly.

He winks at me. "I'm a bit of a grape head."

My cringeometer ratchets up a few points, genuinely debating whether just to call this meeting now. But Cecily's words of encouragement ring in my head: *Just try and feign interest and eventually something will click. Fake it till you make it, baby! Investors like to be wined and dined a bit first; getting straight to it reeks of desperation. You need to act like you don't need their money, that you're doing them a favor.*

But we do need the money. *Really*, really need it.

Swallowing my pride, I place my chin in my hand, open my eyes really wide, and nod. "So how did you get to be so knowledgeable about wine?"

He clears his throat. "From the boss, a lot of after-work drinks."

"Your job must be really stressful," I speculate.

He stretches like Superman ready to save a child from traffic . . . "Nothing I can't handle."

Searching for a way to steer this ship back to Wyst, I ask, "Do you have a lot of clients right now?"

He shifts awkwardly.

Shit, was that a weird question to ask? "What I mean to say is, you seem really important at work."

My leg bounces under the table as he continues to talk about himself. Listening to this guy brag about his six-figure-job-before-bonuses, I feel my soul and bank account draining. I could be reaching out to investors right now or researching new grant applications. Instead, I am listening to this man talk about his favorite films (*Pulp Fiction* and *Fight Club*, obviously), how Jack Kerouac inspired the post-university travels he is still hoping to relive despite hurtling toward his mid-thirties, and informing me that Tame Impala is *actually just one guy.*

I down the last of my drink, glancing at the waiter in the hopes that she will either bring the bill or drop an anvil on my head.

"So what do you do at that company again?" He looks at the table, running a finger over the wood grain.

The question halts me; we're twenty-five minutes into this meeting and this is the first question he's asked that didn't directly lead into a fun little anecdote about him. I resolve to give him the benefit of the doubt; maybe he's just the chatty kind of nervous. Maybe we can turn this thing around.

"I founded the company. We're in the prelaunch stage right now but have some exciting expansion plans coming up soon. It's a great time to get in on the ground floor." I fiddle with the stem of my glass.

"Mmmm," he replies insightfully. "I like to dabble in crypto."

He tells me about his cyber wallet and how he was one of

the few people in his office who "didn't fall" for the NFT fad because he only bought "one or two."

"That's great. My company is more in the FemTech space," I say, my leg bouncing harder under the table as I prepare to present my case.

He scrunches his face as though I've just told him I don't think male stand-up comedians are funny. "What's FemTech?"

My lips creep into a smile. "It's shorthand for technology addressing mainly women."

His shoulders lower. "Oh right, yeah, like periods and shit."

I swallow my indignation. "FemTech *does* encompass menstrual health, yes. But Wyst, my company, is a platform for women to talk to therapists, counselors, and doctors for free about all sorts of women's issues."

"Right." He nods his head like he's interested, but I can see his eyes starting to glaze over. Maybe it's the wine. "So how is that meant to make any money?"

"Advertisers, and we rigorously vet every advertising partner. Branded content. Usually sanitary products, fitness brands, health and wellness products." I nod, feeling my defenses rising up like tide dams. "With the aim to move to a tiered premium subscription model later down the line." He doesn't ask a follow-up question, but I push on while the microphone is on my side of the table. "Which is why I reached out to you, to chat about potential investment opportunities."

"Right." He sighs. "I just want to be straight with you."

"Okay . . ." I lock in, ready for some unsolicited business advice I've likely heard already from a mean man's mouth before, sometimes with a *sweetheart* thrown in for good measure.

He shakes his head. "I'm not really interested in the 'career woman' type."

My hand freezes against my glass. "Excuse me?"

He laughs. "I know that's not like progressive or whatever, but I'm really looking for someone who is more of a homebody, who is happy for *me* to be the breadwinner."

I study him, a long deep line between my brows.

He sighs, like he assumed I wouldn't understand. "I just don't think a relationship can work if both parties are working all the time. Who's going to make meals and keep the house in shape? Look after the children?"

"What?" Seemingly I have lost the ability to speak in full sentences.

"I get having your own life and hobbies, but I just don't think this would work."

I blink at him in silence, flabbergasted, until finally my brain reboots to ask, "Do you think this is a date?"

He furrows his brow, looking at me like I'm insane. "What else would this be?"

I scrape my chair across the floor, moving out from the table. "A meeting, to discuss you investing in my company."

"Oh." He huffs a laugh, clearing his glass. "You were serious about that? I thought you were just shy."

My mouth hangs open. "We connected on LinkedIn?"

One corner of his lip snarls up. "I know, right? Dating apps are so crap these days, too many weirdos and time wasters. I was on Ignite for a while, but it never ends well for the nice guys. It's so hard dating in the city."

"This is *not* a date," I clarify one last time to get it into his skull.

He lowers his eyes and grins. "Come on, you don't need to be coy just because we aren't compatible from a relationship standpoint. I still think you're a good-looking girl. We could just, ya know, keep it casual?"

I can't help the way my mouth twists into a disgusted scowl, but then my mind starts second-guessing everything I've said and done up to this point. The messages I sent, my leg brushing against his as I sat down, maybe I should have worn a suit instead of a dress. "I'm sorry if I gave you the wrong impression, but this isn't a date. I'm not dating or 'keeping it casual' with anyone right now."

And even if I did have the emotional or mental capacity to date someone, it certainly wouldn't be this guy.

His eyes squint for a second. "Right, well. That's fine. I'm not that attracted to you anyway; not a fan of brunettes." He sits back in his chair. "Especially when they don't look like their profile picture."

It takes everything in me not to question why he even came here, but I don't want to continue this conversation.

His eyes crease curiously. "It's weird because now I've seen you in person, you do seem quite familiar. You went to business school, right? Do we have any friends in common?"

"No," I say on reflex. A champagne cork popping makes me jolt out of my skin as a familiar dread rises in my stomach, curdling the wine into vinegar. "No," I repeat quietly.

He leans in, scanning my face. "Are you sure? You went to Goldsmiths, right? I have a few mates who went there."

The blood draws from my face, metastasizing into hives across my throat. "Probably not, it was a big school."

He clicks his fingers in front of my face, eyes wide. "Wait,

I know what it is. You worked at Graystone. Were you there when that grad scandal happened? That was crazy. I can't believe the poor guy got fired over a couple of photos."

My chair scrapes against the terra-cotta tiles. "Excuse me, I'm gonna use the bathroom." My mouth forms a tight smile as I leave the table and meander through the crowd to the back of the bar.

The moment I close the bathroom door my chest begins to heave.

My brain is throbbing so hard it feels like a computer lagging and overheated. Flashes of memory appear as black dots in my vision.

Walking into the office, everyone staring.

My friend's face as she pulls me aside.

Seeing the photos, my world imploding.

The sex was consensual, but not when Malcolm took those photos. He convinced me after that they were just for him.

Heart racing, I check LinkedIn for William Salter. My hand freezes on the screen, my skin cold and clammy. He was right; we have seven mutual connections. Four through university, but my three former colleagues at Graystone bash alarm bells against my skull.

Eyes stinging, I sit on the toilet seat and put my head between my legs, breathing through my nose like the YouTube videos taught me, and stare blankly at the upside-down layer of dust accumulating around the bottom of the porcelain basin and count to sixty—the world's most efficient panic attack. After my breathing's normalized, I wash my hands, roll my fingers across my bottom lashes and then through my hair.

Before I exit the LinkedIn app, my eyes snag on a post by

Odericco Investments, one of my dream investors at the top of my funding spreadsheet.

Open call for start-up pitches, ending tonight at midnight GMT.

Due to scheduling conflicts, a space has become available for this year's TechRumble competition.

A link to an application form sits below the post. The original deadline for this year's TechRumble finalists was months ago, back when I was in the final stages of talking to another investor. The deadline passed, and our investor called me "petal," then ghosted me. I bookmark the post, mentally steeling myself for the more pressing issue—getting back to this car crash of a meeting. As I swing open the bathroom door and head back to the table, William has vanished, along with his coat. All evidence of our "meeting" gone, except the unpaid bill sitting on a small silver tray in the middle of the table.

CHAPTER 2

Business Account (WYST) BALANCE: £13,216.57
Personal Account BALANCE: -£1,960.63
Recent Transactions:
The Withering Vine London: £150.00
Transport for London: £2.90

Thirty minutes later, after a mortifying amount of "your card was declined" attempts at the bar, I shove through the heavy office door with a half-drunk bottle of wine in hand. The draft guard hisses against the carpet as I see Cecily's and Pacha's heads pop up from behind their computer screens. The familiar scent of lit TK Maxx candles that, according to Cecily, "smell just like the ones from Anthropologie" hits me as I nearly trip over a box of promotional T-shirts to get to my desk.

"How did it go?" Pacha asks, his green Adidas tracksuit looking particularly neon today.

"Have you not told him?" I ask Cecily.

She shrugs. "He's been locked in for the past few hours."

Pacha is fluent in JavaScript, not in office small talk, but we soon found his no-nonsense ways the perfect antithesis to my and Cecily's ability to talk about literally anything for hours on end.

I throw my bag down and slump in my office chair. "He thought it was a date and stiffed me with the bill for a £150 bottle of wine."

"Such an arsehole," Cecily replies, "but I will happily take that off your hands." She picks the bottle up out of my grip.

"Why did he think it was a date?" Pacha asks, his focus already half back on his computer.

Cecily shouts before I can, "Because she has a vagina and therefore is incapable of presenting a business proposal!"

Pacha looks at me, perplexed. "Really?"

I give him a look. "Are you shocked about the business proposal or the vagina?"

Pacha screws up his face and slides his over-ear headphones back on.

Cecily relaxes into her seat, handing me a coffee in a light purple Wyst-branded mug. "If you were a man that would have gone a lot differently."

I rub my temples. "If I were a man, a lot of things would be different. Look at this."

She peers at the Odericco Investments post on my phone screen.

Her eyes widen. "Are you going to apply? The deadline is midnight."

"I have all the pitch decks ready." I click through to the application portal and, as I start to type in my name, huff out a laugh, toggling over the different options on the prefix drop-down menu. "Maybe I should select 'Mr.' Cole just to make sure the entirety of Odericco Investments knows I'm not asking them on a date."

"It would probably get their attention too," Cecily surmises while picking at her manicure. "Everyone loves it when a man is championing women's issues."

Rolling my eyes, I say, "Especially massive companies like Odericco."

Odericco Investments is a leading investment firm with offices all over the world. TechRumble is hosted at their annual Summit of Innovation. Rookies can only get in if they are competing in Odericco Investments' *Hunger Games*–esque, multi-round, knockout competition. Thousands of young companies enter every year, and there is first-, second-, and third-prize money, earning £500K, £250K, and £100K respectively, as well as the backing and guidance from Dominic Odericco himself. Dominic is notoriously cutthroat, but it's serious cash. But even if you don't win, just being there, receiving an invitation to get up on that stage and compete, puts you in front of big venture capitalists and investors who are there to discover the "next big thing" in the tech world. Opening doors I've been scratching at for two years.

As I watch the upload bar slide on my presentation, my phone dings with a LinkedIn message from Will. I click it, in the hopes it will be an apology for running out on the bill. Now that sleeping with me is off the table, maybe he'll actually be interested in hearing about the investment opportunity.

One new message from William Salter.

I remember where I know you from.

My ears begin to ring as I freeze, immediately going to block him as another message pops up on my screen.

Guess I should have stayed ;)

And there it is.

The demon on my back. The specter that doesn't *always* pop up behind me in the bathroom mirror, but just often enough to make me flinch every time I look.

The sound of the telecom jolts me back into the room. Followed by my brother, Spencer, flying through the door like a car running a red light. I glance back at my phone, blocking Will's account before he can send me anything else.

"Please don't talk to me," Spencer announces, throwing off his green angora check scarf and matching beanie hat. His dirty blond hair bounces in the air as his body drops down. "I've been up since 3 a.m., and I think my bones have transformed into icicles." His face, still with a sheen of last night's stage makeup, gleams in the fluorescent lights.

London is freezing. An out-of-context cold that should be enjoyed curled up in a cottage in front of a roaring fire, with a glass of red wine and a good book. Only occasionally looking out the window and commenting, "Maybe we could make snowmen before dinner," as some sort of small furry cat or dog curls around your thick-socked feet. Instead, you are forced to battle royal for an inch of space on the Tube, as those who usually walk or cycle avoid spending a moment more than necessary outside with the bitter wind, murky slush, and 4 p.m. darkness. Like going from freezing to sweating to freezing ten times over in the world's angriest Austrian spa before you've even made it to the office.

"So the shoot went well?" I ask with an arched brow.

He shakes off his layers of North Face padding and throws them onto his desk at the opposite side of the room. "I thought I was getting a featured role, but all I did was walk pensively from one side of the street to the other. Then, when we were *finally* wrapping, a PA noticed one of the extras wearing his Apple Watch with his Elizabethan three-piece suit, so we had to all get back into costume and reshoot for another three very long hours."

I cringe. "Nooo, did they get fired?"

He nods solemnly. "Shot on sight."

"Any celebos?" Cecily asks, wide-eyed.

"Jennifer Lawrence bought everyone fancy hot chocolate." He shrugs nonchalantly, but a subtle smile appears on his lips when Cecily gasps with excitement.

These small, seemingly insignificant details have all of our friends and family eating out of Spencer's hands. I have never had that, an innate ability to charm people so naturally it's like breathing. When we shared a womb, the charming, confident, and good public speaker genes went wholeheartedly to Spencer. His latest acting gig, a minimum wage featured-extra role in a period biopic, Hugh Jackman's directorial debut starring Jennifer Lawrence, was the hero piece of the annual Cole Christmas newsletter. Subject line: Spencer the Superstar!

Wyst has never made it into the family newsletter. My mother assures me once I secure seed round funding, she would include it, but for the time being she doesn't want to "embarrass" me in case the business fails.

While Spencer's natural charisma and career trajectory followed a trail of breadcrumbed hopes and dreams, my skill set mostly came in the form of sheer will power. A willingness to prioritize achievements over sleeping, eating, self-care, and, as my father likes to say, "Being an active member of this family."

"Mum keeps asking me to send her pictures of my costume for her Facebook page," Spencer remarks.

He avoids saying it's not explicitly *her* Facebook page, but a Facebook page she runs *for him*, posting updates of his latest work and "exclusive behind-the-scenes content." In Spencer's defense, he didn't ask her to set it up, but he never asked her to take it down.

"Oh, so she is alive," I say. She hasn't returned my calls for the past two weeks after I turned down Dad's job offer from his mate Darren who is looking for a new line manager at his local waste processing plant:

"You want me to literally manage shit shoveling?"

"There's plenty of career growth; the waste industry is booming right now."

"So is FemTech," I countered.

"If it's booming so much, why are you always struggling?"

Spencer wheels his chair over to my desk. Light from the third-story window illuminates his face as he crosses his legs and laces his fingers together on his knee. "So I actually came to talk to you."

"You just said, 'Please don't talk to me,'" I remind him, remaining focused on copying and pasting the company information into the application.

He smiles a cheesy grin. "That's fine because I just need a nod of the head from you."

I say nothing, as previously instructed.

"You know how you are my *favorite* twin sister?" he continues.

"One: I am your only twin sister. Two: Are you suggesting if you had any other non-twin siblings, I would not be the favorite?"

He refuses to play ball. "I was thinking now the movie has wrapped, I could up my office hours a bit?"

In between acting gigs, Spencer helps out replying to user emails, tidying the office, creating expense sheets, and answering the phones. Essentially a glorified intern with a company email address, but I can only afford to give him sixteen hours a week.

Swinging my chair round to face him, I say, "I'd love for you to find us a mountain of cash?"

"What happened?"

"A potential investor turned out to be a date," Cecily says.

He shoots me a look of concern you would give a child who just fell over while running. "Oh, Jess, surely you're not that desperate?"

I throw a pen at him. "No! I just wish we could have had something in place for the meeting with Dr. Bernie tomorrow." My mind goes blank for a few seconds as the voice echoes in my head:

Maybe it's your name, maybe all previous investors recognize it just like Will did—that's why they keep rejecting you. Maybe Dr. Bernie will see you just like everyone else: a woman who made a stupid decision that cost two people their promising careers.

"Maybe we should reschedule," I say to Cecily, anxiety rising like dry heat up my throat.

She looks offended. "Do you know how long it took me to just get a sniff of a meeting with Dr. Bernie? There's absolutely no way we can reschedule."

"Who is Dr. Bernie?" Spencer asks, pouring himself a 2 p.m. glass of the very expensive wine.

Cecily gapes at him. "How do you not know Dr. Bernie? She only has the best podcast of all time. I've sent you episodes!"

He spins back and forth in his chair, chewing on his lip. "The one where they talk about niche SewingTok internet drama?"

She shakes her head. "No, the other one."

He looks to the ceiling, racking his brain. "The one where they rewatch the entire filmography of Krysten Ritter?"

I point a finger at him. "No, but that one is good, though."

Dr. Bernie is my white whale. I have been trying to get a meeting with her about being the face of Wyst for months. Her podcast *How Have You Been?*—a concept therapy podcast focusing on women's mental health and relatable experiences—tops the health and wellness charts every week. And when she has the occasional celebrity guest talking about their struggles, it's almost guaranteed to hit the number one spot across categories. Clips are always going viral on social media for the candid, raw offering she brings to her advice. She is one of the major inspirations for Wyst, and just getting in the room with her would be a dream come true.

Spencer asks Cecily, "How did you get her?"

"I followed her personal assistant's TikTok a few months ago and have been watching it like a hawk. She was tagged in a video with a London-based hair stylist, so I followed *them* on

Instagram and they posted a story at the hotel. I went there for breakfast and *just so happened* to bump into her PA and pitched Wyst to her. She must have passed it on to Dr. Bernie because the PA literally DM'd me a few weeks ago to say she'd be in town if we wanted to chat." She points the phone screen toward me so I can read the message.

Once again, his mouth hangs agape. "Whoa. You are certifiably insane and I love it."

"Every evil genius needs a crazy henchman." She winks at me and leans back in her chair, triumphantly placing her stiletto heels on her desk.

Cecily makes the inaccessible accessible. A social media stalker extraordinaire, she has a reach the depths of which I can never fully fathom. I deleted all my social media platforms three years ago and never looked back. I jumped back in last year with an anonymous private account to watch any coverage of Wyst and stumbled across Dr. Bernie's podcast. Something about her snagged my attention among the eons of home and lifestyle content (my studio flat with damp mold could never), random dance videos (cannot dance), and cooking tutorials (anything beyond beans and toast isn't in the budget). Maybe it's her soft but assured tone of voice, her kind but stern demeanor, or her penchant for expensive jewel tone velvet suits and pussy-bow blouses, but something about her stuck with me during a time when no other voices could get through.

Nerves rage through my stomach at the idea of coming face-to-face with someone as established as Dr. Bernie. She could make or break a company like mine. During a YouTube interview with *GQ* outlining her "favorite things," she emphasized her love for a self-heating coffee mug. It was from a small female-founded start-up, and they sold out within minutes. They now have a permanent space in Selfridges, huge social media presence, and a waitlist a mile long. The influential market power of Dr. Bernie is not to be taken lightly. When an indie artist was interviewed about the trauma of being dropped from her label, her new single went viral on TikTok. Dr. Bernie interviews authors, and they turn into bestsellers. She has the Midas touch for anyone looking for mass appeal to women. She could turn us from nobodies into somebodies.

Spencer interrupts my train of thought with a throat clear. "So, ummm, about those office hours?"

My stomach twists. I'm usually able to help him out. The whole twin thing makes the guilt even worse. "Sorry, I can't give you more than two days a week at the moment." Read: Every rent payment is sending me deeper into my overdraft, the bank keeps leaving me threatening voicemails, I'm already trying to pay off business and student loans, and I'm considering dropping out of my studio rental because why pay for a bed when our tiny office has a decent-sized sofa?

Spencer slumps but plows on, studying his fingernails. "It's just that I owe quite a bit to the theater, and I could use the cash in between jobs . . ."

"They don't accept Jennifer's fancy hot chocolates as payment?" The rush of regret hits my cheeks almost instantaneously. "Sorry," I add before I've fully taken a post-sentence breath.

He huffs a laugh, barely a laugh. Laugh lite. "No, and to make up for it, Hugh gave everyone a lottery ticket and declared"— Spencer throws his hands in the air like a spectator at a football match—"'You make your own luck, boys!'"

Something sparks in his eyes and he digs his hand into his pocket. "How about this." His lips wind into his pre-famous grin. "You give me some additional hours this month, and I'll split whatever my winnings are with you. Fifty-fifty." He wiggles a shiny blue and gold square in front of my face like he's Charlie Bucket and I his crotchety grandfather.

I cock a playful eyebrow. "Is this before or after the director's 15 percent?"

"You two are idiots." Cecily laughs from across the desk.

"I'm sure he'll live; wanna scratch?" He points the card toward me with a pursed lip.

I reach for it, before hesitating. "No, it was given to you. It's bad luck if I do it."

The TechRumble application burns in my periphery while Spencer takes a penny and begins to tear away at the first shiny patch, the metallic shavings littering the pristine white surface of my desk.

He gasps as a cherry fruit emoji appears under his fingers. "We need five in a row to win the grand total."

"What's the grand total?" I ask.

"Fifty K," he says, deadly serious. He rubs the next patch clean, revealing a second shiny red cherry.

We glance at each other, sucked in with the suspense as he drags the bluing coin across the third circle. A third cherry.

"What will you do with your twenty-five grand?" Spencer asks, wiggling his eyebrows at me in childish glee.

My mind runs wild with the fantasy of a debt-free life. No more calls from the bank about my overdraft, my student loans paid. It wouldn't cover my studio rent, office rent, and everyone's wages, but it would give me some breathing room as I locked in advertisers and finalized the website for a beta launch. Money like that would take me from scrambling to stay afloat to actually enjoying what I'm trying to do. Money like that would change my life. I wouldn't need to apply to things like TechRumble, begging for just the chance to *compete* for funding.

Before I've had a chance to answer, he sighs wistfully. "I've always wanted to go to the Maldives." He lifts his chin like he's trying to smell the salty sea air before continuing to scratch.

"Oh, shit." Cecily rolls her chair in closer, crunching a Diet Coke can in her fist as Spencer wiggles the coin aggressively across the fourth spot to reveal another cherry.

My stomach knots. A sliver of hope warming my nerves against the blizzard forming outside. What if this is real?

It's not like we are on the poverty line. I'd like to think our parents would help us out if we really, *really* needed it. Especially Cecily's, whose generational wealth makes the royal family look penniless. But I could never ask her to do that. They want her to either join her family business or give them several grandchildren, and unfortunately one of our few shared personality traits is stubbornness and pride, and disappointing our parents is the worst-case scenario. I can't disappoint my parents, not again. Maybe, for me, it's the twin thing; having a sibling in the same school year, same classes, and the same stages of life has always made the natural comparisons so easy. I was always better at exams and schoolwork; Spencer was always popular and beloved. I've never asked my parents why they didn't encourage me to help Spencer with school and him to introduce me to his friends, but our differences ate away at our childhoods, the bite marks still showing now.

Spencer's hand trembles as he pulls the coin across once to reveal a blast of red underneath the gray, shiny surface. I can already feel the tears of relief stinging my eyes.

He excitedly scratches the remainder off to reveal a big red cross. A visual game show–style buzzer screaming "EH-EH." My chest deflates, letting the dream ride a one-way journey on the CO_2 out of my lungs.

We sit in an embarrassed silence for a few seconds, until finally, Spencer's green eyes flick to mine. "Do you think that waste plant is still hiring?"

With a sigh of resignation, I press submit on the TechRumble application without another thought.

CHAPTER 3

Business Account (WYST) BALANCE: £12,120.57
Personal Account BALANCE: -£1,960.63
Recent Transactions:
Office rent: £1,096.00

The next morning I stare at the latest post on Dr. Bernie's Instagram. Our meeting with her is in an hour, and my nerves are getting the better of me. Scrolling through her posts I stop on an image of her looking immaculate in a deep purple velvet suit sitting on a panel holding a microphone. A quote surrounds her in a trendy font like she's a new age prophet: *Without failure, there would be no progress.* I have to laugh because if that was the case, I'd have a Fortune 500 company by now.

As Cecily and I finish packing our bags and decide the best bus route to get to the hotel, Spencer's head pops up from above his computer. "Hey, this email might be a scam, but I'm gonna forward it to you just in case. If you click the link and it's porn, it's not my fault."

I furrow my brow and click on the fresh email as it pops into my phone's inbox.

FWD: investment@wyst.com
From: Odericco Investments
Subject: Your Application

Dear Mr. Cole,

Thank you for your application to TechRumble's open call for start-up pitches.
   We would like to schedule a call to discuss further.
   Please select a preferred time for a call tomorrow:
   2:30 p.m.
   3 p.m.
   3:30 p.m.
   4 p.m.

Mr. Kavanagh
Odericco Investments

Everyone turns to me as I gasp, "Oh my god!" My hands shake as I reread the words "discuss further" over and over again.

Cecily jumps up to see what's on my screen. "Oh shit! You got an interview?" She takes the phone out of my hand and immediately scowls. "Wait, Jess . . . You know when we were saying you should change your prefix to Mr. and apply as a man?"

"Yeah." I laugh at the ridiculous idea, high on approval adrenaline.

"You know that we were joking, right? That was a joke." Her eyes flick back to me, a mix of confusion and dread on her face.

My stomach drops, my body tingling with a different kind of adrenaline. This is the kind you'd feel if you bungee jumped off a bridge and realized halfway down you've forgotten your harness.

Eyes widening, I scan the top of the email again. The application, I sent it from "Mr. Cole."

I turn to Spencer, who is sat on the other side of the room yawning and typing emails with one finger. He senses me staring and sits upright, clearing his throat.

"Sorry, was it porn? Let me know if it's good."

A FEW HOURS later the bus trundles along the cold concrete as we head to Soho for the Dr. Bernie meeting. I tap my finger against my phone screen, reading and rereading the draft of an email reply to Odericco Investments.

"What's a professional way of saying, 'I accidentally pretended to be a man when submitting this application; can I still go ahead despite trying to dupe you please?'"

"Hmmm, that's a hard sell. Admin error?" Cecily offers.

"I don't know which sounds worse to a company like Odericco; I'm careless enough to make this kind of stupid mistake or reckless enough to subconsciously do this on purpose."

She puts a hand on my arm. "Maybe let's focus on Dr. Bernie for now. She's a real, viable option."

"You're right." I sigh, sending the half-written email reply to drafts as the bus lurches to a stop.

We enter the hotel lobby with nervous energy, gilded columns and raspberry-red walls giving the space a maximalist grandeur that suits this occasion perfectly. I etch the details into my mind almost as though I know this is a core memory as it's happening. An out-of-body experience where I can't fully feel or hear what's happening around me, like I'm recalling the moment as I'm living it. This could be it, a defining moment for Wyst.

Our heels click on the marble tile floor as Cecily and I weave our way through the lunch crowd of freelance creatives on their third spicy marg. According to her assistant, the only time Dr. Bernie had available today was her thirty-minute "Caesar salad slot" in between a radio interview and filming *The One Show* to promote her latest self-help book, *Permission to Feel*. As well as hosting a chart-topping podcast, her books are front and center in every airport, train, and chain bookstore.

As we approach her table, I put on my confident CEO persona. "Dr. Bernie? Jess Cole. So lovely to meet you—I'm a big fan."

Cecily shakes her hand. "So, so great to meet you; thank you for making time for us."

"Hi ladies, please sit." She waves at the two chairs in front of us in a way that somehow doesn't come off entitled. She's definitely used to the praise and doesn't have time for it today.

Sensing her urgency, I jump straight in. "Let's get down to it, shall we?" I open up the folder with the pitch.

"Sweetie." She rests a soft, perfectly moisturized hand on mine, silver rings with turquoise stones cold on my skin. "Firstly, we're not in session; please call me Bernadette. Secondly, I would like *you* to tell me, not a pile of paper."

Cecily gives me an encouraging nod, her eyes suggesting this is a good sign.

"Sure." The folder creaks as I close it and slide it off the table onto my lap; my fingers brace the cardboard edges like it's a sled and I'm about dive off a snowy cliffside.

"Wyst is, at its core, a discovery platform. A way for women, girls, and people who identify as women to have a constantly evolving resource on everything to do with women's health.

"As I'm sure you already know, women's physical and mental health is, the majority of the time, not taken seriously. How many times have we heard 'It's because of your period,' 'Try losing some weight,' or 'Come back if the pain gets worse'? Then with search engines losing their potency in the wake of AI integration, most users are resorting to Reddit or Quora. Which is the Wild West for misinformation."

She nods her head so I power on. "We are launching a completely free-to-the-user resource where women can access clear, professionally vetted, judgment-free advice from leaders in the industry such as yourself. We already have a wait list of twenty-five thousand users for our beta. Women *want* something like this."

Cecily chimes in, "With you as the face of Wyst, it brings credibility and global recognition to our mission."

Having reached the end of the rehearsed section of my pitch, we wait for her response. Bernadette's jaw twitches as she studies me. "Why are you the person to build something like this?"

My brain reverts back to sales-pitch mode. "Because I care about women of all ages having access to information about their own bodies and minds."

"Don't we all." She smiles into her tea, then purses her lips as her blue eyes cut back up to mine. "But as the founder, why *you*? With your background at Graystone, you could have had a fruitful career in finance. Why this? Why you?"

I freeze. Literally freeze in every sense of the word. Does she know what happened? My mouth is open mid-thought, my blood sends a shiver through my veins, my hand begins to shake like it's just been stuck in a bucket of ice.

"I . . ."

Sensing my hesitation, Cecily jumps in. "Jess is incredibly passionate and hardworking and—"

Bernadette's hand comes up, immediately silencing Cecily.

My finger traces the rim of the cup. "I had a . . . situation . . . during my time there, which resulted in me leaving the job I'd worked very hard for. In hindsight, I wish I'd had a resource like this to help me figure out my next steps. How to talk about it, how to handle things better. So I didn't feel so alone."

Cecily squeezes my hand under the table.

Bernadette nods, as though confirming a suspicion she'd had from the moment I sat down.

I lean back, my heart pounding as she flicks her silver-gray hair over her ear.

"I read your pitch deck this morning, and I like what you're doing. I am willing to discuss this further; my only other question is can you afford me?"

The numbers in my bank account flash before my eyes; the answer is no, but the moment I admit that this meeting is over. The draft email to Odericco Investments burns a hole in my side. The rejections folder bashes against my temples. I am blacklisted because of what happened.

Cecily begins to proclaim the PR'd version of the truth. "Well, we are in the process of seeking fu—"

I interrupt before she can finish her sentence. "We are in talks with investors who have a keen interest in Wyst. The funding we are discussing with them will take us through to the public launch and help us expand our growing team, as well as partner with a high-profile ambassador such as yourself."

Bernadette sips her tea and nods lightly. "When will you have funding?"

"I'll know more in a few weeks." I nod, lying through my teeth. I wonder if she can tell because she gives me an almost imperceptible look like she knows I'm scrambling.

Bernadette taps her perfect fingernails on the table. "You know I can't say yes to anything without a definitive contract?"

Cecily's smile falters into seriousness as she follows my lead. "How about a deferred payment schedule?"

"I'm an international bestseller, I don't do IOUs," she says smoothly. God, I wish I was her.

We attempt to bow out gracefully, saying our pleasantries, goodbyes, and we'll-be-in-touches while both knowing we don't currently have the money to make this happen.

Stepping out of the hotel onto the pavement, Cecily takes my arm in hers. "So you know that thing you said about funding? That wasn't referring to what I think it is, right?"

I avoid her gaze, focusing on the traffic light. "The Odericco competition? Yes."

She shakes her head in disbelief. "But what are you going to say? 'Sorry, I wasn't paying attention during the application process and I'm actually a woman'?" If I say that, they might wonder why I did it, then realize who I am. What if exactly the same thing happens as it did with William at the bar?

"Nooooo," I drawl nonchalantly, "Odericco Investments is cutthroat. They would never give us a chance after a mistake like that." And the moment they find out I'm in charge they're going to use this "clerical error" as an excuse not to give Wyst a chance. But I can't lie, can I?

If you were a man, you'd probably have funding by now.

I look at her, the sheepishness unavoidable across my face. The only way out of this hole is money. And it's just a call. I'm an idiot for getting myself into this situation, but I'd be an idiot to let it slip through my fingers. Do I really have a choice? I have an in; even if we got knocked out of the first round of the competition, the platform might attract other smaller investors. Being on the world's stage is money-can't-buy levels of exposure.

We stare at each other, unsure of our next move. Until Cecily finally breaks the silence with a nod. "Fake it till you make it, right?"

I shrug. "It's just a call. It probably won't go anywhere anyway."

As we cross the road, the winter wind blowing against our faces, I pull out my phone and delete the drafted email before starting a fresh reply.

Dear Mr. Kavanagh,

Thank you for your request. I have some other calls with potential investors this week. Would another member of my team be able to take the call?

Best,
Jess Cole

Shit.

I delete my first name, type *Mr.* instead, and press send before

I can think about it. This is fine, just a slight fudging of the truth to cover up a stupid mistake to hide an even stupider mistake.

A reply comes back almost instantly.

Dear Mr. Cole,

Mr. Odericco would prefer all candidates to be vetted personally. If you are not available at the listed times, we will unfortunately have to consider that a pass on this opportunity.

Mr. Kavanagh

"No, no, no!" I say into the screen.

Cecily reads the email. "Shit."

Despite the chilled air, my hands start to sweat as they plow against the keyboard.

Dear Mr. Kavanagh,

That is completely fine. I am more than happy to take the call personally.

Best,
Mr. Cole

I stare at the message for a few seconds and glance up at Cecily before pressing Send. Just a small lie to cover up the last.

No big deal.

CHAPTER 4

Business Account (WYST) BALANCE: £12,058.89
Personal Account BALANCE: -£1,960.63
Recent transactions:
Charlotte Street Hotel: £45.69
FemTech Monthly magazine subscription: £15.99

This is going to work, right?" I say mostly to myself before leaning back in my chair, the nerves fully taking flight. An anti-nausea tablet and that yellow "herbal remedy" throat spray would usually give me the placebo courage I need to get through a phone call like this with no trouble. But the added factor of deception on the phone to a potential investor is clawing through any medicinal walls built to house my anxiety.

Pacha stands over me, his neon yellow tracksuit glistening in the speckled sunlight. "My program? Yes. Your plan? No."

When I asked Pacha if he could create a voice changer software for me, I did not imagine he'd be able to do it so quickly, no questions asked. This plan came out of pure unadulterated panic, and he didn't say anything, but I think he could see it on my face. I've been holding on by the tips of my fingers for the past three years, and this might be my last chance. All that money, time, and energy. I have to do this.

My stomach gurgles like a washing machine on a heavy load as the voice changer spits out my voice at a lower octave. There's a second-long delay, which I blame on my old phone's crappy signal. I have no doubt Pacha would have been able to create some sort of all-out AI man-face filter for me, but I'm still thanking the tech gods Odericco Investments didn't want a video call.

As the clock ticks toward 3 p.m., my hands vibrate against my phone. Cecily answers the intercom and receives a gigantic bouquet of pink, yellow, and purple flowers. She admires them in the kitchen for a few seconds and then breaks the bunch into four mini bouquets, placing them in used jam jars.

This is a fairly regular occurrence. She will deny the existence of sugar daddies in her life but if I had four or five adoring men who want to take me out for dinner at the hottest restaurants, buy me flowers, and send me for massages and facials at the swankiest hotels in the city, would I really be saying no? I've heard people in tech say "never spend your own money," a phrase I clearly didn't take to heart. Cecily's parents have more than enough money that she doesn't need to work a day in her life, but it doesn't mean she has to spend it. After a while, Cecily started referring to them as her personal "investors," because is what we're doing really any different? No. Is she much, *much* better at soliciting financing from men in fancy suits? Yes.

She brings one of the bunches to me with a warm smile, the pink roses, violets, and yellow ranunculus vibrant against the dull gray, black, and white of my desk setup.

"You're going to be great," she says, squeezing my shoulder as I plug my headphones in.

"Thanks." I tap my pencil on the surface until my phone begins to shift under vibration. I let it ring once, switch the voice changer on, and answer the phone. There is an odd sense of camaraderie radiating from both Cecily and Pacha at this moment. It's not like they haven't been supportive of Wyst getting funding in the past; they are wholly aware that eventually Wyst's cash flow, aka their salaries, will eventually run out if we don't. But maybe it's me edging on a panic attack, my excitement at the email invitation to this call, or maybe the desperation of this plan that is hinting at something not being quite as fun and exciting as these kinds of opportunities used to be. It feels dangerous to fuck this up, rather than exciting to go forward. This feels and probably to Pacha and Cecily looks like a last chance. A Mary I'd only be hailing if things have really gone to shit.

"Mr. Cole?" a smooth, self-assured tone asks.

"Yes, this is he," I reply, bringing down my own voice just in case the voice changer doesn't work. I catch the feedback of my lowered tone, genuinely thinking for a second that Spencer is also on the call. Cecily sucks in her cheeks as I try not to acknowledge the ridiculousness of this situation. But we're in it now, no going back. With nothing else to do, I go into business pitch mode. "Thank you so much for the opportunity to talk to you about Wyst, Mr. Kavanagh, we are big supporters of Odericco Investments and would be thrilled to be thought of among your top-tier portfolio."

"That's great." Mr. Kavanagh seems unfazed or perhaps completely uninterested by my compliment. "I'd like to start by hearing a bit more about Wyst." His American accent doesn't surprise me. The call came through from a blocked number, so this guy is probably calling from the New York office. Odericco Investments have offices in London, New York, Paris, and Hong Kong and do business in just about every other country in the world.

I guess we're getting straight down to it. I take a deep breath and explain the entire concept, probably going into way too much detail, but I'm so pitch practiced at this point, I might as well throw every morsel of information onto the plate. By the time I'm finished, I realize I've been talking for over a minute and the man on the other end hasn't said a thing. The urge to hedge the conversation, to say something to soften my domination of the conversation, like "but I'll stop waffling now ha-ha-ha," bubbles up within me like a geyser ready to blow. But this is a man speaking; Spencer is sure, certain, and unflinching in his words even if they are wrong. A man would not hedge; I finish my sentence and hold for his response.

After a few seconds of excruciatingly painful silence, only punctuated by the sounds of phones ringing in the distance and the whirring of an air-conditioning unit on his end, he finally asks, "And what about daily functions? Can you explain your current setup?"

"Sure. We're based in London, a dedicated team of four." I'm lying about Spencer and Pacha being full time, but it's par for the course at this point. "We are on the final push to get our beta version live, and we are in talks with a major figure in the health and wellness space to come on board as the face of the brand." I scrunch my face, regretting saying it the moment the words slip off my lips. *Please don't ask who. Please don't ask who. Please don't ask who.*

"Who?" he asks.

Shit.

This guy really doesn't mince his words. I can't tell if he's simply disinterested or genuinely thinks he's too important to speak more than ten words an hour. My gut twists, flip-flopping over the two potential roads to go down like a fish trying to get back to water. If I tell him, reveal the name of the big-time, influential figure who is intrigued by the concept, it's adding another lie on top of everything else I have just said. But what's *one more* lie. I've already lied about where our initial funding came from, the amount of employees we have, my own fucking identity; compared to that one, this feels like a shiny little maraschino cherry on top of a yummy Neapolitan sundae of deception.

"Hello?" he asks, his voice a furrow of the brow. I can just imagine him, sitting in his big fancy chrome office, thousand-pound Herman Miller chair—probably one of those obnoxious wooden captain's desks all men of a certain corporate caliber love to own to give them the illusion that they aren't a tiny cog in the machine; they are the captains of their own four-by-four office space. His voice is smooth, so I imagine his look would be too. Sharp suit, clean haircut. A classic New York Finance Bro.

"Dr. Bernadette Reid," I say, teeth clenched. My fingers snake through my hair, gripping at the scalp. What am I doing? This is so stupid. I need Dr. Bernie to be in with a chance of getting funding, but I can't have Dr. Bernie *without* funding.

"That's a big name," he says, tone unaffected. No opinion, no emotion, just a fact that yes she is a big fucking deal, three million followers across her social media platforms, a bestselling book, and a podcast that holds a permanent place on the top ten charts.

"It is," I agree. Maybe this is how businessmen talk to one another, instead of feigning interest and politely smiling, nodding and laughing in all the right places. One thing working at Graystone taught me was that the way I conducted myself, and probably still do, was not the "correct" way of doing things. To be a successful businessman you must be callous, calculating, ruthless, and emotionless. That is, if you completely ignore the fact that anger is actually an emotion. Even in my business school classes, I knew being a woman would hold me back. It would make men put their efforts into holding me back, a physical hand on the lower back at a bar, pushing me out of the way, establishing contact when there was no need, even when I wasn't truly a threat. Me just being in the room was a threat.

For a second I think about the last time a man considered me a threat in the room, but I pull myself back into the phone call with a shepherd's crook.

We speed run the next few questions:

"When will the beta be live?" he asks.

"In a few weeks," I answer.

"And what are your projections for daily active users?" he asks.

"We already have major registered interest from twenty-five thousand users who will be part of the soft launch," I answer.

"Is there a reason you're soft launching?" he asks. I can hear a pencil being rhythmically tapped across the line.

Yes, because we don't have the money for a full balls-to-the-wall campaign rollout.

"It's . . . a savvy audience. We want to encourage our users to feel like they are part of an evolving community, not having a product being thrust upon them," I answer.

"Right," he says. I hear typing in the background. He's taking notes.

"But once our beta test has worked out any potential kinks, we will be going full steam ahead with a countrywide roll out as soon as possible." I nervously click my phone to check the time; it's only been ten minutes.

"Okay." He types some more.

"And the U.S. will go live straight after," I offer.

He stops typing. "Excuse me?"

"The U.S. will go live afterward," I repeat.

After a brief pause, he asks, "Who am I speaking to?"

I glance down at my phone, and my body is briefly shuffled off this mortal coil, then jolted back to life when I realize the app is no longer running. *Fuck, fuck, fuck.* My finger stabs at the screen, trying to reload. I click the icon, my hope soars, then plummets once again as it opens, then immediately crashes. My body goes rigid; he just heard my real voice.

"Hello?" Mr. Kavanagh says as I wave my arms out to gain the attention of Pacha on the other side of the room. His eyes are focused on his screen, finishing the code to our forum pages.

I clear my throat and lower my voice to a point of cartoonishness in an attempt to match the software. "Errr . . . My apologies, that was my assistant . . ." I glance in a panic at the flowers in the jam jar in front of me. ". . . Violet. She's . . . enthusiastic." I pick up a packet of salt and vinegar kettle crisps from Cecily's desk and hurl them in Pacha's direction. They hit the back of his computer screen with a *thwk*, and he pops his head up over the gray, shiny edge.

I mouth "Help!" at him, still waving frantically and pointing to my phone while Mr. Kavanagh begins to speak.

"It seems like you have a lot of people who really believe in this vision." If I'm not mistaken, I can hear a creeping smile on his stern voice.

"Indeed," I say in my man voice, cupping the headphone's microphone in my hands to muffle any other sound as Pacha pads over to me. My man voice is coming out less like a normal twenty-first-century human and more like Lord Byron. Thankfully, the monosyllabic nature of our conversation is actually working to my advantage. Pacha picks up my phone and holds it up to my face to unlock it as sweat begins to coat my brow.

"Great, well, I think I've got everything I need. Please send your financial projections and presentation pitch over to the link provided in my original email as soon as possible. As I'm sure you're aware, there is a sense of urgency as the competition begins next week." The sound of paper shuffling on Mr. Kavanagh's end loudens.

"Of course, will do," I bellow, closing my eyes at the sheer idiocy of this plan. Pacha clicks away at my phone and then finally gives me a thumbs-up. "Thank you for your time." My real fake voice kicks in again. "We really appreciate your interest in Wyst. The FemTech space is a fast-growing, lucrative industry; this would be a great opportunity to get in on the ground floor."

"I'll pass that on to Mr. Odericco," he says, hinting that it's not actually him making any decisions. The realization elates and deflates me at the same time. "Goodbye."

"Have a good aft—" The line clicks off before I can finish.

I crane my neck to look at Pacha, neon yellow arms crossed in defiance.

"My program works; your phone is just shit." He gestures to my iPhone 8, its scratched screen and dirty phone case very past its prime.

"Be civil, children," Cecily interjects, holding a steaming hibiscus tea between her fingers before placing it down in front of me. "If your insane plan works, that's all that matters."

"I guess we'll find out soon," I say, sitting back in my chair, a bead of sweat sliding down my lower back. "But he didn't seem *that* interested." My internal to-do list yawns awake; there are so many things to do ahead of the beta launch.

Within seconds, a new email appears. My hand trembles as I move the mouse to hover over it.

Dear Mr. Cole,

Thank you for your time; it was great to speak with you.

Mr. Odericco would like to extend an invitation to attend and present at the Odericco TechRumble Round One. Itinerary and invitation are attached. As mentioned, if you will be in attendance, please have your assistant send over materials for a presentation.

Mr. Odericco hopes you can make it.

Regards,
Mr. Kavanagh

I let go of the mouse as the green and yellow PDF invitation fills the screen. "Holy shit."

Odericco Investments invites you to compete at this year's
Odericco TechRumble.

In partnership with Wyatt Regency Rome.

"We got in?" Cecily squeals, leaning down and wrapping her
arms around me. I clutch at her forearm as her Baccarat Rouge
envelopes me.

"We got in." The swell of emotion immediately lances
through me. Hope laced with anxiety curdles like oil and milk.

"Shit." Cecily's arms loosen as she reads the invitation. "I *so*
didn't think we'd get away with it I forgot about what would
happen if we *actually* got away with it. You're going to Italy!"

I rest my face in my hands and say through my fingers.
"Worse. *Mr. Cole* is going to Italy."

And who the hell is Mr. Cole?

CHAPTER 5

Business Account (WYST) BALANCE: £12,058.89
Personal Account BALANCE: -£1,986.62
Recent transactions:
St. Martin's Underground Theatre: £25.99

A stone archway cocoons the entrance of the performance space. The walls are aged and crumbling, cracks leaking cold wind from outside. I pull my coat in tighter and traverse down the steep, uneven staircase until a man in all black scans my ticket. He guides me through the aisles of other audience members as a wave of heat hits me. There is practically no ventilation down here, so the air is warming with every shaky exhale from the audience. The space looked amazing from the outside, a Gothic church in the middle of the city, but as signage pointed the audience down two sets of stone stairs, it was like wading into a vacuum cleaner bag.

Some of the faces in the crowd ring familiar to me. Mostly friends and family of the performers with a few Shakespeare enthusiasts littered among them. Spencer and his fellow actors sent out requests to every casting director and agent in town in the hopes that one of them would show up for their World

War I reimagining of *Macbeth*. I wouldn't know them by face, but this is the last show of the run, so I hope there is someone here. Spencer is a great actor and has been in the business for five years without professional representation. This led him to take matters into his own hands, organizing troupe-run productions like this one. According to Spencer, ticket sales have been just enough to cover the four-week run. Everything has been done by the actors, including sourcing costumes, finding venues, and promoting the play. The crowd is silent as I duck down and creep toward my seat. The room is pitch-black except for a spotlight haloing the center of the stage. This performance space is a crypt in a church basement in the middle of the city. It's ironic really; if Spencer doesn't agree to my wild plan, my company is six feet under.

A man dressed in a fitted green tweed jacket steps into the light, briefly making eye contact with me as I squeeze past an aisle of annoyed onlookers to get to my assigned seat.

"So, thanks to all at once and to each one,

"Whom we invite to see us crown'd at Scone."

I am late. Mostly deliberately to avoid chatting with my parents before the show and a little bit accidentally after putting the final touches on an updated pitch presentation before "Violet" sent it off to Odericco Investments. I slink into the seat beside my mum as she tuts and whispers something to my father.

"Sorry, I came straight from work," I mouth, wriggling out of my puffer coat.

"Why are you wearing a T-shirt and jeans in the office? Aren't you in charge?" My dad grumbles, the shine from the spotlight skimming his bald spot like a halo.

I purse my lips, glancing down at my Debbie Harry T-shirt

and patchwork denim before schooling my mouth into the polite smile I reserve exclusively for taxi drivers who start ranting
about the "state of things nowadays" when there's still fifteen
minutes left to the journey. "Nice to see you both."

Neither of them reply, focusing back on the stage instead.
As quietly as humanly possible, I readjust my body into a com-
fortable position and settle in for two hours of Spencer and
Company.

My brother laps up the crowd; he is never more comfortable
than when he's on the stage. And luckily, he's also very good at
what he does. He has this natural quality that makes you truly
believe what he's saying. It's almost eerie, watching someone
you've known your whole life become a completely different
person.

When the applause subsides, the cast reappears from behind
a red velvet curtain. I also came to opening night, when the
tails were bushy but the flow was clunky. Now, as their shining
faces line up and glance at one another to synchronize the final
bow, the looks of sadness and relief are potent.

Spencer played Macduff and was the understudy for the tit-
ular role, something he was disappointed to not have had the
chance to do during this run of shows. He practiced the iconic
"Is this a dagger which I see before me?" monologue to Cecily,
Pacha, and me so many times we all know it by heart, mouth-
ing along with him like some thespian cult groupies singing
B-sides.

"Why did you cut bangs?" Mum says as we leave our seats,
standing face-to-face for the first time this evening. My parents
always frame insults in the form of a question. Like this is their
way of being interested in my life. No "How's work?" "What

are you up to?" "How's the love life?" We don't hug, but then again, the Coles are not famous for expressing their emotions through body language. Or any other language for that matter.

I consider replying, *Because that's what you do in a life crisis*, but don't gather up the nerve. It was either my homemade bangs in the bathroom mirror with a pair of office scissors or getting a part of my body pierced that isn't my ear. Curtain bangs were free and seemed way less likely to end in an infection.

Before my parents leave, I watch them say their hellos, goodbyes, and well-dones to my brother and his fellow actors as they scatter into the crowd, how proud they are of him for saying lines in a basement. If that sounds mean, it's because I'm bitter. They don't know about the numerous times I've bailed him out, the times he's refused a full-time or even part-time job at a local coffee shop or restaurant because he needs to be available for background acting on *Made in Chelsea* at a moment's notice. But after tonight, he will have a huge piece of dirt to hold over me as sibling mutually assured destruction. So maybe this will be a good thing for our relationship?

Once the crowds have filtered out, I follow Spencer backstage.

"Remind me again why your play *had* to be performed in a crypt?" I ask, grasping my puffer coat for warmth.

Spencer peels off his military jacket, arms glistening with sweat underneath, and hangs it on one of the metal clothing racks lining the walls, "For the om-bee-ance," he declares in a French accent.

"The zombi-ence?" I tease, holding up a Styrofoam skull.

He rolls his eyes. "The ambience, you philistine."

I run my finger across a wooden shelf, opening a line in the dust like Moses parting the Dead Sea. "This ambience is going to be stuck in the back of my throat for several days."

Spencer rolls his eyes as I wipe my finger off on my coat. "So I wanted to talk to you about something." I lean against a stone structure covered with the cast's leftovers from lunch.

He pauses, staring at the stone behind me and awkwardly grits his teeth. "Yeah, I think there might be an actual body in there."

"Ew, dude," I say as I tidy the sacrilegious paper coffee cups, plates, and napkins off the surface and dump them in the bin.

"And if this is about the missing desk lamps, I promise I will bring them back now we've finished the show run," he says quickly, as though saying it fast will cause it to fly over my head.

"Not that, but yes definitely bring them back; they are the building's, not mine. It's about work."

"Of course, when isn't it?" He sighs.

I contain my jab that we are literally having this conversation in a plague pit because he insists on us coming to every opening and finale show.

Just accept it; you're about to ask him for a huge favor.

"You know that email I got the other day? The one you thought might be a scam?"

"The porn one?"

"Yeah, that one . . ." I take a breath. "It was from a potential investor."

He steps behind a changing screen. "Weird of them to send you porn." A set of wool trousers and suspenders fold over the top of the taut beige fabric.

"It wasn't porn!" I say louder than anticipated; the word *porn* echoes around the cylindrical hall like a whirlpool of cringe. "It was an invitation to compete in this big tech competition in Rome."

"Oh cool, when are you going?" His shadow asks.

My lips thin to form a straight line. "In three days."

He pops his head above the screen. "And what does that have to do with me?"

"Well, it's kind of a funny story . . ." I laugh nervously, trying to find the right words. "On the call with a guy from the investment company . . . I kind of, maybe, *definitely* insinuated that *a man* is the CEO and founder of Wyst . . . not me." I shouldn't tell him about the voice changer situation in case he concludes I'm legitimately crazy, so much so he has to tell Mum and Dad.

He steps out from behind the screen, now dressed in a loose Fleetwood Mac T-shirt and frayed jeans I'm fairly certain are mine, his face set in a deep scowl. "I'm sorry, you did what?"

My fingers interlace as I try to come up with a viable reason. "I made a mistake on the application, selected the wrong gender, and I guess I just . . . went along with it. And now they think a 'Mr. Cole' runs Wyst." I look him up and down and sigh. "And you're the closest thing I have to a Mr. Cole."

He shoots me an incredulous look. "I literally am Mr. Cole."

"Fantastic! You're hired!" I clap my hands together.

Spencer eyes me with both sympathy and confusion. "If you needed a man, you could have just made someone up? Or hired an actor?"

I step forward, placing my hands on his arms to try and bring the focus back to the most urgent part of this conversation. "That is exactly what I'm doing. I need *you* to come to

Rome with me next week and pretend to be the CEO for a few days. And do a presentation."

He takes a step back, shaking his head and laughing. "No way, this has to be a joke. There's no way you, Jess Cole, would be this stupid."

I shrug defeatedly. "Everyone has their moments. Like that time you cut a right angle into my hair because you thought it would look cool?" I'm hoping reminding him of the ways he has slighted me throughout our twenty-seven years together will ease us toward a yes.

"I was nine!" he shouts, arms flapping against his sides.

"And you still haven't made it up to me, so now's your chance!" I flail my hands out to suggest "Oh, wow, I can't believe this opportunity has landed right in our laps!"

He crosses his arms, coughs out a laugh, and stares at the floor.

"Listen. I'm begging you; this is a once-in-a-lifetime opportunity," I plead.

Spencer's attention lifts. "Once in a lifetime? So you think you're going to win?"

I suck my teeth. "No way, I don't think we have a chance in hell of placing."

He flaps his arms out in exasperation. "Then why do you wanna go?"

I glance around, trying to think of a way he could understand this. "It's like your play. You didn't do this whole production to win an Olivier Award. You performed with the hope that someone in the audience would see your talent and be willing to give you a chance." I sigh. "Wyst is *never* going to win, but if we put on a good enough show, the smaller investors might start paying attention."

His shoulders ease. "But how would I *pretend* to be a CEO?"

Gesturing around at the piles of props, a hastily thrown together makeup station, and racks of costumes, I say, "Hmmm, I wonder how?"

"It's not acting if there's no script," he counters. "And I hate doing improv."

Seizing the moment, I reach into my bag and hand him a lilac Wyst-branded folder with the presentation and notes. "Au contraire . . ." I am nothing if not prepared.

He whips the folder from my fingers and spends the next minute silently flicking through it, the laminated sheets crinkling as he throws them one by one to the left.

He shakes his head at the folder, then swipes his eyes up to mine. "I don't understand this."

"Which pages?" I lean to see where he's looking.

"The ones with words on them." He snaps it shut. "How am I meant to present something I don't understand?"

I wipe away the dust from my hands. "You're telling me you understood everything you said onstage tonight? You understood the meaning of every line of Shakespeare?"

He purses his lips and blinks. "What about questions? We don't do a Q and A on sonnets and iambic pentameter after the show. How am I meant to answer things these nerds ask me?"

I smile. "Do you remember that scene in *Freaky Friday* when Lindsay Lohan is onstage miming playing guitar with the band, but Jamie Lee Curtis is actually the one slamming it offstage? We can do it like that, with wireless headphones. I'll call your phone before you go on, that way I can pep talk you throughout if necessary and answer any questions live. You just have to repeat what I say." My words come in a calm, managed tone, but in reality I have no idea if we'll be able to pull off this part of the plan.

"Riiiight. But . . . what do I get out of this?"

"Apart from a free trip to Rome? The joy of helping your favorite sister," I deadpan.

He leans against the wall, arms crossed, and lifts an inquisitive eyebrow. "Besides that."

"I'll let you keep my jeans." I point at his legs.

He scratches his thigh. "They're kinda itchy anyway."

"I'll let you use my flat as rehearsal space?" His open-plan warehouse shared with four other creatives has a strict rule about unsolicited performances in the common spaces.

He grimaces. "Nah, we started using Jeremiah's dad's apartment on Old Street while he's at work."

I dig deep; if I know my brother . . . what he wants more than anything in the whole world is to be famous for his craft. He needs exposure, and I know exactly where I can get him some.

"I'll get Cecily to post about your next show." She's not an influencer; she just *has* influence. Her one hundred thousand followers are obsessed with her candid posts. If she says she'll be at an event, ticket sales immediately increase. It's honestly where a lot of the digital word of mouth originally came from for Wyst.

He presses off the wall with a flourish. "Ladies and gentlemen, we have a winner!"

"Great." I immediately pull out my phone and open the browser tab with two easyJet flights to Rome already in the basket.

"I'll need to get working on my lines right away." He starts pacing, a plan forming in his head. "And develop the physical presence of the character. Who are we flying with? BA?"

"EJ." I tense, hoping he won't catch on.

"Okay, sounds good." He nods with a finger on his chin. "So if I'm the CEO"—he stretches his neck like he's seeing if the costume fits—"who would you be? My security?"

I purse my lips. "I need a reason to stay close and the guy on the phone thinks the CEO has an assistant called Violet, so I guess it makes sense that she would be me." The best lie is a consistent one after all. "Does this mean you'll do it?" I try to stop the upward tug of my lips, the hope creeping into my chest.

He rolls his eyes, trying to hide the excited smile curling over his mouth. "Fine."

"Thank you, thank you, thank you!" I pull out my phone, excited for the first time in months about what the future might bring. "So there are a few hostels to choose from, but I'll book the accommodations tonight and—"

"Whoa, whoa, whoa." Spencer throws his hands up, back straightening. "No way. I will do this *massive* favor for you, but you're not making me play the part of a fancy CEO, then putting me up in some dodgy Italian hostel."

"Well, we can't really stay in the conference hotel; a hostel is all the budget allows," I reply, using the business lingo that loosely translates to "I'm fucking broke." I'm probably going to have to take out a credit card to pay for this trip.

"You just said this is the *big leagues*, Jess. How is it going to look if everyone else is staying on site and I'm rocking up in crumpled clothes after bunking with a bunch of students."

He nods to himself assuredly as he starts to pack up his bags, clearly thinking through his argument as he goes. "And I want my own room."

I purse my lips; okay, he does have a point. "We can stretch it, but we'll have to share a twin room."

He crosses his arms. "Sorry, that's my main condition. You know how many tech bros are closeted?" He juts his chin out like it was so obvious, the trademark twinkle in his eye remaining even under sputtering light.

"I'm not booking you a shag pad; you're there to play a professional," I remind him.

"So in that case . . . why would a *professional*"—he spits the word in a mocking tone—"be sharing a room with his female assistant?" Knowing he's made a second great point, he starts heading toward the stairs back from the subterranean level. I can practically feel the money draining out of my account, like blood being leeched from my veins as I follow him up the stairs.

"All right, you can have your own room." I stick out my lower lip, nod my head, and add another room to the bookings page.

He turns, throwing his army uniform over his shoulder as he bounds up the stairs. "I'll only go if I get a suite!"

CHAPTER 6

Business Account (WYST) BALANCE: £9,502.56
Personal Account BALANCE: -£1,986.62
Recent transactions:
easyJet flights to Rome: £181.98
Wyatt: £2,374.35

The yawning automatic doors slide open as we drag our suitcases across the mezzanine, past the row of well-dressed drivers with names on whiteboards like penguins in a police lineup, out onto Rome airport's uneven arrivals exit tarmac. My head is pounding due to the three crying babies scattered so perfectly throughout the cabin no seat was untouched by the bloodcurdling screams. The only in-flight entertainment came when everyone turned on the man who shouted, "Will you shut that kid up?" to his nearest baby. The camaraderie was frankly heartwarming.

Originally, we had time to get to the conference hotel, check in, unpack, prepare all the materials, go over the presentation plan, get zhuzhed, then leisurely head down to the welcome drinks hosted in one of the hotel's event rooms. Instead, due to a three-hour weather delay, we are running to the shuttle bus in the rain. We step around puddles and past the line of tired-faced passengers waiting for taxis and head toward a sign with giant red letters spelling *Bus navetta*.

"Come on." Spencer waves at me as the long bendy bus covered in images of the statue of *David* and the Trevi Fountain creaks around the corner of a dilapidated public toilet, sighing to a stop. "The next one is in an hour."

Following the flow, I run toward the double doors. Tensing my arms to lift my suitcases—one full of clothes, one full of marketing materials—I slam them onto the bus's black terrazzo floor and squeeze in between an old Italian woman wearing a red babushka headscarf and a couple with matching chestnut hair shouting at each other in Italian.

The bus vibrates to life, and we lurch forward with a long high-pitched moan, the entire crowd of standing bus passengers rocking back and forth in unison like a jar of dill pickles.

After an hour of winding roads, horns beeping, and road rage, we arrive at the hotel. The raw-edged wood and chrome beams give the hotel a distinctly masculine vibe that makes me immediately shrink as I step foot into the wide lobby. Leather chesterfield sofas and armchairs are littered around like burned marshmallows.

Spencer examines the lobby before turning to me. "I thought it would be busier than this."

"We must be early; the actual TechRumble competition doesn't officially start until tomorrow, but it's some obligatory welcome drinks thing tonight."

He fixes me with a look. "I imagine all the important people have better things to do than be here this early."

My back straightens in defense. "The rooms are expensive! I wanted to get my money's worth."

He sighs. "I think I'll go to the spa; it's been a long day."

I slip Spencer the Wyst company credit card. "You'll need this to check us in." Thankfully, it doesn't have my name on it. When I booked our rooms, I decided to use my conference alias, Violet Leigh, to book mine.

"Here's your key card, Mr. Cole. The executive suite gym and spa facilities are on the basement floor; you'll need your key card to access those. Complimentary breakfast is served on floor one between six and nine. Oh, and here is your TechRumble literature and complimentary drink tickets." The pretty receptionist smiles, handing a matte black key card in a decorative cardboard case and a TechRumble-branded folder to Spencer as a man dressed in a three-piece suit offers to take his bag.

"And yours." A considerably less pretty smile is afforded to me as she passes over a white shiny key card.

She types something on her computer before looking up once more. "We just need to see your passports please, to have on file."

A basketball-size knot forms in my stomach as I attempt to school my face into neutrality, faking looking through my handbag to kill some time. The last thing we need is someone questioning my identity the night before the competition even starts. Next to me, Spencer hands his over without a second thought.

I let out a nervous laugh of an inexperienced assistant. "I think mine is at the bottom of my suitcase. Can I bring it later?"

"Ummmm." The receptionist looks at the man behind her, with a demeanor that suggests "manager." Spencer glances at me, cottoning on to my dilemma.

He shifts his demeanor into CEO mode, faking a loud laugh

and adopting an accent considerably posher than his own. "I can certainly vouch for my own assistant's identity; don't you worry!"

After receiving a nod from her manager, the receptionist gives us a tight-lipped smile. "Of course, sir."

"Thank you," we both reply in unison. I quickly thank the genetic gods that Spencer and I don't look that similar, because we just sounded identical.

The receptionist gestures her palm out to a nearby teenager in a red blazer. "Our bellhop will bring your bags up to your room."

"Great, thank you so much," I reply with a relieved sigh. Once we're in our rooms we'll be safe.

She smiles again, this time with teeth. "Oh, I'm sorry, a complimentary bellhop is just part of the suite package. Your suitcases are over there." She points a long finger at my two suitcases stacked in the far corner of the lobby.

Spencer holds in a laugh as he slides his passport back into his jacket pocket.

The receptionist nods her head at Spencer. "Enjoy your suite, Mr. Cole."

"I'm sure I will," he replies, as I drag my suitcases toward the elevators, one handle in each fist.

As we walk, Spencer flicks through the bright green TechRumble folder until he stops at the judging panel page. "Whoa, is this the Big Kahuna?"

I glance to the side, seeing an image of a man who is known as the epitome of tall, dark, and handsome. "Yeah, that's Dominic Odericco. He took over Odericco Investments from his father five years ago and introduced the whole concept of TechRumble the year after."

"He looks like that guy Regé-Jean Page," he says, examining Odericco's strong jaw and sharp cheekbones. "I did not think tech nerds could be this hot." Spencer's voice bounces off the walls as we make it to the elevators.

I look around to see if anyone overheard before bringing my voice down to a whisper. "Can you keep it in your pants please; we are here to be serious business people."

"Don't worry, I am *very* serious about that bod." Spencer has already googled Dominic Odericco and is clicking through long-lens paparazzi photos of him half naked, drinking martinis on a yacht with a small gaggle of models. His toned golden-brown chest with a smattering of dark hair glinting in the sunlight.

"Oh my god." I throw my hand over his phone screen as a pack of men in suits walk by.

Spencer laughs and clicks the button for his special little elevator with swirling gilded doors reserved for the top three floors of the hotel.

As it dings open, he shouts, "See you, cheapskate."

I glare at him, running a hand over my face and slinging my handbag over my suitcase before pulling both my bags toward the normie elevator. The much less exciting silver doors immediately start to slide open. All I want to do right now is shower and chill out in a king-sized bed.

Before I've even stepped a foot into the elevator, my eyes scrunch shut as a large body barrels into me like a freight train. A freight train grasping a cardboard holder of coffees, which promptly lose their flimsy lids and release their contents all over me. Like a targeted tag team assault, the iced coffee with whipped cream splashes over my face and hair while the matcha latte hits me directly in the chest. The two cappuccinos fall out of the holder and explode in every direction as they slam into the ground with a wet thwack.

"Shit!" a disembodied voice shouts.

"Fuck!" I wipe my blurry eyes and stumble backward, immediately feeling the lobby go upside down as I trip over one of my bags. As I fall, I grab blindly at the nearest object to try and save myself, but all I do is pull the shirt of whoever slammed into me over the top of the other suitcase until they are on the ground next to me.

Everything scatters across the lobby—my phone, key card, coffee cups, the entire contents of my handbag, and the other person's over-ear headphones.

As the assailant and I peel ourselves from the floor, our eyes finally meet. Mine squinting through the coffee, his wide form just hitting the floor at full speed. His biceps flex under his white shirt as he pushes himself off the floor, sitting upright with his hands on his wet thighs. His eyebrows meet as he stares at the crowd around us slowing their pace to gape. To be fair, I would also stop and stare at the brown and green explosion staining the perfect marble floors.

His hazel eyes scan the scene once more before flicking up to me. "Are you kidding me?" he says in an American accent.

"Am *I* kidding *you*?" I say, completely bewildered at his tone. "I'm not the one who just launched themselves into another human being without looking where they were going." I glance around too. Great, just half the people in the lobby are looking at us now, but my heart is still pounding. Several members of the janitorial staff are already cordoning off the area so other patrons don't step in the mess surrounding us and quarantining our embarrassment.

Gathering up the contents of my handbag, I take no real notice of the man next to me until he shakes his head in bafflement. "You know, it's common courtesy to let *other* people out of an elevator before you and your twenty bags enter. I thought the British were meant to be polite?" The front of his chestnut hair flops forward as he assesses where the coffee hit him. He wasn't originally in the splash zone, but his fall landed him face-first right where the two cappuccinos exploded. His jaw tightens as he winces and stands, then offers me a hand up.

Does this guy think because he has a face like that, he can just ram through life however he pleases? I don't take the offered hand, instead choosing to place my palm in a puddle of cooling coffee and get up by myself, causing a ripple effect in the liquid. He barks out a humorless laugh and shakes his head, choosing to watch me lift my suitcases off the floor by the dripping handles.

"It's common courtesy to look where you're going when you're carrying two liters of latte like a loaded weapon." I wipe at the bright green and brown stains covering my coat.

"Just perfect. Exactly what I needed today," he grumbles to himself, wiping his wet hands on his suit trousers before checking his watch.

I throw my arms up in exasperation, gesturing to my torso. "And this is exactly how I wanted my day to go! This is the only coat I packed!" I gesture to the rain clouds building outside.

He winces, eyes softening as he takes in my state for the first time. My face is wet, my light beige coat now looks like I'm making a cow print fashion statement, and my hair has a smear of whipped cream in it. Compared to me, he barely has a scratch on him. He runs a hand through his hair. "Shit, I'm sorry. I'll pay for your dry cleaning."

"No, it's fine." I gather my things and shove the loose, soggy contents of my handbag back into place. The laminator Cecily got me for Christmas thankfully saved my folder of presentation notes, narrowly avoiding complete and utter disaster.

"I insist." He picks up one of my suitcases. "It's one of the hotel services, so you'll have it back by tomorrow."

I glance up and down at him, and he easily stands half a foot taller than me. "Are you seriously holding my suitcase hostage? After you've thrown coffee all over me?"

His face softens. "Is it working? If not, I'll have to send you a cutoff handle in the mail with a ransom note."

I roll my eyes, determined not to crack a smile. Reluctantly, I shake off my coat to reveal a fitted purple Wyst-branded T-shirt and jeans underneath. They both have residual wet patches on them, but they are salvageable. He assesses the stains and raises an eyebrow in question, creating a crack in my resolve. "I am not starting this trip off by stripping in the lobby."

"Weird, that's how I usually prefer to kick things off." He tilts his head, a smile tugging at one side of his mouth. He waits for my reply, but I just stare at him, trying not to blush. "Just the coat then." He nods as I place it over his gesturing arm. "I'll ask them to leave it at the front desk when it's clean. What name should I put it under?"

I'm about to speak, but we are interrupted by three angry janitors holding mops and *Wet Floor* signs.

"Sorry, guys, thanks." Coffee Assailant looks sheepish as he slips one of the men a twenty-euro note.

"Sorry," I repeat, wincing for effect as I pick up my bags and drag them into the elevator.

Instead of giving me my suitcase back, he rolls it into the elevator, standing next to me.

His hazel eyes lock back on mine. "What floor?"

I readjust my bags and dig the still-wet key card out of my pocket. "Three."

"Same as me. Assistant or intern?" He's definitely American, but can I detect a tiny hint of an English accent?

The doors slide shut with a dull thud. "Why do you think I'm either of those?" I ask.

His eyebrows crease ever so slightly as he lowers his chin to meet me, gesturing to my key card. "Because you're in the cheap seats."

I go to protest, to say I'm neither, but the plan kicks in. *A good lie is a consistent lie.* "Assistant. Are you one too?" I clear my throat, not quite comfortable at swallowing the truth.

"Unfortunately." He straightens his broad shoulders, making me realize how much space he takes up in this tiny Italian elevator. "I hate having to come to these things, having to wear a suit at all times." He gestures to his stained attire, and I feel my cheeks go pink.

He stretches out his hand as we come to a stop, offering for me to leave the elevator first as it pings on the third floor. We awkwardly pace over the red and brown geometric-patterned carpet in the same direction until I can't stand the silence.

"You come to these events a lot?" I say over my shoulder, my bags taking up all the space in the corridor so he has to walk behind me. The overhead lights cast his cheekbones in sharp contrast.

"Yeah, part of the gig." He starts to slow down, reaching his room.

"It's my first time," I say, immediately regretting the turn of phrase.

He smiles, eyebrows raised, lines forming in the corners of his mouth. "Well, at least you've got the hazing out of the way," he says, glancing at my stains. He raps a knuckle on his room door before sliding the key card into the scanner. "My apologies again."

"Thanks." I smile back, lips tight.

The security light on his door goes green, and he pulls down the handle, then hesitates. "Hey, ummm, tomorrow night, once the big cheeses have gone to their dinners, the assistants are throwing a night-off party at this dive bar a few doors down . . . if you're free."

I freeze and laugh nervously. "Oh, I think I'll probably be busy working, but thanks." I use my head to gesture to all my bags, only now realizing I'd come to a complete halt to continue talking to him.

His smile falters from genuine to rebuffed but polite. "Oh, right, yeah. No problem. Okay, well, see ya." He jumps into his room.

"Bye—" I say as his door clicks firmly shut.

An hour later, I've showered off the coffee and airplane, hair and makeup are done, and I'm lying in a robe on the bed, looking through my notes for Spencer. When Coffee Guy described this floor as the "cheap seats," my expectations plummeted, imagining a budget-friendly airport hotel vibe, but even the cheap floors in the really, really nice hotel are comfier, airier, and better designed than my London studio flat.

My phone vibrates across the fluffy cotton duvet.

"Ciao!" Cecily's voice echoes down the line. I can hear the faint sound of pounding techno music in the background.

"Ciao," I reply. "Where are you?"

"At Spin, just getting ready to go in. How's it going?"

I get up and pad toward the wardrobe and scan the array of shirts and sensible trousers I packed. "It's going well, I think . . . I successfully lied to a guy in the elevator; he even invited me to an assistants-only after-party tomorrow."

In hindsight, even if I was being awkward and weird, he'd have no reason to think I'm lying. When people lie about their career, it's usually with upthrust, not demotion.

Cecily gasps with joy. "You deceitful little trollop, congrats!"

"I'm not gonna go, though." I click the call onto speakerphone, undo my robe, and step into the dress.

"Why?" She goes to a whisper. "Was he ugly?"

I laugh that *that* is the only reason she assumes I wouldn't go, my mind briefly slipping to his crossed arms under the fitted white shirt and his bright hazel eyes. "Definitely not ugly."

"So you think he's hot?"

I sigh defeatedly down the phone. "He has those kind of ooey-gooey eyes and nice floppy hair, but a guy is the last thing I need to be focusing on right now."

I can practically feel her rolling her eyes over the phone. "Jess, you're meant to be an assistant right now. Why not live a little?"

"Because my focus is on getting Spencer through this; he seemed stressed about it on the plane. I don't want to just abandon him to go and flirt with some guy I'm never going to see again after this trip." My fingers fiddle at the zip for a few seconds before pulling it shut.

"And where is my new boss, Spencer? He hasn't posted anything on his Instagram story today. I was getting worried about him."

I sigh, clicking the speaker off. "He's on a complete social media ban while we're here, and he's hopefully behaving himself in his suite." I never wanted to plaster my name all over Wyst. Who knows what investors had heard about the Malcolm incident or not. It always felt safer to fly under the radar. So we made Spencer new profiles and populated them with some Wyst content just to make sure anyone googling would be pointed in the right direction, but it doesn't mean I'm going to give him free rein of them. "I'm going to pick him up in a second for the welcome drinks thing. Everything okay there?"

"Yeah, Pacha brought his daughter in today, and we taught him how to braid hair." I can practically hear the smile on her face. "We also got an email from Dr. Bernie's agent asking for a meeting about the collaboration. I've told them you are away on a *very* important business trip with Wyst investors and you will be back in a few days."

"Okay, well . . . I guess that's not the worst lie we've told this week."

"So true—listen I've got to go. Instructor Talia has arrived, and you get publicly shamed if you're late to your bike."

"All right, thanks for the update," I say.

Cecily sighs. "Just . . . make sure you don't spend the entire trip stressing, okay? You deserve a break. You've made it this far, nobody there knows who you are, and you should let your hair down for once."

My shoulders sag. "Maybe I'll have a drink at the hotel bar after the first round of the competition tomorrow."

"You go steady, girl! Okay got to go, kisses!"

The line clicks as Cecily hangs up, leaving me standing in front of the long skinny wardrobe mirror. My hair up in a French twist and makeup perfect for a day in court. I'm dressed like a CEO. I need to look like a casual but smart assistant, like Coffee Guy. He looked smart in a fitted shirt and trousers but not stuffy.

I pull my dark brown hair out of the claw clip, letting it dance over my shoulders and curve into curls at the ends. Finally, I swipe on some extra eyeliner and red lipstick for good measure, taking a picture in the mirror and sending it to Cecily with the caption "Hair? Down" before heading out the door.

Spencer's suite has simple meringue-cream walls with white moldings, antique dark wood furniture, and the biggest bed I've ever seen.

Two beautiful sparkling chandeliers hang from the fresco ceilings, painted with cloudy skies. The small balcony hosts a twisted cast iron seating area with puffy cream pillows, overlooking Rome. Tops of the basilica, metal crosses, and two gods on chariots adorn the purple, orange, and pink dusk skyline. For the first time since arriving, I realize I'm actually in Italy. It's like I've been on stress-induced autopilot since this morning . . . maybe since first receiving the invitation to come here.

My arms prickle with goose bumps from the cold evening air, listening to the sound of cars passing by below, doors opening and closing, and men in suits greeting one another as they step into the lobby. This feels like the start of something. Whether it's good or bad, I haven't decided yet.

CHAPTER 7

Business Account (WYST) BALANCE: £9,485.44
Personal Account BALANCE: -£1,986.62
Recent transactions:
Rome tourist tax: £17.12

From 9 a.m. the next morning, the hotel lobby is littered with men in suits. People have come from all over the world to take part in this competition. Some look like businessmen, gripping briefcases or delegating to a nodding gaggle of minions, while others seem more like journalists, gathering camera equipment or jotting things down on a notepad and sporadically looking back up to the person sermonizing about the benefits of AI integration. My chest tightens as I squeeze through the immovable crowd; this competition is going to be packed. As I emerge from the cloud of heavy cologne, I straighten my posture and adopt the "power walk" I saw on YouTube, hoping to give the air of someone who belongs here.

I stride past the front desk until I hear an "Excuse me, miss?"

My head turns back to see the same woman from yesterday waving at me from behind the concierge desk. "Could you come here, please?" she asks.

My stomach drops; maybe they are going to ask for my passport again. I can see it now—they either force me out of the hotel for refusing to hand over any identifying paperwork or they kick me out for being a fake.

"Helloooooooo." The word extends out my mouth like I'm pulling a piece of chewing gum.

"Good morning, I trust your stay has been enjoyable so far?" she asks with a sickly sweet smile across her face.

She knows. She definitely knows. I'm twelve hours in and have already been found out. Sweat runs down my back as I try to come up with any reasonable excuse that won't have further repercussions. I could tell her I lost my passport on the way from the airport to the hotel, but a fancy hotel like this would quite happily book a car to send me straight to the British embassy. I need to be here monitoring and managing Spencer instead of being on a wild goose chase for nonexistent identification.

"Yes, everything has been lovely. Thank you so much." I don't know why I'm thanking the woman who was rude to me at check-in, but politeness seems to be the best way to get away with this.

"Excellent, I have a delivery for you."

"What is it?" I ask cautiously.

She hands over a white dress bag with the hotel logo on a silver metal hanger. "Your dry cleaning."

"Oh, great, thank you." Relief flows over me, lowering my shoulders by several inches. Hopefully, she's forgotten about the passport.

"I have a note for you also." She flicks through a pile of papers on her desk until she finds a handwritten note and hands it to me.

*If you change your mind, I'd love to buy you an apology drink.
L'ultima Goccia 6 p.m.*

—Oliver

I feel my cheeks redden as I scan the note, a small thrill
bouncing in my stomach like a cat with a ball of yarn. Spencer
and I didn't stay for long, but my disappointment at the welcome drinks and competitor mixer last night had to be majorly
tamped down when I didn't see Oliver, formerly known as Coffee Guy, at the event. But something inside me warms at the
thought of him looking out for me too.

Suits on suits on suits glide into the auditorium like lem-
mings off a cliff. I slide backstage, getting prepped for Spencer's presentation. I slip on a blue Odericco-branded baseball
cap from Spencer's complimentary goody tote bag. I feel like I
need to be hiding my face, but no one here will even know my
face to misidentify. I'm completely anonymous. Unlike Spencer, who is sitting on the stage in a row of contestants in front
of a huge audience.

Despite my pessimism about this plan as a whole, I can't help
but imagine how this would all play out if we were successful.
If we were to win this competition and gain the backing of one
of the biggest investment companies in the tech industry. I was
never really the "face" of Wyst, but Pacha has done a great job
of scrubbing my presence from our website and Cecily has ed-
ited or deleted any relevant social media posts. It's like I never
existed. Will people forever see Spencer as the heart and soul
of Wyst? Will I ever be seen as the original creator? Would

anyone ever believe the truth if we came clean? Could a fledgling company survive a scandal like this?

From the side of the stage, I watch the lights in the auditorium change color, projecting green spotlights up the walls.
Dramatic music descends upon the spectacle, green lasers
flowing over the crowd and twisting into a formation around
the stage. A man with the sharpest suit and whitest teeth I have
ever seen steps into the spotlight; he must be the competition
presenter.

Out of the corner of my eye, I spot Dominic Odericco strid-
ing past me backstage, a gaggle of Odericco employees following behind.

"Where's okay?" he asks, voice booming.

"Somewhere around here, sir," a Brooks Brothers minion
replies, a sheen of sweat licking their brow.

Odericco looks around for something with a furrowed brow
as he straightens his collar and checks his shirt cuffs. Maybe
he's used to a nicer entrance than stepping over wires backstage. The other support crews for the competitors are scattered
around backstage, running around looking at clipboards and
whispering into phones. It feels like we're all putting on a play.
This is certainly a performance. I briefly thank my lucky stars I
have a real actor in the midst of this pantomime.

The presenter taps against the microphone, sending a static
whine-inducing feedback screech across the room. The crowd
groans as the sound bursts from the speakers. "Sorry, sorry!
Hello and welcome to Odericco Investments' TechRumble
Round One!" The crowd politely claps as their hearing returns
to normal. "Our first round of investor pitches is about to be-

gin. We encourage you all to photograph, film, and post all of our incredible competitors across social media; their handles and information are in the brochures under your seats along with . . ." He pauses for effect, pulling the microphone almost into his mouth. "Odericco Investments baseball caaaaaaps!" This gets the crowd going, with a few whooping at the free merchandise. Most of the men in this crowd are probably used to this kind of event, so it's not exactly exciting. They are here for the potential investment opportunities, not the branded clothing.

This is the main reason I wanted to be involved with TechRumble, the idea of getting Wyst in front of thousands of business people in the tech space. If we get knocked out of the competition today, there's a chance someone here will be interested in Wyst. Exposure is everything, but I know seeing images of Spencer in the position I always dreamed of being in will hurt more than I care to admit. But if I'm really honest with myself, I doubt I would ever have the courage to get on that stage.

"Now, without further ado," the presenter shouts, "please welcome the founder of TechRumble, Dominic Odericco!" The crowd roars as Odericco straightens his suit jacket lapels, rolls his neck, and steps out onto the stage.

"You good?" I ask into my wireless headphones from the edge of the stage.

"Mm-hmm!" Spencer hums, his mouth still shut to not draw attention to the beige wireless headphone in one of his ears, which is just covered by his fluffy hair. He glances over to where I'm standing and shoots me a quick smile.

"We can do this," I say more to myself than him.

He gives me a subtle nod in response as the crowd starts to die down.

After an hour of clenched buttocks, listening to group after group pitching their ideas, it's our turn. As we are the latest addition to the group of competitors, we are the last of the day to present. A good 50 percent of the crowd has already filtered out of the auditorium, which makes my shoulders sag with both relief and disappointment. Hopefully, the majority of the absent consists of company team members, off to celebrate or commiserate the success of their endeavors, instead of the smaller investors and journalists.

"To finish things off for the day, we have a debut contender, representing the FemTech space. Presenting for Wyst, Spencer Cole." A considerably less enthusiastic reception than the screams for the baseball-caps flitters around the auditorium.

Spencer steps into the spotlight, taking in the audience. He clears his throat, and it's like he flips a switch. His shoulders straighten, chest broadens, and chin lifts. I can't find a trace of the nerves I could see in his eyes earlier.

"Hello. My name is Spencer Cole. I am the founder and CEO of Wyst, and I'm here to tell you a story."

He takes a breath, then clicks the remote in his hand, and I throw to the first slide in my binder. We rehearsed this part to death over the past few days, but every muscle in my body is tense as Spencer heads into the presentation.

"This is Charlotte; she's sixteen years old." He gestures to a picture of a young girl with flowing chestnut-brown hair. "Her peers have all had 'the talk' from their parents, but Charlotte lives in a strict Catholic household. She has no access to sex education beyond what she was taught in one class when she was twelve by her school's embarrassed PE teacher."

He clicks to another slide. "This is Janice. Janice is worried because her child has come out as nonbinary, and she has no idea how to connect with them and support them through their journey of self-discovery."

I quickly scan the crowd; most are politely paying attention, but a few are typing away on their phones as Spencer continues. "This is Florence; she is struggling with her mental health at university, but the wait list for free student counseling is months long." Spencer injects a moment of seemingly genuine emotion into his voice. Wow, he's really good at this.

"What all these people have in common is they need help, support, and a safe community. This is what we are providing at Wyst. A new kind of social media platform run by professionals in their field."

He approaches the edge of the stage, no longer flicking through the slides. "Charlotte can talk to medical professionals, anonymously asking the questions she's too scared to ask anyone else. Unlike searching Wild West forums like Reddit and Quora, information on Wyst is asked for by the community, but provided by leaders in their fields. Janice can talk to LGBTQ+ mentors about how to foster a positive communication style with her child. Florence can get immediate access to mental health specialists and be set up with the help she needs. This is what we are providing through Wyst. Peace of mind that there will always be someone to talk to."

These users are made up to protect the anonymity of the users, but also to sell something like this to a room full of men, who for some reason need to think of women as their mothers, sisters, and daughters to actually give a shit about them. Even with these stories, I can tell the audience is less interested than when the presentation started.

Despite the reduced attention span of the audience, Spencer is killing this. He's doing better than I ever could. He belongs on the stage, regardless of whether it's Shakespeare or business jargon.

Just as he reaches his conclusion statement, the five-minute pitch timer goes off.

"And that's your time. Thank you, Wyst!" the presenter says off to the side. "We'll now move on to the Q and A with our panel of judges."

The audience claps as the panel sits on plush red chairs in a semicircle on the stage.

Spencer talks quietly behind gritted teeth, barely moving his lips. "I think I started to lose them at the end."

Not wanting to derail his confidence, I lie. "No, you had them eating out of your hand. You smashed it. Final hurdle now, you've got this. Just repeat after me." We rehearsed a few standard questions I thought might be asked, but quickly came to the realization we needed me to do the thinking and Spencer the talking to avoid any inconsistencies in his answers.

A short American man wearing an untailored suit goes straight in with the questioning. "What's the difference between Wyst and the current market of therapy apps?"

I say the answer down the phone line as Spencer repeats it word for word. "This is not a one-to-one therapy app or a platform to talk to a well-trained chat bot. Think of this as a directory. A community-built, professional-managed social platform. We intend to hire more and more vetted profession-

RISKY BUSINESS 77

als to expand our unified reach; we aim to become a premier entry point for all FemTech B2C businesses."

The man nods, semi-interested in the response.

"Thanks, Spencer," the host says. "Dominic, would you like to ask a question?"

Dominic crosses his legs. "How do you plan to expand your content? How big is that delta?"

Spencer's eyes flash wide; he has no idea what that means. I barely know what that means, but luckily, thanks to my time at Graystone, I'm partially fluent in bullshit.

"We plan to scale up and expand our pages to cover a range of topics affecting women, while launching in as many territories as possible," I say down the phone.

"We plan to scale up and expand our pages, while simultaneously launching in different countries and languages." Spencer pauses for a second, assessing the crowd. His shoulders relax as he adds, "We also intend to launch a full-scale multimedia platform."

My entire body freezes as the crowd murmurs approvingly. Some finally looking up from their phones. My fingers scramble through my folder. "Spence? That is not on the fucking cue cards." The folder slips out of my sweaty hands and clatters on the floor. My thighs tense when I bend down, my knees pressing against the cold vinyl flooring as I gather the loose white papers scattered like petals.

I watch from the ground as he steps closer to the edge of the stage toward to the crowd. "We will have video content and podcasts hosted by a wide range of celebrities and professionals."

"What the fuck are you doing?" I say in a strained voice, tapping my finger against the headphone. "Can you not hear me?"

My vision locks on the screen above the stage, Spencer's beaming smile and dilating pupils projected for all to see. He isn't panicking; if he can't hear me, why isn't he panicking? Maybe he's been disconnected and is winging it.

Another judge asks, "What's the go-to-market motion here? How do you find people with this specific pain point and how do you convert them into users?"

I pull a headphone out of my ear, bring it close to my mouth, and say slowly, "Through content marketing, affiliate programs, high-end influencer marketing, highly selective brand collaborations."

Spencer's words match mine, but he paraphrases slightly. My brow furrows; so he isn't winging it—he's just going off piste because he feels like it.

The only woman on the panel of six clears her throat. "Obviously, if you don't mind me saying, you are a man. What jurisdiction do you have in the FemTech space?"

Spencer sighs and puts his hands in a prayer position against his lips, before bringing them down to gesture to the panelist. "I am passionate about women. I believe that all women and girls should be educated and autonomous with their own bodies. By creating this company, we are putting the power in their hands. Ultimately, it doesn't matter who I am—what matters is our users and community."

I roll my eyes as raucous applause flies from the audience, and I watch on the big screen as Spencer's irises turn liquid black.

He shoots a wide grin at the crowd. "In fact, I've been an advocate of feminism for years, before it became the mainstream thing endorsed by celebrities. And with my idea, we can bring feminism into the future."

Oh my god, what does that even mean? I scan the crowd; it's a sea of men, and they are eating this up. If it were women in the audience, they'd see right through this embarrassing display of pseudo-support. But these men haven't had a lifetime of figuring out if a man is an actual feminist or whether they are just saying things to get what they want. And what man in the crowd, in the face of all his colleagues and industry leaders, would denounce supporting women?

The applause continues. Spencer clasps his hands together and lowers his head toward the ground. Spencer fucking *bows*. My hands shake with frustration as I pick up the remaining few pieces of paper off the floor.

A cocktail of emotion roils in my chest; I'm glad this is going well, but he's making promises I can't keep. He's making a mockery of my plan. My heartbeat races, bouncing around my rib cage like a knocked-over basket of tennis balls. This is my fault. Why did I do this? Why did I let him go out there? Why did I risk everything for this? If this doesn't work, it will all be for nothing. The bad thing will all be for nothing.

If a woman got up and said they support women's rights, nobody in this room would give a shit. Because it's a man, all of a sudden "giving women the same respect and access as men" makes him look like the Second Coming. My head pounds and spins at the same time, like a snow globe full of needles.

An energetic murmur settles among the crowd as Spencer returns to his seat on the stage.

My hands shake as my phone begins to vibrate aggressively.

Social media notifications catapult across the screen. Over one hundred mentions from accounts and publications covering the event. Shit, is the competition live streamed? Spencer went off script and it was recorded in 4K. My throat goes tight, an invisible hand cutting off my air supply until I see dark spots.

I know we're lying, but now he's straight up LYING.

I shrink into the edges of the side stage until I'm shrouded in darkness, the constant flashing light from my phone screen making me even dizzier. My back presses against the cold concrete wall, and I slide down until I hit the floor; my heavy head hangs in between my legs as I try to breathe slowly.

Punctuating the ringing in my ears, I hear footsteps approaching me.

"Are you okay, miss?" An Italian man places his hand on my back, making me jolt upright.

"What?" I ask, my voice slow and cracking.

"Are you all right?"

Wiping the tears lingering on my lash line, I squeak out, "Yeah, I'm fine." My head whips around, looking for the fire exit. My hands move over the walls, searching for some sort of door, until I find a crease and push the door open.

Once I'm outside at the back of the concrete parking lot, my breathing sharpens, trying desperately to get air beyond the barrier in my throat into my lungs. After a few minutes crouched in the corner, my body and brain start to calm down.

The panic and urgency curdle into outrage. I've spent the past few days worrying so much about whether Spencer will be okay. I never thought to worry about if he would deliberately fuck everything up. Why would he go rogue like that? He has no reason other than humiliating me and sabotaging the company to make himself the star. When we were children, he used to push me out of the way so he could have all the attention, and he's still doing it. Except this time, he put my company, my entire life on the line.

My loafers slap against the patterned carpet as I stride back through the hotel. I would go back to my room, but I need to pace. In fact, I need to get out of here. Before I can think twice, I'm out the door, walking down the darkened street. The sounds of cars and people chatting and laughing settle on my chest as my warm anger breathes out of me, immediately neutralizing against the chilled evening air. It's 6 p.m. and the sun has just set, but as Italians don't eat early, most restaurants are still empty. The quiet is a welcome reprieve from the competition.

My feet stomp down the road for a few minutes until I realize I have no idea where I'm going. I slide my cold hand into my coat pocket and feel a crinkle against my phone. Pulling out the note from Oliver, I open Google Maps and look up the bar written in scratchy handwriting. It's an eight-minute walk away.

You know what? Fuck Spencer and fuck this. Cecily was right; I deserve a break.

CHAPTER 8

Business Account (WYST) BALANCE: £9,485.44
Personal Account BALANCE: -£1,986.62

The windows of L'ultima Goccia glow in shades of red and yellow, the flicker of candlelight a stark contrast to the bright tubular fluorescent fixtures and sharp green spotlights of the auditorium. It looks cozy, the comforting bursts of laughter and song spilling onto the street, easing the tension in my chest within seconds.

I just want to sit in silence and have a drink, maybe some meat and cheese.

The creaking wooden door is barely audible over the raucous noise filling every corner and crack of the battered brick walls. My eyes snag on a couple of empty seats at the edge of the bar. I take the farthest one on the right-hand side, where the bar top starts to curve along the edge.

Pretending to respond to emails on my phone, I watch red baskets lined with yesterday's newspaper appear from the swinging kitchen door, fried calamari piled high. As a plate of burrata, carpaccio, and grilled eggplant makes its way to a table, a tall figure fills my periphery.

"You made it." His low timbre coats the seething anxiety flowing through my veins.

I turn my chair on the swivel, laying my phone face down on the bar and cocking my head to the side. "Disappointed?"

Oliver stifles a smile, chin lowering to meet my eyeline. "Far from it, I was hoping you'd show." His fingers pinch the sides of a sweating glass.

I balance on an elbow, glancing at the drink. "So you can throw a beer on me and finish the job?"

"How about I just buy you one instead?" He gestures to the empty seat beside me, and I nod, rolling my eyes and crossing my legs. He doesn't hold himself with the same buzzing energy most in this room do, like they are desperate to impress their bosses and one another. He has a commanding presence, a mixture of laid-back and authoritative that I can't quite get a handle on.

He settles into the chair and leans his forearms onto the bar, his shoulder muscles tensing under the crisp white shirt. I feel a quiet thrill in his company, like an echo of adrenaline.

His chin shifts to me, the tea lights in red jars on the bar casting his cheekbones in a devilish glow. "What made you decide to come?"

I shrug, glancing awkwardly from him to the shelf of bottles with brightly colored Italian labels. "I was having a mental breakdown in the area so thought it would be rude not to."

He huffs a laugh, hazel eyes twinkling. "Bad day?" The words roll off his tongue so smoothly that I imagine he was a cigarette-lighting bartender in another life.

I contemplate lying, but something about him is making me want to tell him the truth, to drop the pretenses. I lean my elbow on the bar, resting my chin in my palm. "Bad year."

He whistles, almost impressed. "We better make it a double then." He gestures to the bartender with two fingers.

I shake my head, the background noise returning to the room with a pop as I come out of the minor trance. "You don't need to buy me a drink."

He shoots me a fake-appalled look. "Listen, I'm just trying my best to charm you over from the actively disliking me camp to a more neutral zone. I owe you at least one." He holds up a shiny black credit card. "Besides, this is my boss's card." He hits me with another winning smile.

"Oh, well, in that case, I'll have a Negroni." I sit back, relaxing into the chair. "How come your boss lets you run amok with his credit card?"

He taps the short edge of the plastic on the wooden bar. "Because I'm the only one who knows how to get his coffee order right, and knowledge is power."

"The keys to the caffeinated castle," I add with a nod.

He points at me with the shiny card. "Exactly."

"If only you could deliver them in one piece," I add, brow arched.

"Well, then I'd be running the whole company, and nobody wants that." He turns to the bartender as they approach. *"Due Negroni, per favore."*

"He knows coffee and Italian?"

Oliver lets out a breathy laugh before running a hand through his hair and lowering his eyes. "Exclusively fluent in food and drinks."

"Negroni, margherita, risotto, pasta alla vodka, gelato!" I count on my fingers before shifting into jazz hands.

"Fast learner!" He gives me a light applause as I bow my head cartoonishly.

A blond man with navy suit trousers and a light blue shirt half undone approaches us and slaps him on the back. "Hey, man. Has he gone to dinner?" Another American, this one with more of a Southern twang.

"Yeah, I'm off for the night. This is . . ." He squints at me curiously. "You actually never told me your name."

"I'm Je"—*fuck*—"uuust Violet," I stutter. "Just Violet." Shit. *Violet, Violet, Violet.*

"Hello, Violet, I'm *just* David." The man holds out his right hand for me to shake.

"I'm guessing you already read my note but . . . Oliver." My drinking buddy holds out his left hand. I use my free hand to meet his, a jolt shooting up my arm as his fingers grip firm but soft against my palm.

I crack a wide smile as they both continue to shake my hands and our drinks are placed on the wooden bar in front of us. I lean down to the bar and take the little red straw in my mouth.

The cool air hits my palms as they release my hands, laughing.

"So are you an assistant too?" David asks.

I take a large sip of my Negroni. "Mmm-hmm." I nod. If I don't say anything, it feels slightly less like lying.

"Great, that means she qualifies," he says to Oliver.

"Qualifies for what?" I ask.

Oliver sighs, reluctant to clarify. "Pong Rumble."

I give him a look before he retorts, "It's a working title."

David takes another sip of his drink before explaining. "Every year at TechRumble, the assistants and interns have a beer pong tournament on the first night of the competition. But there is limited beer in this place, so it's usually the cheapest, nastiest aperitif spirits they have behind the bar. We all put money in the pot and the winning team have their drinks paid for the rest of the competition."

My eyes grow wide. "Oh, shit, that's a good prize."

David continues, even more exuberant now as he slaps Oliver on the shoulder. "And his teammate just went back to the hotel with a bad case of jet lag, so he's gonna miss out if he doesn't find a new partner."

Oliver wipes his hand over his mouth. "I should have warned you; you don't have to if you're just here to chill."

"But your team will be disqualified if you don't find a partner in the next . . ." David looks at his watch with the face of a father whose son is about to miss a qualifying game. "Ten minutes."

Oliver turns in his chair to David. "She's had a rough da—"

"No, I'll do it." I look between the two of them, my preternatural urge to prove myself useful kicking into high gear.

Five minutes later, we move to a back room of the bar, where more young people are half dressed in business attire. Blazers are thrown in a pile on a wooden chair, ties shoved into trouser pockets, and shirt collars unbuttoned like the last hour of a wedding. The space is tight, and we have to shuffle along the walls like cat burglars circumventing laser beams to avoid knocking into the scuffed Ping-Pong table occupying most of the room's square footage.

"Have you played before?" Oliver asks as we make it to the end of the table, holding up an old, dusty Ping-Pong ball with a small dent in the side with two fingers.

Having attended a business school with a high percentage of

international students, beer pong was the universal language. If the students have never played it, they've at least seen it in a movie. Also, the rules are pretty easy to pick up when there's just two: throw ball, drink.

I pluck the ball from his hand and throw it across the table. It's a slam dunk into the middle of a cup, and the chorus of cheers urges our opponent to down their drink.

Oliver coughs out a laugh as I smile sweetly. "I think the more pertinent question is can you keep up?"

He stares me down. "So you're . . . good?"

Our competitor, an Italian man whose baby face is so prominent he could be two children in a trench coat, throws his ball toward our cups, missing every single one.

I look up at Oliver, trying to hold in a satisfied smile as I place the ball back in his hand. "And competitive, don't let me down."

He grins, briefly glancing at my mouth, then back to my serious stare. "Yes, ma'am."

His neck muscles shift as he limbers up, eyes darkening as he locks onto his target of the central cup. The crowd cheers again, and I awkwardly high-five him as a wave of relief visibly washes over him. Is he scared of not impressing me?

I'm too busy catching his eye to notice the competitor's ball slamming into one of our cups so hard it wobbles in place. As I go to pick up the cup, Oliver's hand meets me there and pulls it toward his mouth. His eyes glimmer as he knocks it back and winces. I can't help but laugh at his face cringing at the sharp liquor as he says, "Thank me later."

It comes out as a joke, just a phrase you say after doing someone a favor, but the way my body reacts, you'd think he just told me he wants to push me up against the dusty wall behind us. It dawns on me that for once I'm not thinking about Wyst. Not thinking about my past or money or the people relying on me to keep it together. All I'm thinking about is getting a ball in a cup and the humming in my blood as Oliver's hand playfully squeezes my shoulders and he whispers tactics in my ear like a coach hyping up an athlete.

We play for another two rounds before we're defeated in the semifinals and pour back into the main room of the bar. I'm greeted by spectators and invited to join a group of Italians and Brits. We sit in a bundle in the corner, talking, laughing, and sharing stories of horrible bosses. But the majority of my brain cells are taken up by monitoring where my doubles partner's attention lies. Maybe I'm overthinking it, but it seems like he's slowly gravitating toward me. Why am I even focusing on him? Sure, he invited me here but not like as his date or anything. This is a casual hang between assistants.

He double cheek kisses a woman before making his way over to me. I study him, and I know I'm not the only person in the bar doing so. He's the kind of handsome that makes you look twice, once for evaluation and once for indulgence. The slope of his nose pulling focus toward his warm hazel eyes, framed by the depth of his brow, his full lips encasing a wide infectious smile—it's all mesmerizing. I've seen lots of pretty men, but the way he holds himself in complete comfort without managing to look like a cocky bastard is rare. My skin tingles as he strides over to our group, and instead of taking the empty seat on the opposite side, he drags an empty chair from another table and places it next to me. The gesture makes me blush like a teenager.

RISKY BUSINESS   89

As I'm listening to a group debate the difference between Aperol and Campari, I overhear David ask Oliver, "You're coming with later?"

Oliver glances briefly at me, but I pretend not to notice, remaining hyper-focused on my drink.

He shrugs, a slight tug at the side of his lip. "Maybe, I'll see how I feel."

"Sure, brother. Have a good night." I give David a tight smile as he nods goodbye to us both.

Oliver turns back to me.

"He seems nice."

"He's a good guy. Works too hard, though."

"Do all the Americans form an alliance at these things?"

Oliver laughs into his glass as it balances on his bottom lip. "Yes, and if it gets too British, we naturally have to throw you all in the river. Where in the UK are you from?"

"London. Well, born and raised just outside of London, but it's a place nobody's ever heard of."

"Try me," he dares.

"Welwyn Garden?"

"Never heard of it." He smiles, leaning back against the wooden back of his chair, his elbow resting against it. "Sounds nice, though. Maybe I'll go when I get back."

The bitter liquid catches like a hook in my throat. "You live in London?"

He laughs. "Yeah, couldn't you tell? My accent is fucked now. I say 'quite' and 'a bit' more than any American ever has; my siblings take the mick all the time." He goes to sip but stops. "There's another one."

"How do you like living in London?" I ask, feeling more

sheepish now for some reason. Like the conversational stakes have risen knowing we share smog.

"It's great. I love the walkability, the restaurant culture, and it's nice to experience the seasons. But it drives me crazy whenever all you Brits have a single pint and say my name. *Olly Olly Olly, Oi Oi Oi!*"

I snort a laugh. "Oh, I'm about to break out into song any second now."

He holds in a smile. "I knew there was a reason I threw coffee on you."

I take a long breath before bringing the subject back to him. "So what else does your job in London entail, besides coffee orders?"

He opens his mouth, closes it, licks his lips, and says, "I don't want to be rude, but as interesting as filing, printing, and Microsoft Excelling is, I'd love to not talk about work right now. It's been a long day of talking to so many assholes." He emphasizes the last three words.

"Assholes are chatty?" I furrow my brow.

"Believe it or not, even more than mouths. But please, I'm even happy to sit here in silence"—Oliver hangs his head dramatically—"just *anything* but work."

I purse my lips, my shoulders sagging with relief that I don't have to lie. I drag my straw around the edges of the glass in silence for a few seconds. Finally, I ask, "What's your stance on Aperol Spritz during the winter months?"

He considers, his thick brows furrowing. "Far right." He twists his chair toward mine. "What do you do for fun, Violet?"

I consider, staring at the bottom of my glass. "I think . . . nothing?"

"You don't do *anything* for fun?" His hazel eyes pick up flickers of the candlelight.

I jut my chin out towards the beer pong table. "This is the most fun I've had in a while. I think I only do things for money or glory," I half joke.

He tilts his head in question, eyes glittering. "Want to carry on the fun?"

I scrunch my eyebrows, scanning him up and down.

"Not in a creepy way—there's, like, twenty of us sneaking into the executive hotel pool when they throw us out of here."

I pause, swishing the final lick of liquid in the glass before knocking it back.

My finger taps against the glass. "Buy me one more drink, and I'll consider it."

FORTY-FIVE MINUTES LATER, the alcohol blanket keeps me warm as we walk back to the hotel. Oliver and I hang back from the gang of Americans, British, Italians, and three Dutch people we've collected along the way as they sing down the road.

"Olly Olly Olly!" one of the British guys shouts over his shoulder as he approaches the automatic doors at the front of the hotel.

"Oi oi oi!" I shout in unison with the rest of the group.

He cuts a side glance at me. "Told you."

I nod solemnly. "It's a disease."

"Your coat looks good by the way; did dry cleaning get all the stains out?"

"Yeah, thanks for sorting that. How did the front desk know it was for me?"

He leans into my side. "I told them it belonged to the pretty brunette who got decimated by several cups of coffee in the lobby yesterday."

"Oh god." I cup my face in my hands, partially to hide the embarrassment of the scene but also to cover my blushing cheeks at being referred to as pretty. It's not that I think it's a lie. I like the way I look. I just don't usually like the way I'm being perceived. But something about the casualness of his compliment, like to him it's just a scientific fact, makes my skin tingle.

Sneaking through the hotel, I glance at my phone. Still no messages or calls from Spencer; that little wuss is too scared to come face me after what he did.

We pile into the fancy elevator, a thrill tingling around my body as I'm briefly packed against him at the front of the crowd. "You're, like, King of the Assistants," I assess as we exit on the pool and spa floor.

He leans down toward my ear, his voice lowering as he deadpans, "A responsibility I take *very* seriously."

When we exit on the spa floor, he unlocks a door with a key card that looks a lot more like Spencer's than my third-floor one.

As the final person goes through, I raise an eyebrow, "King of Thieves too?"

He shrugs, hazel eyes twinkling. "Whichever the Queen of Beer Pong wants me to be." His lips curl as he uses his broad shoulder to hold open the door.

My stomach does a flip, but I roll my eyes, sliding through the door and brushing past his large frame. This close to him, his peppery scent mixes with a wash of chlorine air emanating from the pool.

This pool isn't just a pool; it's a full-on spa. One you could imagine diplomats and First Ladies frequenting. The steps down to the water open like a *grande maison* staircase. Greek columns line the edges, circling around a Jacuzzi at the very end of the pool. The walk down can only be described as a promenade. I glance into the water to see a Medusa-esque face in the mosaic floor shimmering under the surface.

The two Italians pull out their backpacks, handing out miniature bottles of liquor, presumably from their boss's minibar, as well as beer and wine from the local co-op. Everyone throws off their clothes, removing silk shirts and trousers until they're laid bare in matching underwear sets and Calvin Klein boxer shorts. I flinch, my body rapidly coating in sweat.

"Come on!" a man shouts to the crowd as they slide into the water.

My arms slink around my body, pinching the fabric on my forearms to check it's still there as my chest begins to heave.

What if someone takes a photo of me?

"Coming in, Oliver?" A pretty redhead blinks, perky breasts in a white lace bralette bobbing just above the water like two little ice caps. My eyes fix on her. Does she know everyone has their phones out? Strangers? She notices me watching her and gives me a suspicious look. My chest collapses inward.

Oliver glances to me, then at the striped forest-green and cream pool loungers. "I'm good. Think I'll chill here for a while." Bringing his eyes back to mine, he gestures to the loungers while clasping two small bottles of red wine in his hand. "Wanna join me for some luxury living?"

I scan him suspiciously. Does he sense my hesitancy? His face doesn't give it away, but my stress begins to thaw regardless.

I force a word out of my mouth—"Sure"—urging my tense body to move.

We sink into the loungers, flicking back and forth between chatting and flirting as we watch everyone else frolic in the pool. A man ducks under the water, launching a woman into the air on his shoulders.

"Thanks," I breathe out, as he unscrews one of the bottles before passing it to me.

"You know, I think TechRumble is going to be the end of your bad year," Oliver surmises as he takes a long swig.

I take it, our fingers lightly grazing as I grasp the bottle. "What makes you think that?"

"You've got *it*."

I glug the wine before mimicking him. "*It?*" The booze goes immediately to my legs.

"Ya know, you've got, like, fire in your eyes. Not everyone has that in places like this; they just want to make as much money as possible and then sell at the highest price before moving on to the next thing."

I make a "hmmm" sound, not meeting his eye. My shoes clatter to the ground as I kick them off.

He leans forward, eyes scrunching ever so slightly. "You don't agree?"

I throw an arm behind my head and close my eyes for a second, considering while squealing and splashing echoes around us. Oliver doesn't say anything, just watches as I open and close my mouth, stopping and starting what I feel like getting off my chest.

I open one eye. "This doesn't leave the pool?"

He puts up three fingers. "Scout's honor."

"I had an idea, a good idea, I think. Anyway, I'm not getting the recognition for it, and it's pissing me off." I let out a breath, feeling the weight of relief washing off me and sliding down the pool grates.

His shoulders shift. "Someone is taking credit for your idea?"

"Well, kind of. They are the better person to showcase it in the industry, but they don't actually care about it."

"So is your passion about the idea or getting credit for it?"

My brows lance together as I part my lips in retort. Before I can say anything, our eyes catch on someone bashing on the locked door. David jumps out of the pool and opens it, leans in to talk to the person, and then turns back toward the pool.

He swivels his head around to the rest of us. "Security is coming!"

Everyone in the pool frantically swims toward the steps, grabbing from a pyramid of rolled-up towels stacked like firewood and running into the changing rooms.

Oliver grunts as he leans upright. "We better go. If they find us, we'll get thrown out of the hotel." He says it so casually like it's more of an inconvenience than anything.

My eyes widen in disbelief. "What? You didn't think of mentioning that when we got here? I can't get chucked out."

"We'd better get a move on then." The Britishisms sound even weirder with his accent.

We grab the empty bottles and pace toward the door, but when we get to the door handle, Oliver backs up and reaches out for me behind him. Before I have a chance to think, I grab onto his hand, his warm fingers curling around mine.

He whispers, "Without sounding like a Scooby-Doo character, we've got company."

The fluorescent lights flick on in the corridor on the other side of the door, the light making me squint as we both step back.

"Everybody put your clothes on and get out," a booming Italian voice echoes out from the changing room, followed by light whines, protests, and feet shuffling en masse.

"Shit. I can't get kicked out," I whisper, squeezing his hand.

"Then we have to hide," he says.

My head spins around the spa until my gaze drops to the Jacuzzi circled by large Greek columns. Without a word, I drop our bottles and my phone and gun it for the tub, pulling Oliver behind me as I carefully step in. I've been in a body of water fully clothed and shoed, and I hope to never again, but this hiding spot feels like a no-brainer; it's shrouded in darkness, so they'll think they've caught everyone already.

My clothes bulge with air as I become submerged up to my chin, gesturing for Oliver to get in too. The Jacuzzi is right at the very end of the pool area, and with my back to the columns, we can't be seen by security if they don't explore the entire space.

His face contorts in confusion as he joins me under the rippling surface. "I thought you didn't like water? Or couldn't swim or something."

"No, I just didn't feel like taking my clothes off in front of a group of colleagues," I snap. As a whisper, it sounds incredibly sarcastic, but before the security guard gets here, we don't have time for me to explain how I'm not judging everyone else's choices, just living with the regret of my own.

He flattens out my inflated shoulders, the touch making me

shiver despite the hundred-degree temperature of the hot tub. "If it's any consolation, the Michelin Man look suits you," he murmurs.

The security guard's footsteps get closer and closer, the sound like a ticking clock as he rhythmically scans the area. My fist forms around Oliver's shirt, pulling him out of view and next to me at the edge. His eyes flare when his side bashes into mine. He floats closer to me, the water rippling and hiding most of my body with his. We both duck down, mouths just above the water as though the clear liquid will camouflage us. The light skims over the floor above, just narrowly missing the tops of our heads. Oliver rests his head over my shoulder and I turn my face toward him, hoping the cover from his dark hair will shade my features even further than the shadows.

As the footsteps get slower and closer, a cold shot of adrenaline courses through me. My chest heaves again, this time for a different reason. My mind runs through all the consequences of getting caught, but the potential scenario that blares loudest is getting kicked out of the competition. All of this for nothing.

Two flashlights chase each other over the tiles, showcasing parts of the room in a violent white light. I swallow, my heartbeat pounding so hard I'm shocked it doesn't make ripples in the water. We stay completely still, only my occasional held and caught breath punctuating the silence.

A quiet buzzing sounds from the pool loungers where we were just sat. My body atrophies as I realize it's my phone. The two men turn their lights away from the edges of the hot tub toward the loungers.

Oliver whispers into my ear, "Try to breathe normally," the warmth of his mouth a calm compress against my anxiety.

"I am," I whisper; my pulse runs with a mixture of icy fear and sweating desire. "And this isn't some professional crusade."

"What?" he mouths, barely a sound coming out over the echo of their footsteps and the continuous muffled vibration from my phone. I wonder for a second if it's Spencer calling to apologize.

"What you said over there." I glance in the direction of the illuminated loungers. "I'm not out to get credit; I just want to do things the right way." He stares at me, almost impressed that I can manage a stressful situation and still have a bone to pick with him.

Finally, my phone stops ringing, plunging all four of us into a humming silence.

"Do you mean *your* way?" he asks into my ear; I can hear the fucking smirk on his lips. "Ever heard of a compromise? We all have to do things we don't want to do."

My eyebrows meet in the middle. I want to ask what he means, but before I have a chance to, my whole body jolts as the sound of a walkie-talkie's static blasts through the air. The water sloshing around us, I press in closer, his taut body holding me steady.

"*Tutto okay?*" a crackling voice asks down the line.

"*Va tutto bene,*" the man standing just feet from our floating foreheads confirms as his footsteps slowly dissipate toward the door. Waiting until the door clicks shut, Oliver lets out a breath, then huffs a laugh, lifting his head so we're face-to-face.

He runs a wet hand over his face, then through his hair, and I don't know if it's the wine or the adrenaline or this day or his full lips, but I'm worryingly close to making out with this man in a hot tub.

"You okay?" he asks, inspecting my face.

"Yeah," I say breathily, "just a bit wired."

"I know how we can work all this adrenaline off." He wiggles his eyebrows.

"Seriously?" I say, rolling my eyes as an electric thrill chases the blood pumping at top speed around my body. The feeling marbleizes in my chest.

"I feel like it would do you a world of good." He steps forward toward me, then sinks into the water until fully submerged. After a few seconds, I hear a muffled shout under the surface, bubbles appearing on the surface.

I laugh, close my eyes, go under, and scream. Letting everything from the past couple of days out into the warm abyss.

Eventually, we both come up for air. My mind is empty of stress, like a fresh lump of clay ready to mold to whatever comes next. Panting and laughing, which quickly disintegrates into shallow breaths and held stares. The way he's looking at me turns my blood into strawberry jam.

Maybe I'm riding the high of not getting caught, but before I can think of a reason not to, I tug his wet shirt toward me and kiss him. I'm unsure of anything as his hand runs up the back of my neck to pull me in closer.

The kiss grows deeper, rougher, and more wanting than exploratory as I urge him closer. Our tongues graze, tasting the sweet, bitter red wine and Negroni that fueled us at full velocity toward this situation. A soft moan releases from my chest when his fingers grip my hair a little tighter until I come up on tiptoes to meet him. He nudges his thigh between mine and eases me against the edge of the hot tub. The cold tile above the surface at odds with the heat of the water surrounding us.

His erection presses against my thigh, water dripping from his hands as he runs his thumb over my cheek. He pulls back, surveying my body like I'm fucking edible.

My head spins as I try to catch my breath under his dark gaze. I know I should stop, but Cecily's words ring in my ear: I need a break, I need a night off from myself, I need fun.

My voice comes out low, soft, and breathless. "Wanna get out of here?"

CHAPTER 9

Business Account (WYST) BALANCE: £9,485.44
Personal Account BALANCE: -£2,000.60
Recent transactions:
L'ultima Goccia: £13.98

We sneak through the men's changing room toward the elevator, leaving a trail of pool water behind us like breadcrumbs. The air-conditioning is blasting throughout the hotel, keeping the temperature at a neutral sixty-six degrees. Since checking in, I haven't noticed this at all. But now, soaking wet in this morning's clothes, my whole body starts to shiver. The bell dings at our floor, and, once checking the coast is clear, Oliver takes my hand, leading me into his hotel room down a familiar hallway. Twenty-four hours ago, the idea of sneaking around with someone seemed unfathomable, but now it's like the universe knew this is exactly what I needed.

His hand loops around my waist as we step through the door with our clothes squelching. I'm freezing cold, but the desire to have him all over me again feels like a bonfire that's raging a little too hard for comfort. The contrast has goose bumps skirting across my skin. He turns the lights on, revealing his room. It's slightly nicer than mine but not as neat. His clothes are still bundled in a suitcase, whereas mine are all hung up in the wardrobe. Some of his towels are draped over the bathroom door to dry, whereas mine are arranged neatly in a pile by the sink. His bed is rumpled, like he was lying on top of it earlier, whereas mine looks like the maid already came for turndown service.

Things were already getting heavy in the hot tub, but this feels new, like the stakes are higher now we are somewhere private. Somewhere there won't be a flashlight shone in our eyes at any second, nothing to stop us.

"Sure you're okay with this?" Oliver asks, his eyes dark as he searches my expression for any sign of hesitancy.

It's like Cecily said, I just need to let my hair down for one night.

I nod, lifting my chin back up to kiss him.

His large hand takes the side of my face and eases me against the door, our wet clothes dripping onto the carpet in rhythmic thuds. He leans in to place his mouth on mine, but I rest a hand on his warm chest. "We need to take our clothes off."

Looking sheepishly at the floor, Oliver's hazel eyes eventually flick back to meet mine. "Okay, sure. Whatever you wanna do."

I stumble over my words. "I—I don't mean like that; we're both soaking. We're going to die of hypothermia."

"Well, if it's a matter of life and death." He smiles wide. "Come with me."

I try to contain a blush as he leads me into the marble bathroom. His is bigger than mine, with a freestanding tub and a walk-in shower with dual showerheads on opposing sides of the wall. He takes me by the hand and stands me just shy of the shower, holding out his free hand and running the water until it's a warm temperature. My heart pounds, watching his back muscles shift under his shirt as he adjusts the showerhead.

My rigid shoulders ease the moment I step into the warm water's path. Letting it seep into my shirt until the painful cold melts away. I try to focus my eyes on anywhere but him as he steps into the opposing stream of water and sighs, running his hands through his hair and undoing his shirt one torturous button at a time.

Despite the water, my mouth goes bone-dry when he turns his back and slides his shirt off, exposing the tanned muscles underneath. His hair looks darker under the soft shower lights, messy and undone compared to the more work-appropriate look it's usually styled into. I try to breathe normally, but my heartbeat has reached the back of my throat, blocking off regular air supply.

Okay, you haven't taken any of your clothes off. You could step out of the shower, go back to your room a few doors down, and never see him again.

Maybe that's the excitement, knowing we are in another country and I'm never going to see him again. That he doesn't even know my real name, his phone is somewhere in his room. The door is shut, no cameras. In here, I'm safe from scrutiny, from consequences. Little did Oliver know, this is the perfect place for me to feel comfortable. I close my eyes and run the steaming water through my hair, triggering goose bumps to run wild over my body. When I open them again, I find him staring at me. His eyes flick up from my chest to my face without a word. I glance down, my nipples hard against the wet cotton of my shirt. A thrill runs up my spine, following the path of fire his eyes made on my body.

Slowly, with trembling fingers, I start to unbutton my shirt. His mouth twitches as he watches me, water pooling between my hands as they fumble on the slick buttons. His hands are by his side, fingers itching to move. His breathing deepens, matching mine, as my lace bra is exposed under the water. It's almost completely see-through at this point but still feels like the final thing keeping my resolve in place. My shirt drops to the floor with a slap.

His straight mouth curves into a satisfied smile when I gesture at his trousers with my chin. I can already see the outline of his erection. I felt it in the hot tub before we ran here, but as he undoes his belt and unzips his trousers, dropping them to the floor and kicking them to the corner of the shower, my heart starts to palpitate so hard I can hear it in my eardrums. I want this. I want him.

I undo my trousers and they drop to my ankles with a thud. Trying to kick them off my feet almost knocks me over, not the sexy move I had in my mind. One swift movement would have had me standing gloriously in my mismatched underwear, but of course, I nearly fall over trying to get them off me. My foot slips, and I catch the soap holder before feeling a hand on my calf, easing the wet fabric away from my skin. I look down to find molten hazel eyes looking up at me, framed by dark wet hair and soft lips. His hand is soft but calloused, brushing down my leg before throwing the lump of clothes we've both taken off into a pile in the corner.

"I never liked business casual anyway," I say, unable to think of anything vaguely sexy.

"Me neither." His hand smooths across my leg and grips the

back of my knee, bringing it to his lips like a prince would do a gloved hand. "But now I'm a *huge* fan."

My laugh comes off as more of a scoff than I intended it to, and I look up at his showerhead to avoid the alluring stare coming from below until I feel him shift. A soft graze of the hand slowly moving up the side of my thigh until it reaches my waist, and a shadow forms over my cheek. Our eyes meet, tiny droplets of water coating his eyelashes like frost on morning grass. I shudder under his gaze, soft but intense. He hasn't asked me outright yet, but I can feel his demeanor shift as he starts to think I'm regretting the decision to be here. Like he's desperately trying to read me, but the book is in a language he's never seen before. He inches back until just the tips of his fingers stroke my waist. I feel his heart racing, pounding hard against my hand, and for some reason that eases any uncertainty I had left.

"Hotter now?" his voice teases as his eyes gleam.

"Much, much hotter now," I say. I slide my hand around to the back of his neck and pull him closer to me. His palm drifts through my hair, using a gentle grip to maneuver my face upward toward his. At the same time, we pull each other into our orbit, our lips grazing chastely like we haven't just been drunk and messily making out in a hot tub. In hindsight that seemed like a playful moment we could easily forget about. Chalk it up to needing to let off steam after a bad day at work, the adrenaline of not getting caught, or the rejuvenation of being away from home. This feels different. This feels like it's seared into my memory before it's even begun.

The smallest fraction of sense shines through, and I pull away. "I'm clean and on the pill."

"Get your mind out of the gutter; I'm just in here to shower," he says into my mouth, a laugh erupting from us in unison. "I'm clean too," he says before kissing me again.

We turn frantic, like we know this is the first and last time we'll be here so we might as well go on all the rides. He pulls urgently at my waist as his lips trail down my neck to my breasts, kissing over the wet lace as his hands smooth up my back to the clasp. Like a pro, he handles it with ease. He leaves me to take the fabric off like a piece of fruit being peeled before it can be fully consumed. He draws in a deep breath as he revels in me, mouth opening, then closing as he tries to find a sentence but comes up with nothing. Instead, he moves his mouth back to where it was, this time with barely a scrap of fabric. His tongue plays with my nipple as he cups my breast. My hands balance on his hips, running over the elastic waistband of his boxers and tracing the outline of the smattering of hair below his navel. He moans as my hand travels to the front of his boxers, pressing lightly against the cotton fabric to find he's rock-hard. My mouth salivates at the thought of him inside me, pressing me up against the tiles and fucking me until I can't see straight. His hand dips under the side of my thong, making me jump as he snaps it against my hip. He smirks, taking my chin in one hand as he uses the other to dip between my legs, running a finger against the fabric.

"These are so wet," he says.

"How can you tell?" I ask, my voice ragged.

"I meant from the water." He smiles, kissing the matching smile from my mouth as my cheeks go hot. My teeth pull on his lips. I have never wanted anything so badly in my life.

He spins me around so my hands are pressed against the

wall; the water runs down my back for a few seconds then stops as his figure blocks out the stream. He kisses down my back as he eases the underwear off me, kissing up the back of my legs so slowly I want to scream. I want to touch myself because he isn't doing it. By the time his lips meet my upper thighs, I feel his fingers running from my ankles, following the same route his mouth has just taken. His lips make their way to my shoulders, up my neck before reaching my ear.

"There's no water on you now. Shall we see if you're still wet?"

I swallow and nod as his fingers wind up my inner thigh, slowly dipping in from behind until I'm shaking with anticipation. I can't help the noise from escaping my mouth, the whimper that leaves me as his fingers dance over my skin. The low ache is almost painful. He works me, slow rhythmic circles back and forth until I realize I'm the one moving my hips to the same rhythm, helplessly using him to get myself off in a way I've never done with anyone before. His free hand smooths over me, guiding me even more as he adds more pressure, pressing harder against me. It slides over my hips as he works me from the front; I grip his forearm for support, feeling the muscles moving under my taut fingers. Feeling the way he touches me *as* he touches me. Coming out of my own body and seeing what he sees, feeling what he feels as the sensation builds and builds within me. Rubbing circles around my resolve until I'm about to collapse.

Fuck is the only word in my vocabulary as he's effectively holding me upright, working his mouth against my neck and behind my ear. "Just keep—" I can barely get my words out as he breathes a laugh against my ear.

"Stay like this?" he asks. "Want me to keep touching you like this?"

"Yes, but . . . more," I say, not knowing if that sentence makes sense.

He understands, pressing harder and increasing the pressure. My knees begin to shake as he knocks them apart, spreading me wider as he adds another finger. Plunging in and out, working me into a frenzy so intense it takes me over the edge in waves of pleasure. Drawing a climax out of me that feels like it lasts forever. I'm shuddering as his left hand presses against the glass wall, causing condensation mist to gather, creating an imprint of his fingers.

We pull apart, both out of breath, as the steam from the two showerheads begins to completely fill the space. I turn, leaning my head back against the tile.

"Are you okay?" he asks, sucking in steam with every breath.

"Yeah, I just need a second, dizzy," I say, not fully comprehending whether the cause is him or the steam.

"We should probably slow down." His chest heaves, and his forehead lowers to my shoulder.

I stick my lip out playfully as he turns off the shower and adjusts my underwear back. "Don't worry, there's still a whole hotel room." He points his head to the closed bathroom door. "And I'm not going anywhere."

He smiles through the mist, giving me one last kiss that scatters my resolve across the floor and down the drain.

CHAPTER 10

Business Account (WYST) BALANCE: £9,485.44
Personal Account BALANCE: -£2,050.60
Personal Account overdraft charge: £50.00

The silver faucet tap squeaks as Oliver turns off the shower. As the warm water swirls down the drain, the steam covering us like a blanket dissipates, drifting upward. It hits the marble ceiling, skittering left and right like fog rolling over valleys. My body is vibrating, mostly from the aftershock of one of the most intense orgasms I've ever had, but it begins to full-on shiver as he unravels his wet body from mine.

"Wait here. I'll get you a fresh towel," he says, taking one final look at me. His eyes are glazed and heavy, but his eyebrows lift like he's coming out of a trance; he smiles and shakes his head before disappearing around the corner of the bathroom.

Hearing his bare feet padding across the tiled floor back toward me, I cross my arms, covering my hard nipples as though he wasn't just running his tongue over them. My goose bumps bring clarity; I'm standing here in this near stranger's hotel room, practically naked in the shower. This was so stupid.

I wring out my underwear and slide it back on, the cold sensation unwelcome but the action instinctual.

He reappears with a white, fluffy hotel towel wrapped around his waist and a bare chest, exposing the V's pointing down to his snail trail of hair dancing under his navel. My breathing hitches before I refocus and grasp the other towel he's holding out for me.

He watches me for a few seconds before coming to his senses. "Sorry. I'll get you some dry clothes." He pads back into the bedroom, riffles around in his suitcase, then approaches me with an oversize navy-blue T-shirt. My fingers curve over the soft fabric, our hands brushing as we exchange.

He huffs a laugh as I take the soft T-shirt from him, strategically holding the towel with one hand as the other forms a circle and loops the T-shirt over my wet hair.

I head straight to the bathroom mirror to remove the residual makeup smeared across my eyes. I wash my face, drying it off with my towel. As my eyes refocus, they study Oliver's bare back in the mirror as he looks for his own clothes before locking onto the reflected text on my T-shirt.

I tilt my head, trying to figure out what *stnemtsevnI occiredO* means. I pull the fabric away from my stomach to read it upside down. In white text on a navy background, it says, *Odericco Investments*.

Scrunching my eyebrows, I turn around and say, "We didn't get these in the welcome pack," holding the fabric out like a child showing their parent a new drawing.

Oliver shrugs. "Being Dom's assistant has its perks; you look good in it," he says, his stomach muscles tense as he stretches his torso to put on a matching T-shirt. He catches me looking, transfixed by the ebb and flow of his body, before approaching me, fingers lingering on my waist as he places a soft kiss across my lips. My chest deflates as I sigh into his mouth, pulling on the fabric to get him as close as possible.

Finally, as if on a transatlantic signal delay, my brain catches up to what he just said. I stare blankly at him, blinking as I try to process the words.

"What do you mean?" My mouth hangs open ever so slightly, eyebrows sky-high.

"You look good in my T-shirt," he repeats.

He looks me up and down, studying my confusion with an equal glower. "They give them out all the time at the office." He scrunches his brows together. "You can keep it. I have a ton more I use for the gym."

I press two fingers into the bridge of my nose. "No. I don't mean the bloody T-shirt. You're . . ." I can barely get the words out because honestly I don't want the confirmation. "Do you work for Dominic Odericco?" My voice echoes off the walls.

"Yeah?" He looks at me suspiciously, dropping his hands from me.

"What the fuck?" I jut my chin out in confusion, eyes nearly popping out of my skull as I push against his chest. "You didn't think to mention that?"

He looks as confused as me. "I thought you knew. Everyone here knows."

"Clearly not! My comp—" I stop myself. "My *boss's* company is in the competition that is *hosted* by your boss."

He purses his lips, shaking his head. "So . . . ?"

"You have got to be kidding me." I let out a frustrated growl, pacing the room in my underwear and the Odericco T-shirt; it feels tighter by the second. "It's a huge conflict of interest; thank god we didn't have sex!"

"I mean . . ." He picks up his watch from the side table with a bemused smile. "There's still time . . . ?"

Head in my hands, I sit on the edge of the bed. "Don't you see how bad this is?"

For the first time in this conversation, he looks genuinely concerned. Coming around the bed, he crouches in front of me, gently taking my hands in his. "It's okay—there's like four degrees of separation between us. We're both assistants to the people in the competition. It's not like we're actually *in* the competition ourselves." He scratches the back of his neck and huffs a laugh. "Now, that would be bad."

My stomach roils. *Fuck, fuck, fuck.* If it came out that I'm the real CEO and founder of Wyst, that would be pretty terrible. If it came out that I almost had shower sex with the head judge of the competition's assistant, that would be fucking awful.

"Oh god, I'm going to throw up," I say, leaping up to my feet. A migraine swiftly bubbling its way to the surface. "Why have I not seen you around Dominic?"

He shifts awkwardly. "He's usually sending me out on errands during this kind of event: getting his coffee, booking dinner reservations, managing his luggage. All the lackey shit."

I study him. "And you were openly complaining about those errands to everyone at the bar tonight. I'm surprised he hasn't fired you." That was harsh but what the actual fuck.

"Well." He scratches the back of his head, considering his

next words. "Dominic's also my cousin . . ." His mouth down-turns as he cringes, anticipating my negative reaction. He is correct in the assumption.

A fresh wave of adrenaline hits my chest. "Oh, for fuck's sake, I nearly had sex with *Oliver Odericco?*"

"Oliver *Kavanagh!*" he corrects with an air of desperation, like it's a last-ditch attempt to rectify the night. The name doesn't soothe me; instead, my hands start to shake as it takes me right back to the initial phone call with Mr. Fucking Kavanagh.

Oliver Kavanagh doesn't just work for Odericco Investments, isn't just Dominic Odericco's cousin. Oliver Kavanagh is the sole reason me, Spencer, and Wyst are here. Oh my god, I nearly told him the idea is mine when we were at the pool.

Holding my hands in the air, I announce, "I *seriously* have to go." I frantically pack up my things. My wet clothes are still at the bottom of his shower. I close my eyes briefly, trying to avoid thinking about blissfully ignorant Jess having the time of her life with Oliver, cousin and assistant of Dominic Odericco, under the spray of the warm water less than ten minutes ago.

Scanning on fast forward through everything I've seen and heard at TechRumble, I get stuck on something weird Dominic said backstage earlier.

Where's okay?

It sounded strange when he said it, but now the pieces fall to the floor and lock into place like red-flag Tetris blocks.

Okay. O.K. Oliver Kavanagh.

"Does Dominic call you . . . O.K.? Like your initials?"

He nods. "Yeah, it's a teenage nickname. I used to call him

Dodo as retaliation, but he threatened me with a demotion to office night cleaner if I refer to him as that at work. I think he secretly loves our inside jokes, though." He shoots me a soft smile as he steps off the bed, gently touching the arms at my sides with his warm palms. "Violet, this is fine. I am so *unbelievably* insignificant at Odericco. Dominic barely trusts me to get his coffee order most days." He tilts his head playfully. "Which is fair because I tend to spill them over incredibly attractive women before he can drink them."

That's why he seemed already settled in when Spencer and I arrived at the hotel early. Why he could get the dry cleaning sorted so fast. Why he seemed so disinterested in any of the presentations. Why everyone already knew his name at the assistants' party. Why he had the key card to the executive pool.

My blood pounds into my temples. Every part of this night was because he is Dominic's assistant. Everybody knows him, and everybody saw me with him.

He's the assistant to the King of TechRumble, not to mention his flesh and blood. Everyone probably fawns over him. And I could have been caught heavy petting in the C-Suite hot tub with him.

He holds my crossed arms and lowers his chin to meet me. "Look, why don't we just chill out, I'll order us some room service, we can talk, get to know each other, and maybe if we feel like it, have a couple more life-altering orgasms . . . ?" His hazel eyes twinkle in the low light, swirling gold and green streaks like koi fish gliding around a pond.

For a split second, I consider it. If this was real, I would stay. If I was really an assistant, someone with so little significance in this competition. If I didn't have to watch Spencer like a hawk to make sure the plan and subsequently my company don't blow up in my face.

"No, sorry. I need to, ummm . . . process this. Alone." I swallow, avoiding his eyes.

His broad shoulders slump at my words, but he accepts my decision and he silently steps away from me, hands taut at his sides as I pick up my bag and my bra and slink out the door.

CHAPTER 11

Business Account (WYST) BALANCE: £9,485.44
Personal Account BALANCE: -£2,050.60

After the presentation, I've had time to have a panic attack, go to a party, break into a swimming pool, get hot and heavy with a stranger, then run back to my room to seriously regret getting hot and heavy with a stranger. It's nearly 2 a.m. So why the hell isn't Spencer in this hotel suite by now?

I stole one of his two key cards during the welcome drinks, and I thought the best plan was to ambush the little coward in his room. Instead, my head is pounding as I pace the decadent space alone with my thoughts. Rhythmic pain lances against my temples like someone wrapped a saucepan in a bath towel and is repeatedly smashing it over my skull. *You've done it now, Jess.*

Get it out of my system. What was I thinking? The only reason I needed to get it out of my system was because Oliver was flirting with me. Besides the unfortunate case of mistaken identity, Oliver was kind, fun, attentive, empathetic, understanding. After three years of feeling nothing, he flicked the switch that whirred my sex drive back to life. I should have stopped at the bar. I should have stopped at the pool. I should have stopped at the hot tub. There were so many opportunities to leave, but I was stuck to him like he was a sexy American magnet and I was a rusty nail.

I consume the contents of Spencer's complimentary minibar, since I'm paying for them anyway. Stress eating salted popcorn, smoked almonds, mini KitKats, jelly beans, and some spicy wasabi peas while scrolling through the social media coverage and reactions to Spencer's presentation. Wyst has gained over nine hundred followers on Instagram today, thanks to the positive coverage from Round One of TechRumble. I end up on YouTube, watching the competitors' presentations. As much as I hate to admit it, Spencer did a great job getting into character. Shots of the crowd applauding flash up on the screen, but one frame makes my body freeze. My finger drags across the screen to rewind the footage. That guy in the crowd looks so much like Malcolm. My heart pounds as I take two fingers and zoom into the video. It's pixelated, dark, and grainy—it's probably not him and I'm just being paranoid. Why would he have even been there? He's just on my mind, like he is after every romantic encounter I've had since the day I left Graystone Asset Management. I hate that he's always here, always casting any experience in a dark light. I thought I didn't have time to think about Malcolm after finding out who Oliver really is, but it pains me to see that he's clearly still there, just sitting in my subconscious and making me see ghosts. And besides, the audience has been mostly the teams of the companies that entered into Round One, smaller investors, tech bros, and journalists. It can't be him. There's no reason for Malcolm to be here. This man looks older, skinnier, and disheveled, not the blond-haired trust-funded rake who wore me down, pestering me to go out with him, then ruining my life. I reason with myself that I'm just stressed and it manifests as faces in the crowd.

Eventually, once the stomachache has thoroughly set in, I fall asleep on the gigantic squishy corner sofa that's comfier than any surface I've ever slept on. My sleep is fractured, memories flashing into bright focus, then murky dark, like familiar rooms with lights flickering on and off. Shadowy figures appear and disappear from view as I try to make sense of where I am.

My body leaps awake as the beep of the key card scanner and the door latch echo across the space. The main light switches on, causing me to squint at the bouncy and slightly drunk figure bounding through the door.

He seems almost pleased to see me. "Oh my god, that was amazing." He guffaws, dropping a black branded tote bag full of merchandise and unraveling himself from his black coat. "They *loved* me."

I'm rigid in the middle of the room. "Wow, Spence. I'm *so* happy for you."

This is classic Spencer. Being so blinded by attention, he'll push anyone out of the way to get it. Like when we were seven, he literally pushed me out of the way into a bush when we were trick-or-treating because everyone liked my princess costume more than his Spider-Man costume, ripping my dress and leaving scratches up my arms like I'd been attacked by a baby werewolf.

He doesn't seem to notice my sarcastic tone. He swans to the minibar fridge and takes out a bottle of Acqua Panna, cracking the cap. "I know, right? Everyone who presented today got invited to this exclusive dinner with the panelists for a more intimate chat."

A confusing swirl of feelings runs through me, pulling me in opposite directions like a compass out of whack. I sigh. "And you didn't think that's something I should have been at?"

He looks at me like I've just asked him to run a marathon with me. "Why would my assistant be there?"

I scoff. Is he being serious right now? "Because clearly you can't be trusted to follow the guidelines. What were you thinking, going off script in front of everyone?"

He shrugs and fans his hands out in confusion. "Urgh, that feels like a decade ago. What did you want me to do? Not fucking dazzle them? We were losing the crowd, and I did what was needed to turn it around. You told me to put on a good show."

"What are you talking about?"

"At my play, that's what you said you wanted. I nailed it, and you're welcome by the way."

I spit out a laugh and shake my head. "Did you even realize you were making stuff up in front of the entire world, not just the people in the room? The whole thing was live streamed."

For a blink, his face twitches as he registers the information before smoothing back to normal. "Just think of it more as an embellishment of the truth."

"A lie is a lie, Spencer."

"It was no worse than what you've lied about to get us here." He crosses his arms, eyebrows furrowed.

He's right. When this comes crumbling down, there won't be headlines about what he said onstage. It will be about the woman who lied to get an investment. Shit, is this what committing fraud is?

My mind scours through the potential fallout like a nit comb through hair.

"It's worse because I'm going to be a laughingstock; it'll be Elizabeth Holmes all over again but with less turtlenecks." I put my forehead in my hands, and my body starts to shake uncontrollably.

"Why would you be a laughingstock?" After a few seconds of silence, his face softens, finally understanding.

Spencer had a front row seat to my downfall from straitlaced golden child to the family embarrassment. His presence was helpful, even if he didn't realize it; just his physically being there stopped me from doing something I'd regret or hurting myself further than I already had. I try not to think about what I would have done.

I don't feel like that now, but the memory sometimes returns like a phantom limb, dragging me down when I least expect it. It's like grief. A loss of my former self, the old relationships with my family, my friends, with myself. I used to like myself, some days even love myself. But after everything happened, things were never the same. Spencer looks at me differently too, no less than I was before but just . . . different. Like I've been cloned with a single piece missing and he can't figure out what.

My legs shake; I sit back on the sofa, sinking into the cushions. He sits beside me, holding my hand in his and squeezing it rhythmically.

"It's okay. What happened at your job is not going to happen again," he reassures me.

"How do you know? All those things you promised? Podcasts, TV shows, YouTube channels, books. You think you're just saying words up there, but I'm the one who has to execute and fund it, not you. It'll be my fault if it all falls apart." My voice wobbles. "Do you know how much everything you promised would cost?"

He smiles softly, relaxing on the sofa. "No, I don't, but if we won TechRumble, I think that should cover it."

I wipe my face with a hand. "We're not going to win. We're lucky we made it to Round One."

"Jess, you need to pull yourself out of this headspace." He holds my shoulders, turning me to face him. "I've just spent the whole evening with these business guys; they are forward thinkers and were impressed by everything I had to say onstage . . . including Dominic Odericco." He takes a nonchalant swig of his sparkling water, the bubbles chasing up the side of the bottle.

I pause in place, alongside my racing heartbeat. "You . . . spoke to Dominic Odericco?"

He smirks. "Had a drink with him. He's . . . nice, under that 'I'm a big important grumpy man' persona." He scratches the back of his neck, a little twinkle in his eye. "Even hotter up close too."

I grab his arms. "What did he say?" I sniff the tears back up my nostrils.

He squints and tilts his chin down to me like he's telling me a secret. "We didn't talk much about Wyst. I was playing it cool, ya know? Waiting for him to come to me." I instantly deflate; he missed the perfect opportunity. Until he adds, "But luckily . . . he did."

"Speeeeeeence!" I rub my face. "Just please put me out of my misery already." My chest feels like a balloon filling with confetti, ready to burst and cover everything in sight. Housekeeping will still be finding remnants of this feeling a year later.

He laughs, sitting back on the sofa. "Okay, okay. He told me how much he respects the idea and thinks it's really innovative. He said he couldn't believe the platform you've built with just a team of four. Well, the platform *I've* built." He holds a hand to his chest and shoots me a beaming smile. I throw a beaded cushion in his face.

He sees right through me; it must be that annoying twin telepathy thing. "Look, it's a good idea, a great idea in fact. But how are you going to achieve greatness with no money to get it off the ground? Gotta fake it till you make it, baby!"

The gurgling feeling in my stomach subsides. We'll find out tomorrow whether we made it or not. I guess there's nothing left to do but relax.

I look around at his giant hotel room. "Can I stay here for a while longer? Order room service?"

He gives me a soft look and squeezes my hand. "As long as you're paying."

We sink into the sofa, watching an Italian-dubbed version of *She's the Man*. We know most of the lines anyway. These moments remind me of when we were old enough to stay home alone when Mum and Dad went out. We made popcorn, wore out our favorite DVDs, and ate our weight in sweets we'd bought at the corner shop with our secret stash of coins. We bought ice cream and drank the melted remains like warm milkshakes so we could wash the packaging and hide it in our schoolbags to discard in the cafeteria bins. Once, Spencer had to distract our parents while I hid the remains of our sneaky feasts under our beds. Of course, we both forgot they were there until a sour, tangy smell began emanating from the room. Mum found out, and we had to eat extra vegetables with every meal for a week. She replaced the sweet treats in our lunches with raisins, throwing any playground street cred out the window.

I wake several hours later on the sofa, with a cashmere blanket laid over me, being lightly shaken by Spencer. "Jessie, wake up." I open my eyes to see the morning light peeking through the curtains.

"What?" I ask, my voice groggy. "Shit, is it time to check out?"

"No, it's time to fucking celebrate!" He holds his bright phone screen to my face. I wince, adjusting to the light as I read the black-and-white text:

Dear Mr. Cole,

Thank you for attending the Odericco Investments TechRumble Round One.

We are pleased to inform you that Wyst has been selected to enter TechRumble Round Two. Please accept our congratulations. Details are attached.

Odericco Investments

Opening my phone, I see the forwarded email and click on the attachment.

Odericco Investments invites you to take part in the start-up panel at TechRumble Round Two in partnership with Wyatt Regency Paris.

"Paris!" Spencer shouts, throwing himself onto his bed. My neck cricks as I pull my body from the sofa.

"We got through," I say to no one.

"And we're going to Paris!" Spencer squeals.

Round Two. For a magical moment, I let my brain relax. You did it. You didn't fail.

Then the timeline hits; we have to be in Paris in three weeks. The Wyst beta test launches in a month's time. I'll have to prepare for both, coaching Spencer on the product while making the product as flawless as possible. Maybe we could premiere it *at* TechRumble? Is that too ambitious?

"There's so much to do for it." I pull my laptop out and immediately start typing up a new timeline.

"I think in Paris I'm going to wear a turtleneck instead of a shirt." He looks at himself in the floor-length mirror. "It's more chic."

"Well, that answers my question," I say hopefully. "You'll do the next round?"

He smiles and pulls me in for a hug. "Of course." He sighs, flicking an imaginary lock of hair over his shoulder. "Dominic would miss me if I didn't."

I smile. "We have to prep you thoroughly next time. We'd be launching the week after. There'll be a lot more difficult questions once the beta is live."

He waves a nonchalant hand. "It'll be fine. Prep me all you want. I'll show up and do my thing, and they'll be eating out of my hands."

"*Our* hands," I correct.

"Uh-huh." He nods, fixing his hair in the mirror.

Getting through to the next round of TechRumble means more eyes on Wyst. Informing investors that have rejected us in the past that we got through to the second round. Maybe more sign-ups for the beta launch.

I call Cecily, and once the excited screams have subsided, I come to a wild thought. "Maybe we should go for it. Create a social campaign around this whole thing and push the idea of Wyst being a successful company into the ether."

"It's kind of insane, but it's doable," Cecily says over speakerphone.

"Kind of? It's certifiable," I confirm.

Pulling up our finances, I look at the money eroded by Round One. I've spent way too much already. I didn't factor in the drinks from the assistants party. It's crazy how having a good time can suck up your finances.

I glance up to my brother. "We'll have to be a bit more . . . frugal . . . if we go to Paris."

Spencer shrugs. "I can manage a king room instead of a whole suite."

I purse my lips. "I mean, we might have to share next time."

Spencer scoffs. "But you want me to act first-class? How am I meant to do that in economy?"

I cross my arms. "Fine, I'll try to figure something out."

Maybe I can sleep on the floor in the lobby. To Spencer's point, it would be strange for a CEO and his assistant to be sharing a room. I wish things were easier than this, that I could focus on winning the competition rather than scraping by to be present for the next round. Instead of being occupied with thoughts of how to impress the judges, how to wow the crowds with new and exciting innovations, I'm thinking about how to sneak into breakfast, so we're not charged an extra thirty euros a head every morning.

The details for Paris have yet to be released, but it feels like a competition in itself to be able to drop everything else to attend these events. Maybe it's a test Dominic and Odericco Investments set deliberately to see who truly has what it takes, but I can't help but think about how many amazing ideas and innovations have been ignored simply because they couldn't get the initial funding.

My email dings with an automated reminder from NatWest about exceeding my overdraft. Spencer bounds to his suitcase, pulling clothes to his body and practicing his French accent.

CHAPTER 12

Business Account (WYST) BALANCE: £3,792.47
Personal Account BALANCE: -£1,050.60
Recent transactions:
Room service: £65.00
Staff salaries: £5,619.00
Personal income: + £1,000
Rome airport meal deal: £8.97

'm still reeling from our win as we board the plane back from Rome to London City Airport. Much to Spencer's preferences, the only flights we could find on the way back to London were British Airways. The plane is small but somehow finds enough room to have a business class section, to which Spencer attempts an upgrade for himself.

"I am the CEO of a TechRumble second-round company," he says with a proud smile to the tired flight attendant.

"Oh my god, stop—" I pull him by his collar and drag him toward our economy seats. "You're so embarrassing."

"What? You don't ask, you don't get! The plane isn't even fully booked!" he protests, pointing to the two remaining unoccupied business-class seats as I shove him down the aisle toward economy. I glance over my shoulder, shooting an apologetic look at the line of disgruntled passengers waiting behind us.

The flight attendants tuck carry-on bags into the overhead lockers as the low hum of the airplane provides a meditative background noise. My chest deflates as I relax into my cramped seat; at least after the chaos of the past three days, I can use this time to go over the plan for Paris.

"Welcome, folks, to the British Airways flight 796 from Rome to London City Airport. I'll be your captain, John, and we have Patricia and Jasper on board as your flight attendants for this relatively short flight from Rome. There may be a small amount of turbulence due to some heavy cloud coverage, so please make sure to keep your seat belts fastened whenever you are in your seats. For our passengers in business class, we have a selection of . . ."

Movement among the air stewards catches my attention, and all the noise in the cabin goes quiet as Dominic Odericco steps onto the plane. He doesn't make eye contact with anyone while gliding through the cabin. He is swiftly followed by his assistant, a tall, handsome, tousled brunette whom I last saw almost naked last night.

Eyes wide, I slump down in my seat, praying to the aeronautical gods that they aren't seated anywhere near us. Watching them through the gap between blue patterned chairs in front, I quickly realize that, of course, they are seated up front in business class.

"Why is your face so red?" I hear Spencer's voice permeate the radio silence in my brain.

I turn to face my brother. "It's not."

"You're beet red," he says so loud a woman across the aisle looks over to inspect me too, turning my face even hotter.

Spencer finally spots the source of my discomfort. "Oh, look, it's Dominic. We should go say hi." He stands up, trying to squeeze past me.

I pull him back down into his seat with a thud. "If you make us known to them, I will throw you out of this plane at peak altitude."

"Them?" He looks at me with a sly smile. "Oh." The occasional twin telepathy thing kicks in when I need it least. "What did you do?"

"I didn't do *anything*." I crack open my complimentary bottle of water to try and bring my internal mortification-ometer down. "Okay, fine, I may have ended up in that guy's room last night." I take a nonchalant sip.

Spencer gives me the look, the same look Dad gave both of us after we'd smoked cigarettes for the first time at a party and came home stinking of it.

"Are you serious?" He smacks me with a rolled-up sky magazine. "Who?"

I subtly point at Oliver, who is setting up his laptop for the flight. "That guy." Oliver turns to talk to Dominic, accentuating his dark tousled hair and soft lips. The butterflies in my stomach take flight as I remember that mouth on me.

"Ohhhhh, the hot assistant? Nice," he says loudly, causing several more people to turn around in their seats. "When did you have time to shag him?"

I widen my eyes at Spencer, creeping farther down in my seat and smiling politely at the elderly woman opposite me. "Screaming baboons have more tact than you. We didn't *actually* have sex, but it doesn't matter because it's never happening again."

Spencer arches a brow. "Why? Was it bad?"

I swallow the dryness in my throat from either a light hangover or pure humiliation. "It definitely wasn't bad . . ." My thoughts briefly drift back to my hands gripping his hair in the shower, and my legs turn to jelly. "But it can't happen again because I'm a professional, and even just a casual situation would be way too complicated to take on right now." I throw my hands out and away from each other to emphasize my point.

He shifts in his seat to face me. "Yeah, but if he fancies you, and you fancy him, how is that complicated?"

"He's Dominic's assistant. He's a conflict of interest."

"Forbidden fruit, some might say." He wiggles his eyebrows at me as he slides on his headphones. "Hard to resist a ripe, juicy plum." He pops his lips on the *p*.

"Ew." I roll my eyes and put my headphones on too, clicking play on the most recent Dr. Bernie podcast episode.

We sit in silence for half an hour as the plane takes off, the seat belt signs go dark, and the stewards have brought a glass of orange juice and a snack to all the passengers. Eventually, Spencer starts poking me in the arm.

He blinks at me, eyes wide in hope. "Can I have your pretzels?"

"No." The packet crinkles as I pick them up and move them away from his grabby hands.

He tilts his head and blinks. "But I always have your pretzels?"

I scrunch my face, mouth taut in a line. "What do you mean you *always have my pretzels*?"

"When we went on holiday!" he says, his mouth agape as though how could I not remember.

"This is not 'on holiday,' and the only reason you got them is because you used to cry and cry and cry until Mum *made* me give them to you to shut you up."

"So would that technique work now?" he teases, one side of his mouth lifting.

"Sorry, I don't negotiate with terrorists." I hold them close to my chest.

I spend the next hour of the flight working on everything I need for my meeting later today. I need to freshen up before we land as I'm heading straight into a developer meeting with Pacha's freelance team ahead of the beta launch.

Spencer is fast asleep, his head resting against the closed window. I don't see him in this relaxed state very often anymore; he looks so much younger. Despite me only being four minutes older than him, it feels like we have years between us. Not in an "I'm so much more mature" kind of way, but I have aged faster. He has the privilege of acting his age and being treated as such. I lock my seat upright, place the bag of pretzels and my orange juice on his tray, and get up to go to the bathroom at the back of the plane.

There are some rows of empty seats at the back of the plane that I wish I'd seen earlier, instead of having Spencer take up the entirety of the armrest between us. I rub my neck and shoulders in the aisle and wait for a bathroom to become vacant, sighing as I roll my muscles from side to side.

"Need some help with that?"

My pulse races at the deep tone. For a second, I think I'm imagining his voice. Flashes of his hands gripping my bare waist, pushing me up against the wall and dipping his fingers between my thighs. "I've been told I'm very good with my hands."

I turn around slowly, my gaze traveling up a pair of black sweatpants and a navy-blue hoodie with *Odericco Investments* written across the chest until I hit a pair of amused hazel eyes. The moment our gazes lock, it feels like someone turned off the gravity in the plane. I don't know if that is a thing, but we could be in space for all I care as his smirk turns into a knowing smile.

"What are you doing here?" I ask, clearing my throat to get rid of the shock.

He slides a hand out of his pocket and leans his forearm against the side of the empty back row of seats for stability. "Oh, I'm just here because I heard this place has really good food. What do you think I'm doing here? I'm going home."

I roll my eyes. "No, this *side* of the plane. You're sitting in business." I gesture with my free hand down the aisle toward the front of the plane. I glance and catch sight of the side of Dominic Odericco's face talking to the flight attendant, my stomach dropping. What if Dominic sees us talking and gets suspicious? Do we look like two people who showered together last night?

Oliver doesn't follow my line of sight, his eyes staying trained on me. "Have you been spying on me? Why didn't you come to say hello?" He pouts his bottom lip out playfully.

"You know why." I cross my arms, feeling the heat creeping up my neck ready to color my cheeks crimson. The bathroom door makes a *click* as an older lady steps out, smiling at both of us.

"Ma'am," Oliver says, tipping his chin ever so slightly to the woman, the Southern twang made evident in his accent. For a second it sounds like he should be wearing a cowboy hat and a lasso over his broad shoulders.

Fuck, I am into cowboys now? Let's put a pin in that to over-analyze later.

I give the lady a polite smile, as I pull the bathroom door back open to head inside.

As soon as she's gone, I whip my head back around to him. "I don't want to be seen with you; it's too risky."

His eyes flick to me. "You're seriously overthinking this"—then they flash with a moment of hesitation—"unless you didn't have a good time last night?"

Studying Oliver's sloping jaw, the need to reassure him bubbles up in my chest, but I swallow it down like a mouthful of thumbtacks and say in the most neutral tone I can muster, "No, I had a great time it's just—" I take a long breath. "It was nice to meet you." I hope he will walk away, because I'm not sure if I can.

His rosy lips curve upward into a devilish grin. "I saw that Wyst is coming to Paris, congrats."

"Thanks," I say monotonically as I step into the bathroom, glancing back at him one last time.

He shifts, his head tilting to keep eye contact. "And will *you* be coming?"

"Most likely," I answer with as little detail as possible, still on alert that anything I say to him is potentially high risk.

He smiles, stepping in closer. "Good."

I glare at him. "Not like that."

He glances back down the galley before tucking a strand of hair behind my ear, an electric jolt running down my spine. "Are you sure? Well, I'll be around if you happen to change your mind. Y'know, about round two."

My eyes flare, and I take his wrist in my hand. Before my

brain can catch up, I'm using it as the lever to pull him into the bathroom, locking the door behind us.

I use my forefinger to poke his chest. "Listen, let's get one thing straight, buddy. There will be no 'round two' or anything of that matter because, no matter how good it was, what happened last night was a humongous mistake."

He huffs a laugh as I continue. His peppery scent immediately fills the space, opening up a yawning chasm of want in my stomach.

"*Please* say you haven't told anyone about it?" I plead, hanging my head.

His expression softens as his shoulders relax. "Don't worry. I didn't tell a soul about the 'definitely not bad' almost sex we had last night," he says in a terrible English accent.

I close my eyes and bash the back of my head against the door. I can't believe he heard that.

He runs a finger over his chest in an X motion. "And I'm not planning on telling anyone going forward, cross my heart."

I breathe a sigh of relief. "Thank you. But things aren't 'going forward'. No matter how . . ." I pause to find the best word. ". . . enjoyable it was, it was one and done."

"Sure." He smiles, somehow amused by my protestations. "Whatever you want." His throat bobs as I study him.

Annoyed by my moment of transfixion, I decide to double down. "In fact, in hindsight, I don't even find you that attractive."

His head tilts, his jaw muscles ticking as his smile turns practically devious, like he's discovered a secret nobody else knows. "Don't lie to yourself—you like me." A thrill shoots up my spine as I watch his tongue roll; urgh, his mouth is perfect.

I cross my arms. "I'm completely indifferent." My breath deepens as I realize how close we are.

"Yeah, you seem indifferent, dragging me into *another* bathroom." He tilts his head as his voice lowers to a whisper. "Do you have some sort of kink I should be made aware of?" The light dances in his eyes as he whispers seductively, "Is this your *thing*?"

I close my eyes, hoping it will stop my cheeks from flaming so hot they almost hurt. The problem with closing my eyes, though, are the short-term memories actively turning from soft and malleable to rock-hard in my mind. The feel of the hot water running down my naked back, his tongue brushing against mine, his lips and fingers exploring every inch of my soaking wet body.

I open my eyes. "Oh my god, you are insufferable!"

He steps in closer, his eyes glinting playfully. "You're uptight and a goody-goody."

I press my back against the door, meeting his eye. "You're unserious and unprofessional." My heart races against my rib cage like it's trying to draw me forward toward him.

He lifts an eyebrow. "You like me," he repeats. "And I like you." Imagine being as self-assured as this man. Okay, being insanely good-looking, over six feet tall, and possessing the hands of a god would probably contribute to this kind of complex.

I lift my chin, cutting a glance to his mouth, then back up to him. "You're completely delusional."

"But I'm also right," he quips back, eyes set in razor-sharp focus.

"You have to stop." Our low, shallow breaths dance between

us. He has to stop because I don't think I can. Being near him feels almost like a physical pull, an ache needing to be salved. I want to lean into the feeling, have it envelop me like a duvet so I can disappear under it forever. In an ideal world, I would be running into a bathroom to throw cold water on my face, but that privacy is working to my detriment right now.

His face moves closer to mine, and I don't stop him, our lips almost brushing. "Stop what, exactly? Turning you on?"

"Looking at me like that with your ooey-gooey eyes and floppy hair." I try not to think about when I was holding on to that hair for dear life. My hands are magnetized; they want to float up to him again.

His mouth twists into a smile as an eyebrow lifts. "My ooey-gooey eyes and floppy hair?" He places a hand above my head. "I think that was almost a compliment."

"But not quite." I shake my head.

He studies me for an excruciating few seconds, then presses in closer, his free hand brushing lightly over my waist, making my stomach muscles tense. His voice smooths against my cheek. "Hmmm, I don't know. It almost sounds like you're attracted to me or something . . ."

Like an engine struggling to start, my throat lets out a feeble growl as I pound his chest with the full force of my body, barely making him flinch, but he steps back anyway, nearly stumbling into the sink.

"You cannot tell anyone about last night, I'm serious," I say, ignoring the fact that I can feel his heart racing under my hands. The pounding infiltrates my core, making my knees turn to jelly.

"I won't if you admit it to yourself," he says in a low smooth tone.

I let out a breath. "Okay, fine! I'm attracted to you! But if we're both going to Paris, we'll just have to be . . . friendly . . . with each other."

His jaw ticks as his demeanor shifts ever so slightly. "We spent hours talking at the assistants party; it would be suspicious if we weren't," he says defiantly.

"Sure. We can be friends." I hold my hand out to shake; he glances at it and then takes my hand in his.

Engulfing my palm with his, he says, "Friends who have seen the other naked, but friends nonetheless." His thumb traces the back of my hand.

A crackle of a speaker cuts through the tension. *"Ladies and gentlemen, we will shortly be heading into a section of heavy clouds. Please head back to your seats when the seat belt light turns on."*

I roll my eyes, trying to stop the embarrassed tug at my lips. "What is wrong with you?"

The cabin rumbles, the floor vibrating under our feet.

His eyes drop to my lips as he shrugs. "I can't help it, I like it when you're mean."

"Well, get used to it." I contort my arm up behind me to flick the lock open, but he doesn't open the door. He doesn't want to leave, and if I'm honest, neither do I. I want the walls to squeeze in like an Indiana Jones film, so it's not my fault that we're touching. Plausible deniability. My chest aches at how simple these interactions should have been. I should have been able to stay last night. I should have been able to enjoy whatever this fleeting feeling is, but it's way too risky. Flirting is one thing, but anything further is a risk I can't take for someone who is essentially a stranger. Even if he is a charming, tall, good-looking stranger with a decent job and is good with his hands.

A bump of turbulence rocks us both, causing my back to bash against the unlocked door so hard it clicks open. We hurtle to the floor, him on top of me. As we fall, he pulls me toward him and twists so he lands on his side and I am partially cushioned by his hard chest. The air is thrust out of us by the landing.

After a few seconds to absorb the shock, I pull my head back to meet the gaze of two flight attendants staring down at us with crossed arms.

Oliver huffs a breathy, nervous laugh, his hands still gripped onto me. "Oh, don't worry, ladies. We're just *really* good friends."

Nerves fried, I return to my seat for landing to find a sleeping Spencer and two empty bags of pretzels.

CHAPTER 13

Business Account (WYST) BALANCE: £3,696.50
Personal Account BALANCE: -£1,050.60
Recent transactions:
Adobe Creative Cloud subscription: £40.99
Hard drive: £54.98

The next few days in London go by in a blur of emails, meetings, avoiding calls from Greg at NatWest, and late nights figuring out how my bank account is going to stretch like Play-Doh to get us to the next round of TechRumble.

The air is frigid as Cecily and I stand shivering in the line outside Hackney Town Hall. A gust of icy wind whips past us, taking Cecily's cigarette smoke and twisting it to dance around us. The doors aren't open for another fifteen minutes, but we wanted to get here early to ensure we get good seats. It seems like everyone else had that idea too.

"I knew Dr. Bernie was popular but my god." I glance down at the crowd quickly forming behind us. Hordes of women of similar age to us, dressing in floor-length puffer coats and plaid Acne statement scarves, shiver in the evening air.

Cecily nods. "She's like the Beyoncé of therapists."

The venue isn't exactly small, but Dr. Bernie said in a *Sunday Times* interview that she dislikes massive crowds and prefers to be able to see everyone's faces in the audience to connect on a more "healing" level. I'm riding on her spotting us as our ticket backstage. Bringing the news that we have made it to the second round of investment at TechRumble is a surefire way to get her signed on for the launch. I'm just praying she will see us.

Eventually, the doors open up, and we speed walk to the second row, agreeing the first row would look too intense.

We tear off our coats, gloves, and scarves in unison while balancing the complimentary green juice with the ticket. We sigh and grunt as we plonk down in our fold-out seats. Calming new age music is playing in the background while we slip into our favorite activity: pretending we are talking, but in reality, we're eavesdropping on everyone around us. We can't help it at events like these; this is our target demographic. Wyst is a platform for people of all ages, but the majority who have signed up are women aged eighteen to thirty-five. The exact array of faces we see here tonight.

When Dr. Bernie comes onstage, we cheer and applaud along with the rest of the crowd. Her velvet deep purple suit reflects the light like a chic oil spill, complemented by her silk lilac pussy-bow blouse, her staple and highly recognizable uniform. Her shiny, thick hair cascades down her back, bouncing as she walks to center stage with a jet-black microphone in hand.

After an amazing talk, questions are offered to the crowd and hands shoot up around us.

The audience asks questions about relationships, family dynamics, and careers—the usual topics that are discussed at length on the podcast. Most of her wisdom whittles down to one of her most iconic pieces of advice: "Every conversation is a negotiation."

I lean toward Cecily. "Do you think she's seen us yet?"

"No, she's been mostly playing to the left. I see her agent, Alison, over there, but I've never met her in person."

Checking out Alison, I say, "Maybe she'll think we're stalking Dr. Bernie."

Cecily looks at me deadpan. "That would make sense considering we *are* stalking her, but Dr. Bernie gave us these tickets."

"Pity tickets."

"She gave us these pity tickets," she agrees. "We are practically VIPs. All we need to do is say hello and casually drop that we are in the second round of TechRumble. And maybe get a picture with her for social."

Partially to put the idea of a collaboration in people's minds, specifically Dr. Bernie's, but mostly because we want to measure the reaction across social media. To make sure Dr. Bernie is the right person to bet a huge amount of currently nonexistent money on. Because sure, both Cecily and I practically kiss the ground she walks on, but we can't guarantee our audience and users feel the same without a temperature check.

Cecily posts that Wyst is attending the event, snapping a quick picture of Dr. Bernie onstage with her signature power suit, pussy-bow blouse, and long silver hair flowing to one side.

"Initial reactions are good," she says, flicking her finger across the screen to scroll through the Instagram story replies. "I also put out a poll asking who has listened to her podcast. 57 percent yes so far."

The community Cecily has built across social channels is a

godsend for decision-making. Sure, I have to be firm and decisive, but to have your first-ever business venture include a built-in audience-testing platform is something I find so valuable. The announcement of Dr. Bernie as one of the major faces of Wyst would be a huge deal. A headline-grabbing event we've never experienced before.

"Guess who else I've been stalking." Cecily grins, still staring at her phone.

"Who?"

"Your *lover* . . ." she says, seductively rolling the *l*.

She turns her phone toward me, my brow furrowing as she reveals Oliver Kavanagh's Instagram profile and username @olkav96. My stomach muscles constrict as I immediately feel the phantom press of Oliver's hand slipping up my bare waist before dissolving into thin air.

My eyes widen in both embarrassment and excitement. "Wait, how did you get access? Isn't his profile set to private?"

"Now who's the stalker?" she teases. "I created a fake guy who works at Odericco Investments and requested to follow him."

I scoff a laugh. "Oh my god, you're insane."

"Sorry, here's me thinking *everyone* was lying about their identity nowadays." Her grin transforms into a devilish smirk. "You are a bad best friend by the way."

"How?"

"You failed to tell me that this guy looks like a leading man. An investor's assistant named *Oliver*?" Cecily crinkles her nose. "I was imagining a five-foot-seven scrawny guy with glasses and a bad haircut." She clicks on his profile picture, expanding the photo. It's Oliver, candid and smiling with sunglasses on top of tousled brown hair in a pub garden. The sun shines across him, emphasizing his broad shoulders and taut jawline.

I'm briefly overwhelmed by a sense of longing for my own ignorance. To be back at the bar in Rome, the feeling of recklessness, when pursuing what I wanted had no negative consequences.

I laugh. "Yeah, you were waaaay off with that one." I scroll through the three most recent pictures, feeling at once like an obsessed stalker but also an intrepid explorer.

Cecily nods. "Maybe it's the minimal social media footprint too—that's hot."

She's right. Oliver hasn't posted much, making him even more intriguing. The most recent is the view from what I assume to be the Odericco Investments office, the sprawling London skyline slightly muted and blurred from being taken through a window. The second is a picture taken of him cooking, his back to the camera, a towel thrown lazily over his shoulder as he holds himself over a steaming saucepan. The final post is from over three years ago, a picture of him smiling and rosy-cheeked among a group of friends at a bar tagged in New York.

I'm sure if I wasn't faking my name and my job title, I would have added him, and he would have accepted the follow. So this doesn't feel like it's crossing too many lines. Even so, it feels like a violation of privacy.

"I'm not pursuing anything with him, so it's for the best. You've seen him, you've got your ya-yas out, so you should delete the profile."

She huffs and taps at her phone screen before slipping it into her pocket. "I just don't get why this has to be such a big deal." She crosses her arms. "If you like him, then just tell him the truth; it's not too late."

"In what world do you envision that conversation going well?" I ask, imagining the fallout. Firstly, he'll think I'm insane and won't want anything to do with me after that. Secondly, he'd probably go running to his boss, and we'd immediately be disqualified from the competition. My only hope would be that it wouldn't get picked up by journalists and become an international headline, damaging the reputation of all women trying to survive in the tech industry.

She shrugs. "I just feel like if he likes you, then maybe you could trust him to keep it on the down-low."

I shoot her a look. "Because trusting men I'm interested in has gone so well for me in the past." Even trying to talk about it casually feels weird, my cheeks still flushing from shame.

"I saw that little smile on your face when you were telling me what happened—you do like him; you're just too scared to go for it. After *everything*"—she holds a hand out, referring to what I just mentioned—"you deserve some fun."

"It was indulging in that sentiment that got me into this situation in the first place!" I can feel the blush creeping over my face.

Cecily smiles at me. "I wonder what Dr. Bernie would say about this." Then she stands up, jumping up and down until the bemused event coordinator hands her the microphone.

"Oh, hello," Dr. Bernie says with a flicker of recognition and a smile.

"Hi, Dr. Bernie!" she says as excitedly as the day we first spoke to her. "I have a question about romantic relationships."

Dr. Bernie holds her hand out. "Okay, go ahead."

"My friend . . . Jennifer . . ." she says, forcing the name out. It's so obvious she has made this identity up on the spot. "My friend Jennifer had a sexy rendezvous with a very attractive, funny, smart, single man." The crowd giggles and whoops. "And now she is so obviously into him but is making excuses to get in the way of her own happiness."

I cringe, slinking down in my seat and trying to pull Cecily's sleeve to drag her back into her seat. "Are you serious right now?" I mumble through my gritted teeth.

She clears her throat as she tugs her arm out of my grip. "What advice would you have for . . . Jennifer? How do you think I can advise her to make the right decision?"

Dr. Bernie, to her credit, takes the question as seriously as all the others. "If you believe your friend is getting in the way of her own happiness, perhaps they need to address the underlying reasons why. If this man is as amazing as you claim he is, she is clearly protecting her heart from something deeper. Perhaps . . ." I swear for a second Dr. Bernie's eyes meet mine. "Perhaps your *friend* needs to look inward and address the issues she has surrounding romantic intimacy before she can let someone new into her life."

"And how would she go about . . . addressing that?" Cecily shifts her weight onto her other foot, and the microphone flops to one side. It's crazy to see someone so at ease with everyone staring right at her.

I close my eyes as they start to sting. The buildup over the past few weeks settling on my chest like an anvil.

The whole crowd hungry for her next words, Dr. Bernie considers in silence before responding, "Besides talking to a

professional, being upfront and discussing the issues with a potential romantic partner *before* pursuing the physical relationship would be my best advice."

My disappointment on full display, I stare at my hands and
imagine the catch-22 I've gift wrapped and delivered to my
own doorstep like a flaming bag of poop. I can't talk to Oliver
beforehand because: shower. And I can't do it after because I'm
in the middle of hiding my identity from him and most of the
tech world.

"But specifically for your friend, I would suggest talking to a
professional about these issues. Perhaps avoiding pursuing anything emotionally serious until she has learned to understand
and accept these feelings, instead of denying them."

The idea of talking to a stranger about this makes my skin
crawl. Last time I spoke to a stranger about my problems, it
culminated with me at a conference room table with a bunch
of lawyers negotiating how much money my mental and emotional state was worth.

As the questions from the crowd continue, I plunge deeper
into my seat, melting into the floor as the embarrassment con-
sumes me whole.

CHAPTER 14

Business Account (WYST) BALANCE: £2,841.21
Personal Account BALANCE: -£1,050.60
Recent transactions:
London to Paris Eurostar tickets: £387.00
Wyatt Hotel Paris: £468.29

The morning of our train to Paris started in boxes. I emailed my landlord when I got home from the Dr. Bernie town hall and realized that maintaining a residence was one of my biggest monthly outgoings. If I didn't have to pay rent, I wouldn't have to pay myself a salary. And I have a perfectly good sofa in the conference room of the office, as well as storage space for my stuff. What I did not anticipate was my landlord being so keen on the idea, he emailed saying he would cut my contract short and waive any admin fees if I could be out by the end of the week. Being in Paris for most of this week, I spent the majority of the past twenty-four hours packing up my effects and transferring them via a minivan cab into the office.

As my boots echo across the concourse of St. Pancras Eurostar, my phone starts buzzing for the third time in a row.

I sigh, picking up my backpack and throwing it over my sore shoulder before finally clicking Accept Call. "Hey, Mum."

"Hi, Jess, are you with Spencer?"

"Not right now, no." I glance at my watch—if he hasn't arrived at the station yet, he's going to miss the train. "How are you?"

A loud exhalation runs like static down the phone. "Things have been simply awful. Our neighbors just planted cherry blossom trees in their front garden, the petals are everywhere, and they go all mushy and sticky and stained the driveway. Your father is livid."

"Wow, that *does* sound awful," I say, trying my best to humor her as I continue to scan the crowd of travelers for Spencer.

She pauses for a few seconds before saying, "Well, there's no need to be sarcastic is there?"

"I wasn't. I'm genuinely upset on your behalf. That is awful of your neighbors down the road to plant a tree without discussing it with you first." In my defense, it's difficult to not sound sarcastic when you're humoring a ridiculous person.

Mum and Dad have always been dramatic; I guess that's where Spencer (and admittedly, sometimes me) gets it from.

"So, ummm . . . why are you calling? I'm a little busy right now," I say, pacing back and forth in front of security in case Spencer arrives.

A tall man with broad shoulders and dark hair brushes past me, and for a second I think it's Oliver until the man turns to the side and reveals a smaller nose and less defined jaw. My fingers have been tingling at the urge to look him up online again, to waste an hour going full girlie research mode and finding more traces of his internet presence.

I shouldn't care. But knowing he's going to be in the same place as me today sends a charge up my spine, hitting a nerve I thought long dead. *It's just because he's hot*, I reason. But I can't get over the way he accurately assessed me, the way he couldn't have known how I was feeling about Spencer, TechRumble, and the chaos of keeping up this facade but completely understood how it affected me. I hate to admit it to myself, but I'm excited at the possibility of seeing him again. I've been on tenterhooks imagining I might see him on the Eurostar and play out a *Before Sunset* scenario.

Mum crashes through my wistful train of thought. "I'm calling because Spencer said you've roped him in for some sort of . . . project?" I can feel her flippantly throwing her hand in the air.

"With Wyst, yes," I clarify with as little detail as possible. Telling her we've already been to Rome and are leaving for Paris in thirty minutes will send this conversation down a rabbit hole I won't be able to scrape out of. Even at the ripe old age of twenty-seven, it feels strange and rebellious to leave the country without telling your parents. They don't care where I am any other day of the week, but for some reason adding a passport into the mix adds a level of childishness for which I feel I must be held accountable.

She tuts in the receiver. "Jessica, Spenny has a lot of roles coming up, which he needs to make sure he's prepared for. He has a gift; he can't keep turning down acting roles for you willy-nilly."

I stop in my tracks, almost bumping into a group of tourists wearing matching Union Jack bucket hats. "He turned down a role?"

Her voice hitches up by an octave; she knows she's surprised me. "Yes, and it's incredibly selfish for you to ask that of him."

I furrow my brow. "Which role, exactly, did he turn down?"

"Were you not even listening when he told you? You can be so self-centered; you need to work on keeping your ears open."

My survival instincts kick in, so I do the adult thing of nodding, agreeing, and ignoring. "Okay. Sorry."

"You should be apologizing to him, not me. What is he even doing at your company?" she asks.

I don't think either of my parents has ever said the name Wyst out loud. Like giving it a name would give it life, an acknowledgment of its existence beyond me talking to them about it at obligatory bimonthly family dinners. Usually, these involve Spencer regaling us all with fabulous tales of his brief on-set chat with Ian McKellan about his favorite dried vegetable snacks in between takes and me occasionally mentioning something about Wyst to the sound of sighing.

"Spencer is doing . . . sales," I say as neutrally as possible; it's technically not a lie. I've said a lot of "not-technically lies" recently so I might as well add one more into the mix. A trifle of omitted truths. Before my mum has a chance to question me further, I jump in with one of my own. "Hey, Mum, I was wondering if there was any chance I could come stay in mine and Spencer's old room for a few days. I'm looking for a new flat at the moment and—"

She interrupts me. "Sadly not, we've moved everything out so Dad could fit his gym equipment in."

"Where is it all now?" I ask.

"Where's what?" she asks.

"My stuff?" I try to keep my tone level as I slump into a cold metal chair on the train platform. Picturing my first bunny rabbit teddy Mopsy stuffed into a cardboard box.

"I asked Spencer and he said to give his to a charity shop, so I assumed you'd want the same."

"Right, you couldn't have kept it and checked with me as well? Not just Spencer?" I don't know why I'm even asking, to be honest. This is like when they decided to clean out the attic and threw out all my old school notebooks. I didn't need them for anything besides sentimentality but just throwing away part of my childhood without a second thought felt like a personal declaration of disinterest.

"I guess I'm just the world's worst mother! Your dad's high cholesterol diagnosis was a tad more pressing than a box of old clothes and trinkets, Jessica. His doctor told him he has to be doing cardio exercise every day. Where else did you expect him to put his cross trainer?"

I swallow another five minutes of lecturing before promptly saying my goodbyes. I tap my fingers on the arm of the chair, staring at my reflection in the black phone screen. A notification from my banking app pulls me out of my fugue state. Okay, this is fine. I just need to find a way to get money and shelter. I could enter into one of those flu vaccine medical trials? But then I'd be stuck in a room in a university medical facility for three weeks instead of being in Paris keeping an eye on Spencer. I don't fully trust he won't go rogue onstage again, saying anything to draw in the crowd's attention and adoration.

I could do a million of those paid online surveys or get Pacha to build some sort of AI program to fill out surveys pretending to be me. But the last thing I want is for Pacha and Cecily to think they are working on a sinking ship.

Mum's brother Uncle Rob always goes on about how much he makes in his weekly poker games. Maybe I could give it a go. But that would involve knowing how to play poker . . . Maybe they do other card games, like Old Maid or Snap? Anything you play on the beach between trips into the sea and reapplying sand-covered sunscreen would do.

I could ask my parents for the money. No. I couldn't. That is the absolute last option. If it wasn't for keeping up with Cecily's and Pacha's salaries, I would never, ever consider it. My gut tells me my parents would say no anyway, which has been bolstered by Mum saying no to accommodating me for a few days. And on the slim chance they agreed, it would be the defining moment of Wyst. Something they could hold over me for the rest of my life. Every success would be because they had to step in. Because they had to bail me out when I couldn't run my own company anywhere but into the ground.

I guess I can live in the office for a couple of months, just to get through the launch period. Use my salary to pay for Paris, and who knows, we might make it to Round Three if we're lucky.

SPENCER FINALLY MAKES it through security, and we jump onto the Eurostar with five minutes to spare. Sounds of boarding announcements punctuate our conversation as we shuffle onto the hissing train. I decide to wait to interrogate Spencer until he is trapped in the seat next to me.

Spencer's suitcase is even bigger than last time. He grunts and pants as he drags and positions both of ours onto the almost full racks, shoving them into place. We plonk down in our seats—economy, despite his consistent protests.

"We're going to stay in a literal French castle. I think you can stand a couple of hours with the little people, Mr. CEO."

As soon as the train starts moving, I strike.

"I spoke to Mum earlier. Did you tell her you'd turned down an acting role to work at Wyst?"

He tenses like a puppy caught peeing behind the sofa. "Errr, yeah. I think I mentioned something about it."

I raise an eyebrow at him. "She gave me a lecture about not dragging you down the rabbit hole with me . . ."

"Weird," he says, avoiding my eyes as he starts to dig through the magazine pouch in front of him. "Do they have breakfast menus here? I'd love a croissant."

"Very weird, almost like someone implied I'm *forcing* you to give up roles to work for me. She also said you'd turned down another play?"

He shrugs again. "I'm just getting pretty sick of Shakespeare after the play that shan't be named."

"*Macbeth*?"

"Fuck, seriously? Saying it out loud is really bad luck." He punches me twice in the arm as though to alleviate it.

I punch back once. "Throwing your sister under the bus is worse luck."

"I didn't throw you under a bus . . ." He fiddles with his fingers. "Maybe just like a bike or a scooter or something."

I slump back into my seat. "Spence, you're already the favorite; just once can you please big me up a bit instead of joining them in slagging me off?"

He scoffs. "I am not the favorite. I'm just better at packaging my life into sound bites for Mum to pass on to her friends. You just depress everyone."

The way he says it sounds like a joke, but my stomach twinges at his words. Do I really depress everyone? Does he just mean Mum and Dad, or does he mean *everyone*? The thought sits like a layer of concrete in my stomach. "If you're so good at packaging yourself, why didn't you take the job? Don't lie—you love Shakespeare. How many times did you make me watch that film with Helena Bonham Carter?"

He sighs. "I thought I nailed the audition, so I told Mum they'd practically promised me the role in the room. But when I got the call, I didn't even make the chorus."

My lips spread as I cringe cartoonishly. "That sucks, sorry."

His mouth forms a straight line. "It went to some kid whose dad is friends with the casting director."

I hold my mouth agape. "Surely they have to give it to the right person for the role?"

Spencer shrugs. "In this industry, it's either who you know or who you blow."

I huff out a laugh, staring at the rolling British countryside. "I'm getting the impression that the tech industry isn't that dissimilar."

He shifts, turning to me. "Look, staying on Mum and Dad's good side isn't difficult; you just have to start presenting your life in a more digestible form."

"So you're saying become a better liar?"

"Not lying, just . . ." He waves his hands in the air. "Embellish! Give 'em the ole razzle-dazzle. Next time we're round theirs, I'll help you."

I crack a small smile. "Thanks. And the casting director was stupid not to choose you," I offer. Spencer is a genuinely good actor. Every time I've seen him in something he's gotten even better, from our secondary school's production of *Swee-ney Todd* to a supporting actor in a local indie short film to a featured extra role as a footman in *Bridgerton*. My favorite of his roles was the puppet in a budget production of *War Horse*. They couldn't afford to have a giant stage puppet made, so they hired Spencer to pretend to *be* the puppet being manipulated by a second actor. His ability to play an inanimate object made animate was truly inspired.

We sit in silence for a few minutes as the train speeds toward the Channel Tunnel, Spencer having procured his baked goods and travel snacks while I reply to emails.

"So I've been thinking . . ." he says, shoving my elbow off the armrest between us for his. "About this panel talk thing."

"Uh-huh." I'm half listening while putting the finishing touches on an email for Dr. Bernie's agent to send before we lose phone signal, laying out how we would position her as a major face of Wyst.

"I'm thinking we lean into my idea." His smile is wide and excited.

"Your idea?"

"Yeah. The multimedia verse of it all. YouTube channels, podcasts, maybe even TV shows." He purses his lips.

I shift, folding one leg over the other to lean toward him. "Let me get this straight—you want *me* to go all in on an idea that *you* made up on the spot when you went rogue in front of literally thousands of people. With no market research, no surveying, no testing?"

"Yep." He takes a triumphant bite of an almond croissant, the white powder coating his dark gray cable-knit sweater.

"On what basis?"

He shrugs, taking a bite of flaky pastry. "Vibes, I guess."

I rub my face; this is what years of being coddled by our parents has taught him. "Acrobats take smaller leaps than you do."

"Go big or go home—that's literally the point of this whole thing." He waves a bag of barbecue Popchips for emphasis.

Once we pull into Gare du Nord, we hop on another train toward the outskirts of Paris. Our suitcases hum across the uneven pavement as we pant and groan our way over to the car rental place. Upon arrival, I slap down my passport and booking confirmation for a four-door, five-seater black BMW X3 with trunk space big enough to fit our suitcases and Spencer's ego. The man behind the desk simply nods and leads us to a bright red Fiat Punto with two doors and enough space in the back to fit my optimism for this trip.

Spencer attempts to argue with the man, but he does not speak English and we definitely don't speak French. After fifteen minutes of attempted arguing, I interrupt. Say we are "*très désolé*" and shove Spencer into the passenger seat.

As we circle around to leave the parking lot, avoiding the potholes that will no doubt render this go-cart completely useless, the man holds up his middle finger and yells, "*Bon voyage, putain!*"

The invitation to TechRumble stated "Paris" and continued a partnership with the glamorous and extortionately priced Wyatt Hotels. But upon closer inspection, the hotel isn't nestled among iconic cafés and bustling shops; it's a forty-five-minute car ride from the center of Paris in a tiny French village, nestled between a two-hundred-year-old print shop and a specialist boulangerie that only opens to the public on a Tuesday afternoon.

With my brother being a self-proclaimed *passenger prin-cess* with only a provisional license, I am the one driving us down the treacherous French country roads. We trundle along through picturesque mountains and rolling hills, passing quaint little villages and crumbling châteaus. We stop, on Spencer's request, at a series of vast lavender fields. Specifically to take photos for his Instagram, which I threaten him not to post for several months, as the risk that somebody connects his actor social media presence to Wyst CEO Spencer Cole is too great. He edits them in the car, making the purples pop even purplier on Facetune as I fiddle with the GPS and eventually get us back on track to the hotel in the small town of Lac de Lys. The town is very Parisian despite being twenty-five kilometers away from the city. The hotel, which has a carved wood exterior and iron-patterned windows, looks hundreds of years old.

"Why are we here instead of *actual* Paris?" Spencer asks; clearly this is the first time he's paid attention to where we were going since we left the rental lot.

"I think this might be *his* hotel," I say, ignoring his question. A young man in a cream cashmere quarter-zip sweater runs back and forth between a luxury stagecoach and the entrance, dragging two suitcases at a time over the cobblestones.

As we walk toward the front entrance, I point to a gold plaque shining in the afternoon sun.

Odericco 1967

"I thought this was a Wyatt? Does Dominic own this hotel?" Spencer asks.

"I have no idea," I say, mouth agape at the grandeur.

The man carrying his last set of bags, sweat glistening on his forehead, walks past us. "It's run by Wyatt, but the castle was purchased by Alessandro Odericco, Dominic's grandfather, in the sixties as a holiday home and was later bought by Wyatt and converted into an exclusive boutique hotel."

"Fucking hell," says Spencer, taking in a full 360 view of the grounds. His voice turns dreamy like he's talking only to himself. "He's like Christian Grey."

I cut a side glance to Spencer, not bothering to hide the fully fledged judgment on my face. Spencer comes out of his trance and wiggles his eyebrows at me.

I roll my eyes, gesturing with my purple travel wallet toward the hotel entrance. "Let's get inside. I've been driving for ages and need to shower the Eurostar off me."

"Hmmm, I don't think so." Spencer grips the handle of his rolling suitcase, leaning one leg over the other. "You only booked one room and said we have to be discreet."

"I can only *afford* one room." I purse my lips, but I did say that. Regretting volunteering to sleep on the pullout sofa in the room.

"Oh, it's no trouble, Sis. But to maintain subtlety, I will be taking *this*." He whips the travel wallet from my hand. "And will go check into *my* room." He begins to roll forward, leaving me in the drive before saying over his shoulder, "I'll text you when the coast is clear, and you can bring your bags up."

I scoff, coming so close to turning into a child and stomping my foot on the ground. Annoyingly, he is right. We can't be seen checking into the same room; that would look incredibly suspicious. But I can't help but feel like Spencer is enjoying this a little bit too much.

The floorboards creak under the weight of my wheely suitcase as I wander the seventeenth-century halls. The interior is old, with carved wood and paneled walls adorned with land-scape paintings and a taxidermy warthog, a stark contrast to the sleek, opulent hotel in Rome. An uneasy feeling creeps along my body; the intimacy of the smaller competitor pool means I can't just blend into the crowd like I did last time.

My eyes drag on the sign saying *Gymnasium*, and I push through the door with a hiss into another building. Maybe they have a treadmill I can use to burn off all this nervous energy.

For an old hotel, the gym is incredibly modern. Everyone in here is either a skinny computer nerd doing neck and back stretches or a roided-out tech bro lifting like he's trying to prove a point.

Peeking through the long thin windows into each area of the gym, I spot groups of men playing squash and badminton in state-of-the-art courts. My attention halts on two familiar figures playing on the basketball court, Oliver and Dominic. They are talking and laughing while they play. It's unnerving seeing them be so familiar, like friends rather than the formal boss and assistant roles they play in public.

Dominic's dark gray fitted T-shirt showcases a triangle of sweat spotting his chest. Oliver is shirtless, holding his own against Dominic's natural authoritative demeanor.

I lean against the door as I watch them; Oliver's back muscles shift, sweat glistening as he weaves the ball away from Dominic with athletic precision. I really could have done without the reminder of his hot and wet body. Knowing I'm staying in the same hotel as him is going to make this trip a whole lot harder. I should stay away from him; getting closer can only mean trouble. My tired body presses against the door, only for the latch to click shut, echoing through the court. Oliver and

Dominic glance toward the door in unison, and I drop to the floor, unsure if they saw me.

After a few seconds, I crawl out of the way of the window and scramble away, my suitcase dragging behind me. Maybe instead of a run, I just need a very cold shower.

CHAPTER 15

Business Account (WYST) BALANCE: £2,841.21
Personal Account BALANCE: -£1,850.60
Recent transactions:
Final studio rent payment: £800.00

Most of France is still asleep as Spencer and I stumble half awake toward the grand hall for breakfast. It's quiet in the hotel, but as we turn the corner, the chatter of guests ratchets up.

"Do you remember Buffet Battle?" Spencer asks.

"Of course, I'm the reigning champ," I reply.

Renamed from Who Can Steal the Most Food from the Hotel Breakfast Buffet when we were kids, this competition was the highlight of many Cole family holidays. Sixteen *pastéis de nata* in Portugal was my record, but I'd had the advantage of wearing fuchsia-pink cargo pants and a training bra. It had way more pockets than Spencer's lime-green *Life's a Beach* holiday T-shirt and Quiksilver surfing shorts.

Spencer arches a brow. "Surely I get special recognition for all those boiled eggs."

I cross my arms. "You would have, but then you got disqualified because you left them all in the hotel room. It stank for days."

"Wanna play when we get in there?" he says as we shuffle up the line.

"That isn't CEO behavior; imagine if you got caught." I don't admit that I played each day in Rome, sneaking bread, cheese, and ham to make sandwiches and hiding them in my room's minibar so I didn't have to pay for lunch.

I glance through the doorway as we line up for a table. When everyone is together like this, it's hard to avoid feeling like you're walking into an athlete's training ground. Obvious cliques are forming as people are getting to know each other, like a school cafeteria. Everyone feels more at ease despite the stakes being higher. Maybe people are getting cocky and complacent. In schooltime fashion, Spencer has already declared he is going to sit with the other founders and CEOs. They are sitting at a makeshift banquet table, laughing the loudest to make sure everyone in the room knows they are having a *fantastic* time. The next group of people are taken to a table, and we shuffle up the line. A woman in the group in front of us turns around, and I recognize her from Round One. Her cropped blond hair and short frame are my polar opposite.

"Morning!" She is chirpier than I'd expected her to be.

"Morning." I smile back. "It's Lana, right? From Norton and Associates?"

"Yes!" She seems shocked I remember. "We met at the party in Rome."

I nod confirmation as another burst of cackling laughter

erupts from the CEO table. Spencer lurches his neck to the side, trying to see what the joke is about.

"Wow, I was so out of it that night," Lana whispers, trying to make sure Spencer, aka "my boss," doesn't hear. He had been out partying instead of being safely locked in the fancy suite he insisted upon me paying for.

"I think we all were," I say, flicking my eyes back to her. "I'm sorry, I forgot what you do at Norton. Are you an assistant as well?" The lie is getting scarily smoother each time I say it.

"Yeah. But I'm studying for my law exams right now. I'm taking the bar at the end of the year, so I'm hoping a promotion to a more substantial position will happen after that."

Impressed, I cock my head to the side. "That's amazing."

She leans against the wood-paneled wall. "What about you? What do you want to be when you grow up?"

I huff out a laugh. "I'll get back to you when I figure that out. All I want for now is coffee and as many pastries as I can fit in my pockets."

The breakfast attendant signals to Lana to come forward, and she pushes off the wall. "Good to see you again."

"You too." I smile as her group is taken to their table.

When the attendant comes back, Spencer gives the room number.

The woman runs a finger down the reservation book and frowns. "*Je suis désolée, monsieur.* I have only one breakfast pass for this room."

Shit. I'm crashing on the sofa; there's only meant to be one person staying in the room.

I step forward, interjecting before Spencer can protest. "Oh,

I'm sorry for the confusion. I'm not staying for breakfast. I was just checking in with my boss. I'll be going now."

"*D'accord.*" The woman eyes me suspiciously before shrugging and extending her arm out for Spencer to follow.

Spencer shoots me a confused look.

"It's fine. Go," I mouth, ushering him away and pulling my phone out.

> **Jess:** I didn't put both our names on the same room booking just to be safe. Apparently there's a café nearby so I'll go there instead.

> **Spencer:** kk bring me back a croque monsieur x

After some extensive googling, I discover the cute instagrammable café is up several hills and across a partially flooded field. I return to the room, throw on my running gear, and head out in the brisk early morning air. The mist winds around bends like a curtain to oncoming traffic, so to be safe, I run down the mud-slicked edges. If I get hit by a car while using a fake identity and no phone signal, a broken leg will be the least of my worries.

Wide medieval stone walls, pointed trees, and lavender fields punctuate the horizon, a world away from the dreary gray London winter. Maybe if this plan doesn't work, I could move here, become a lavender farmer. But then I remember I have hay fever and love that there's an amazing Thai food place two minutes away from the office. By the time I'm far enough away to no longer see the hotel, my stomach starts to rumble.

Finally making it back to the road, I notice my phone has

coughed out a single bar of service. I quickly press Cecily's name in my phone log, but the words "Call Failed" force me farther onto one side of the road.

After walking for a couple of minutes, I gain two bars of signal, then three. Then 4G! Yes! Before I have a chance to press Cecily's name again, a rusty green pickup truck speeds past on the other side of the road, its wheels kicking up the mud and flinging it over my back from hair to sneakers.

"Oh my god!" I scream as the icy liquid seeps into my leggings and sweater, through my underwear and T-shirt. "How does this keep happening?" I ask the universe.

"Hi, babe!" Cecily's voice rings through my headphones.

"Cecily! Can you hear me?" I shout into my phone.

"It's a bit crackly, but yes, I can hear you."

"Okay, good, if I die on this road, please delete my internet history."

"Share your location with me," she says.

I tap at my phone. "Done, how are you?"

She sighs. "I'm good. How's it going?"

"Good, yeah, I'm power walking on the side of the road to find a croissant and a decent cup of coffee."

"You wanted to talk about Spencer's 'wrench' or something?" she reminds me. The promises he made onstage in Rome went down so well with the crowd, it feels irresponsible not to at least ruminate on the idea.

"Yeah, the wrench he threw onstage. I've been thinking about it. I think we should start looking into to it. Could you start throwing feelers out to your media contacts?"

"And you're sure you're happy for me to write the pitch?" Her voice softens.

"Yeah, of course. I trust you, and I have a lot on my plate today."

"Great." I can hear her smile through the phone. Delegation is clearly not my strong suit.

The ground changes from dirt roads to cobblestones as I pass into what one might refer to as a "village," as in a place where some humans live. Inhabitants include a butcher shop, a tiny self-pump gas station with a farm shop attached, and a tobacco shop.

"The hotel website said there was a bustling town nearby, but there's barely anything here."

"Where are you? Find my Friends says you're in the middle of a field."

I squint at a nearby signpost. "Lay de Lis?"

"Ahhh, I see. There's an *actual* town half a mile from the hotel in the opposite direction."

My chin drops. "So I just walked two miles for some chewing tobacco?"

"Hmmm, I think there's a café attached to the back of the tobacco shop."

"Merci le gods!" I step around the tobacco shop to find the most adorable café I've ever seen. Vines of ivy wrap around the rustic white one-story building like a warm hug in the winter sun. An optimistic pair of tables and chairs sit like guard dogs on opposite sides of the front door. I snap a photo and send it to Cecily.

"Oh my god, cuuuuute," she coos down the phone. She then proceeds to gasp, then cackle like a witch.

"What?" I ask.

She finally pulls in a breath. "Zoom in on the left-hand side window."

My eyebrows meet in the middle as my mud-splattered fingers drag apart on the screen.

"Oh, bloody hell." Throwing my head back toward the cloudless blue sky.

"Is that who I think it is?" It's grainy, but in the back of the shop by the counter is a tall broad man whose side profile looks distinctly like Oliver Kavanagh.

I groan. "He hasn't seen me yet. I could just—"

"Go over there right now, missy," Cecily interjects before I have time to protest. "Don't let a man, no matter how pretty he is, stop you from getting baked goods."

As if on cue, my stomach violently rumbles again. "But I look disgusting."

"If you're not interested in him, why do you care?" she questions in a taunting tone.

"Because I wouldn't want *anyone* seeing me looking like I've shit myself," I say, twisting my neck to try and see the spray of drying mud up the back of my leggings.

"You're gorgeous, sweaty or shitty. Stop making excuses and get in there."

"Okay, fine, I'm going." I will deny the thrill running through my veins in a court of law.

"Au revoir, mon amie!" The line goes dead before I have time for a retort.

The bell announces my hesitant entrance, several patrons turning to glance at me before returning to their coffee and newspapers. Oliver's back remains side-on to me while waiting in line and his attention remains fixed on his phone.

So I decide to do the weirdest thing possible and stand behind him in silence, building up the courage to say something.

The last time I spoke to this man we were arguing about being friends and falling out of an airplane bathroom, so I resolve to go with a friendly, neutral "Hey."

He looks over his shoulder and parrots an ineffectual quick "Hey" back. But then quickly does a double take and smiles, the look in his eyes shifting away from disinterest. "Hey."

He twists around to face me, studying my dirt-covered outfit and ignoring the continuous string of metallic beeps blasting from his phone. "Did you crawl here?"

"No, I've actually gotten into mud wrestling since I last saw you. How the hell did *you* get here?" I take the opportunity to check him for mud, my eyes running up from his perfectly spotless light brown brogues to his charcoal-gray trousers and crisp white shirt and thick gray wool coat hung over one arm.

His eyes glint, flicking from my leggings to my lips to my eyes. "I used the hotel's car service . . . like a sane person."

I nod. "Ah, so you didn't take the scenic route through the swamp?"

One side of his mouth turns upward. "I'm saving it as aa special treat for the weekend."

"*Oui?*" a bald man with a thick beard asks from behind the counter.

Oliver clears his throat—"*Bonjour, je prends un café noisette, deux cafés américains, et un thé au citron, s'il vous plaît*"—before turning back to me.

"French too?" I ask.

"Croissant, foie gras, coq au vin . . ." He checks off the words on his fingers. "Do you need a ride back?"

Before I can reply, his phone starts dinging again. He rolls his eyes and starts to furiously type.

"Sure," I answer. "Thanks."

While I make my order in an accent that would make my year nine French teacher roll in her *tombe*, Oliver's focus is set on his phone, his brow set in a deep furrow.

I tilt my head, looking up at him. "Everything okay?"

"Huh?" he says monotonically.

"*Le chat* got your tongue?" I tease, my brain firing on all cylinders to regain his attention.

"Sorry, no." He sighs, slapping the phone against his open palm. "But Jocelyn has my balls."

He catches my demeanor shift. "No, uhhh, not like that. I'm just dealing with a minor crisis this morning."

"What's going on?" And why is my instinct to help fix it for him?

He lets out another long breath. "There's this dinner tonight for the executives. One of Dominic's guests, Jocelyn Peters . . . her luggage got lost on the flight over from New York. She doesn't have anything to wear for dinner, but she also doesn't have time to go shopping and—" He stops mid-sentence, scanning my body. "Actually, you might be able to help me with . . . What are your measurements?"

"Excuse me?" My eyes widen as I scoff, defensively wrapping my arms around my waist.

He lowers his voice. "If you'd prefer, I can guess based on memory . . ." He flashes that boyish smile, which really shouldn't do to my core what it's doing right now.

The man places both of our orders down on the counter with an acknowledging grunt.

I huff out a laugh. "Regardless of *that*, you seriously think I own something fancy enough for a high-powered executive to borrow?"

He leans over me, picking up a stack of napkins, wooden stirrers, and the four-cup holder. "Of course not. I have to find her something from one of the rich lady stores in the main town, but she's going to have me murdered and buried in a lavender field if I don't find her something nice."

I let the smooth velvety coffee hit my tongue before I respond. "So you want to take me shopping?"

Oliver cracks a smile, tilting his head. "As much as that sounds appealing, I've already sent one of the interns out with her credit card to just buy whatever expensive work-appropriate dresses she can find in Jocelyn's size. She'll be back in a couple of hours."

I shift onto one leg, placing a hand on my hip. "So what do you need *me* for?"

"I've been attempting to arrange a time for Jocelyn to try on the options, but she's completely booked all day." He lifts an eyebrow at me. "What I need . . . is a mannequin. I obviously can't ask any of the interns to try them on for me; that's an HR violation waiting to happen." He begins to relax, his shoulders lowering as a plan begins to form in his head.

I scoff with faux outrage. "And it wouldn't be if you get me to do it?"

His hazel eyes slice right through me. "If putting clothes *on* you is a HR violation . . ."

My cheeks flare. "And here I was thinking you '*just got the coffees*,'" I say, mimicking his former statement as I swirl my stirrer around in the white foam.

"In Dominic's words, I'm his bitch who can be replaced whenever he wants." He says it like he's repeating it. "So are you interested in helping a poor guy out?"

The response is sitting on my lips. How would a successful CEO use the assistant of the big-time investor who's asking them for a favor to their advantage, rather than just helping a peer out in a tough situation?

Every conversation is a negotiation.

I cross my arms. "What would you do for me in return?"

His eyes crease as he steps in closer, a smirk creeping along his lips. "What would you like me to do?"

I swallow, heat rising up my neck. "No, I mean what am I going to get out of helping you?"

"The pleasure of my company?" he offers, voice still low and smooth. "And I would be very, *very* grateful." His persuasive eyes twinkle at me before his phone starts to vibrate against the wood. "Car's here."

I suck my teeth, running through my options while he packs up his things.

He looms over me as he takes a final sip of his coffee. "Still need that ride? I have to go now to get these delivered for a meeting."

Ignoring him, I say, "I want you to ensure Spencer gets twenty minutes to talk with Dominic at the investor drinks reception tomorrow night, alone."

His eyes widen as he chokes on the hot liquid. "I can't promise that."

I press a finger into his chest, eyes flicking up to meet his as I say slowly, "I think . . . you can."

Oliver lowers his chin, his face contorting into a look that screams, "Are you fucking serious?" But he doesn't say anything, just slides his coat over his shoulders with graceful ease, maintaining eye contact with me the entire time. I imagine him placing the coat over my shoulders, his smell enveloping me as he uses the lapels to pull me in, before quickly snapping out of the daydream. *We're in the middle of a negotiation—stop objectifying him.*

My brain urges me to fill the silent gap as we head out the door toward the waiting black Mercedes. I'm desperate to bridge the conversation, but I hold steady, maintaining eye contact and not flinching when he shifts, rolls his eyes, and says, "I could probably do, like, five minutes."

He grasps the cup holder in one hand and opens the car door for me with the other.

My fingers wrap around the car door as I step around him. "Twenty," I counter, slipping into the warm seat.

He rounds the car, opening the opposite door and sliding into the backseat before looking at me with a playful smile. "You know that's not how negotiating works, right? You can't just say the same thing."

We speed down the winding roads past the massive pools of muddy water I just familiarized myself with.

After a few minutes of admiring the lush scenery, I turn back to Oliver who is doing the same.

He shifts before turning his face toward me. "I can do five minutes."

We stare at each other, both too stubborn to give in. The car screeches to a halt, and before I know what's happening, Oliver's arm springs out over my clavicle, stopping me and my drinks from flying forward into the seat in front.

"*Merde!*" we hear the driver shout as he jumps out of the car onto the road.

"You okay?" Oliver asks, slightly out of breath, his hair disheveled over his forehead.

Before I can answer, a cacophony of *baa*s reach the backseat of the car. We glance out the windows, then at each other.

I unclip my seat belt, put my coffees next to his in the holder, and open the car door before saying, "Ten minutes."

He follows me out, watching as I join the driver in trying to usher an entire flock of sheep around the car and off the road. "What are you doing?" he shouts over the ruckus.

"Helping," I grunt as I run after a lamb who is happily trotting in the wrong direction and herd it back toward the group. I lift my chin and shout across the herd, "You have to get back in time for your meeting, right? Come on!"

"This way," Oliver says to one of the sheep; it stands still chewing on a small tuft of grass.

I cross my arms and try to subdue a smile. "They probably only speak French."

He laughs at me, a full-bodied laugh, and guides two annoyed sheep off the road. "You are ridiculous."

It takes the three of us a few more tries to completely move the sheep out of the road into the valley's field. By the time we get back in the car, Oliver is almost as covered in mud as I am.

"How are you going to explain *this*"—I gesture a finger up and down his outfit—"to Dominic."

He considers for a few seconds. "I got into a very heated negotiation about a one-to-one."

"A negotiation which I obviously won," I announce, folding my arms and relaxing back into the seat. "Because you're going to give Spencer the fifteen minutes?"

He straightens out his hair, trying and failing to hide his amusement. "Maybe I can stretch it to ten."

I beam at him triumphantly. "Deal."

CHAPTER 16

Business Account (WYST) BALANCE: £2,825.22
Personal Account BALANCE: -£1,850.60
Recent transactions:
FemTech Monthly **magazine subscription: £15.99**

Several hours later, I'm grimacing at the past month on my expenses spreadsheet and trying and failing to unsubscribe from *FemTech Monthly* before I get charged again. A brisk knock sounds at the door. I jump to my feet, collecting the papers into a pile and sliding them under the duvet.

Oliver is holding about twenty dress bags over his arm. "Honey, I'm home!"

I'm briefly impressed by his single forearm holding them all before pulling him into the room in case someone sees it. "Why do you have so many?" I stare at the pile as he dumps them on the bed.

His eyes, almost amber in the dim light, cut to mine. "I don't enjoy my job, but I am thorough."

I scan the array of multicolored dress bags covering the duvet like jewels. "There's thorough but then there's . . . Did you tell the intern to buy an entire store?"

With his hands on his hips, he shoots me a side-on glance. "Imagine what I could achieve when I'm actually enjoying myself."

"I don't need to imagine, thanks," I counter, immediately regretting my phrasing.

"I don't know what you're talking about." He smiles slyly at me, and for some unfortunate reason, it's working. I tamp down on the fizzing feeling in my chest and cross my arms.

I roll my eyes, clipping my hair up. "Just shut up and hang them nicely over there."

"Yes, ma'am." His accent pops. I watch his shoulder blades move against his T-shirt as he hangs up the dress bags one by one in the wardrobe. My eyes travel to a pair of black boxer briefs hanging over the armchair. For fuck's sake, Spencer. I thought I'd hidden everything of his before Oliver arrived, giving the impression that I am definitely not staying in the same room as my boss. I whip the underwear off the chair and stuff them into my bag before Oliver spots them.

When he turns around, I cross my arms again, pretending to look at something incredibly interesting out of the window. "Thanks, I'll just be a few minutes." I click on a couple more lamps to counteract the 4 p.m. late January sunset.

"Take your time. And I'll be right outside if you need any help."

"Great, thanks!" I shoot him a sarcastic smile, pushing him out of the room.

When the door clicks shut, I stand in place gathering my thoughts as the tingle of his body dissipates under my fingers.

I unzip the first outfit, a mustard-yellow dress bag with the words *Magie de la mode* written in a white scrawling font over the center. It's a formal black dress, fairly unremarkable, but I can tell just by touching it that the fabric is expensive. I sneak a look at the tag and stifle a gasp. Jesus Christ, thirteen hundred euros. I hesitate, then run to wash and dry my hands before delicately pulling the dress from the bag.

Despite its obvious luxury, the dress looks terrible on me. More like a sack than a dress that costs over a grand. But maybe this is what Jocelyn is going for: a serious business-woman. The opposite of sexy. My back starts to sweat a little. I sigh and shuffle to the door.

Oliver turns around. "That was quick." His face creases in confusion when I just reveal my head. "Everything okay?"

"I've only tried on one." I hide my body behind the heavy door, not wanting him to see me looking like this. "I just need to know what the vibe is, for the dinner."

His face bemused, he confirms, "It's a formal dinner."

"I know, but what does that *mean*? Do you know what the other women are going to be wearing?"

He purses his lips. "It's a Michelin-starred dinner for the executives. Jocelyn is the only woman attending."

My eyes couldn't roll any harder if I tried. "That's both de-pressing and not at all helpful."

He resigns himself, sighing and pulling out his phone.

"What are you doing?"

"Gettying," he says. For a second I'm confused, but quickly realize he's looking up her name on Getty Images. How often does this woman get photographed?

"From what she's worn to other events, I'd say . . . smart but formfitting. No cleavage but you can see her . . ." He searches for the right word. "Curvature. Y'know?" He holds the phone out, showing me a series of event photography with the Getty Images watermark layered over the top.

"Okay, cool, that helps. Thanks." I slam the door the tiniest bit harder than necessary.

I try on ten more dresses at lightning speed, immediately hating each one as I put it on.

Eventually, I stumble upon a ruby-red dress with promise. Once I've fumbled around with the stiff zip, I have to give myself a second glance. It's figure hugging without being skin-tight, enough to show curves without looking too try hard. Long sleeved with a skirt to the knees, but with its sweetheart neckline, it's still flattering. I pull my hair down, moving it to one shoulder to match how Jocelyn seems to style it in the Getty Images. My reflection stares back at me until I decide that this is the one with some accessorizing. I slip on my one pair of black heels and put on gold drop earrings and a red lip to match the dress.

Smoothing down the dress over my waist and thighs, I tilt my head and imagine wearing something like this on the stage Spencer is gracing tomorrow. A smart, confident, elegant woman is something I don't think anyone will ever see me as. When people look at me, they see a reserved control freak who is out of her depth and desperately trying to look the part. I think it's what Dr. Bernie saw in me when we met at the hotel. But wearing a dress like *this*, maybe I could be something different. Someone different. Someone deserving of greatness.

The door clicks open; Oliver looks up from his phone and blinks rapidly. "Whoa."

My cheeks match the fabric as he takes me in, the side of his mouth twitching upward for an instant. Smoothing down the dress because what else do you do with your hands in this scenario, I huff an embarrassed laugh. Hands on hips feels too "look at me" and waving jazz hands and saying "ta-daaaa!" doesn't feel like the chic woman who would wear this dress.

I smile politely. "It's the most flattering . . . I'd go for this one," I say.

He leans into the doorframe. "Yeah, I would too." He runs his eyes over me for a few euphoric moments before clearing his throat, giving his head a light shake. "That's the one; thank you for your help."

"No problem, of course it would be the two-thousand-euro one." I take a deep breath. "Do you need to take the dresses back now?" I gesture over my shoulder with my thumb into the room, my heart starting to pound. I don't really know what I'm actually asking, but safe to say neither of us is thinking about Jocelyn's outfit choices.

"Yeah, I do," he answers, his low timbre and eyes on me making me want to try on a million more things for him. He follows me into the room, his jaw subtly tensing.

"Okay, one sec," I say, taking a long overdue exhale once I lock myself in the bathroom. Him looking at me like that is not exactly the "friendly" behavior we agreed upon. And neither is the feeling between my thighs.

Zipping the dress *up* was hard enough, but as I tug on the metal toggle to pull it down, my stress levels start to spike. Fuck. I tug and tug, throwing my body from side to side as I try to yank myself free. I let out a yelp as my elbow smacks into the metal towel rail. After the longest six seconds of my life, I give up, holding onto the edges of the bathroom sink as I try to calm myself. I'm going to have to pull myself out of this thing one way or another, but the warmth from the towel rails and underfloor heating is making me sweat even more. I step in circles around the bathroom and lift the skirt hem up over my body until it hits my waist.

Okay, this is fine. I can do this.

I take a deep breath in and then fully exhale until my chest is as deflated as can be before pulling the remaining fabric up my waist and over my chest. Except, I don't get it over my chest; instead the seam of the dress cinches inward like a bear trap over my boobs and pins me, arms upraised, in a red fabric prison.

"Shit, shit, shit, shit, shit."

The panic truly sets in when I remember I'm wearing makeup, fucking red lipstick that I stupidly put on to . . . what? Impress Oliver? Now it's going to get all over this two-thousand-euro dress, oh my god. I'm sweating, now I'm sweating. Sweat patches, foundation and lipstick are rubbing all over the front of this two-thousand-euro dress as I fling myself around the room like one of those dancing noodle arm inflatables until the heel of my shoe collides against the metal bin with a loud *gong*.

"Fucking hell!" I growl from inside my 100 percent ethically sourced, sustainably recycled viscose tomb.

A brisk knock is followed by Oliver's muffled voice from behind the door. "Everything okay in there?"

"Uh-huh, everything's fine!" I shout, my voice clearly shaky and panicked. My biceps are cramping from being stuck above my head at this angle.

"Are you sure? Because it kind of sounds like you're in the middle of a fight?" The voice sounds even more muffled now, like he has his face up against the door. "Or is this the wrestling you were talking about at the café?"

"I'm fine, I'm . . . I'm just stuck." My chest is heaving, tightening the fabric around me like a boa constrictor.

He's silent for a few seconds. "Stuck, how?"

"Like, stuck in the dress!" I shout, almost scream.

"Can I help you?" His voice levels.

"No." My voice cracks on the word. I don't want him to see me like this. Exposed like this. He has his phone with him and I'm fucking trapped. My heart pounds at the thought of him seeing me like this.

"Violet, can you please let me help you?" he says, but I can barely hear him over the ringing in my ears. Fuck, fuck, fuck.

I clamp my eyes shut. "Only if you leave your phone outside."

"Okay, sure. Let me in," he says. It's not exactly a request, but he avoids saying it in a demanding tone.

Chest heaving, I swallow my pride and turn slowly toward the sound of his voice in hopes of finding the door. When I do, I bend over until my hands are at doorknob height and pull down on the metal handle.

I straighten as the door clicks open, and for a second it seems like no one is there until Oliver's voice says, "You know you were just meant to try the dresses on, not turn them into an avant-garde fashion project?"

I ignore his attempt at a joke, too embarrassed at being this helpless in front of him trapped in my underwear. "Undo the zip," I say louder than I mean to.

He's seen me like this before, except this time it's not my choice. My eyes sting with undropped tears as I realize I'm completely vulnerable to his course of action.

"Of course, just try to breathe." He goes quiet, clearly sensing my mood. "Jesus, it's so hot in here." He pulls me out of the bathroom into the much cooler bedroom and grips the sides of the dress, heaving it back down my body. My dead arms drop to the side as I pull in a lung full of cold air and his peppery scent.

"You're okay," he assures me, smoothing down my frizzy hair, the look of concern and confusion making his amber-laced eyes darken under his brow. His hands move to my jaw, tilting my head upward to scan my face as a tear finally escapes down my cheek.

I take another long breath, looking him in the eye this time. "I just need to get out of this dress," I say, my breathing regulating but my voice still shaky, turning around and grabbing for the zip.

"It's all right. I got it." He curls my hair around his palm and places it over my shoulder, moving it out of the zipper's path. His fingers leave a trail of heat across my neck, but I barely register it compared to the adrenaline streaming through my veins like river rapids.

After a few failed attempts, he grunts. "All right, just . . . hold onto the wall." He pinches the fabric in the middle of my back as I press both palms against the textured heather-gray wallpaper.

He tugs at the zip, grunting lightly.

"Maybe scissors?" I suggest, mentally tallying how many months' payment plan I would need in exchange for a quick escape.

He hums nonchalantly. "It would be a bummer to cut up a dress you look so good in."

My brain zeros in on his hands, focusing on the feel of his palms against me instead of the dress's tightening grasp.

"Stop trying to distract me," I say through gritted teeth, even though it kind of works.

"Sorry." He drags the zipper down, and it immediately glides over the gathering of thread I got it stuck on. The cool air hits my sweat-laced lower back as the dress folds open like an envelope.

We stand in heavy silence for a few beats too long as his hands smooth away from the zipper and onto my waist.

He squeezes my side and says over my shoulder, "Think you can get it from here?" My body shivers, reacting to the warmth radiating from his chest.

"Yeah, thanks." I nod, unhinging my fingers from the wall and leaning into his hands on me, gentle but supportive. I place my right arm across my waist, the ends of our fingers ever so slightly overlapping. My limbs go heavy as electricity jumps between our fingertips.

Our deep breaths move in sync, calming my nervous system.

He leans in and speaks in a quieter tone. "And if I let go right now, you're not going to drop to the floor?" I can hear the slight twinge of amusement on his breath. He must have seen my shaking knees earlier. My breath hitches as his mouth lingers near my ear. He huffs a laugh, the breath tickling my skin. Maybe he can sense that the last thing I need right now is someone asking if I'm okay.

"What?" I ask, clutching the front of my dress to my chest with my other hand. I turn around to face him, his hands dragging across my middle over the fabric. I tighten my fist on the dress, bunching it in the center of my chest. Unable to slow my racing pulse as his eyes dip to my lips.

His fingers loosen their grip as I move my free hand to grasp his forearm, keeping him in place. His voice is low, amused but self-assured as he glances down at my hand. "Did you get yourself stuck in that dress because you wanted a reason to be alone in a hotel room with me again?" I have to stop myself from biting my lip. My heart feels like it's about to burst through my chest and make a hole through the door like Wile E. Coyote. "No."

We stand in charged silence for a few seconds before my mouth parts on a muted gasp as Oliver slowly moves his hand up to my face, my grip staying on his arm. His warm fingers cup my chin as he drags a rough thumb across the underside of my bottom lip, smoothing out my smeared red lipstick and setting my nervous system alight like it's New Year's Eve.

"It's a shame you want nothing to do with me," he says down onto my lips, almost out of breath.

The need itches like a freshly formed bruise. If I was braver, I would kiss him. Use my free hand to pull his shirt toward me and slam my lips into his. Collide my body against his until his back hits the wall. But I don't. I don't move. I don't do anything. Because that kind of risk is something I can't take.

"I . . . don't." I clear the desire from my throat, reaffirming it to myself as well as him.

The left sleeve of my dress slides down my arm; he runs his hand up my arm, tugging the fabric back over my shoulder, and then, much to my chagrin, he pulls his torso away from mine.

"I'll send an intern for the dresses," he says on a slow exhale. His dark eyes flick back and forth, studying every tiny moment I make like he just asked me a final question.

I look everywhere but his face. "Uh-huh."

He slips his hand into his pocket before stepping away and heading for the door. Leaving me breathless, half naked, and surrounded by expensive fabric.

CHAPTER 17

Business Account (WYST) BALANCE: £2,782.43
Personal Account BALANCE: -£1,857.10
Room service, charged to the room of Spencer Cole: £42.79
Data Roaming charge: £6.50

I was reluctant to believe it in the first round, but Spencer truly is the star of the conference. So much so, I'm not bringing up the smash burger and Kir Royale he ordered at 1 a.m. last night when he thought I was asleep.

"It's kinda strange, really," he laments as we walk to the auditorium for the start of Round Two. "You struggled to get attention on Wyst for like two years, I go up onstage *once* and it's all anyone can talk about."

I try not to roll my eyes as I follow Spencer down the long beige corridor with Odericco Investments banners pointing us toward an ornate conference center. The last thing he needs before he goes onstage is to be berated by me. Carved wood with gilt ceilings would make you assume everyone will be dressed up as French aristocrats. Instead, rows and rows of Banana Republic and Brooks Brothers are milling around in a battle of whose voice can at once be both the lowest and the loudest.

A couple of the men do a double take when they see Spencer, immediately ending their conversations and approaching him with feverish expressions.

"Hey, man, really great to meet you yesterday. I sent you a request on LinkedIn. It'd be great to connect," one of the men says, a hopeful look in his eyes.

Spencer and I freeze in unison.

"Hello, yes. Great, great." Spencer nods way too many times.

As we walk away, Spencer plasters on a smile and says through his teeth, "I don't have a LinkedIn profile."

I'm not sure what scares me more, Spencer lying or telling the truth. Apparently, he was recognized multiple times yesterday, and the other competitors were grilling him at breakfast. I know I should feel excited, but an inkling of dread looms like an iceberg in the distance. What did he say to them and is any of it true?

My brow is already furrowed as I type in "Spencer Cole" to my app. "This smells of Cecily. I'll find out."

There he is; it's all made up but looks legitimate. His fake degree, his fake work experience, interning at a made-up company, then his creation of Wyst three years ago.

Two minutes later, I'm hiding in the corner behind a ficus, waiting for Cecily to pick up the phone. "Did you create a fake LinkedIn for Spencer?"

"Guilty. Did you think your absolutely batshit crazy plan would work without a bit of Cecily magic? When you googled Spencer Cole, it came up with a review article about his one-man show."

I was so focused on hiding his profiles, I didn't think about the social media profiles he *doesn't* have. It never occurred to me he'd be such a hit at the conference that people would be actively googling *him*, not just Wyst.

My stomach drops. "Oh no, the one where he talks about the childhood trauma of playing Bill Sikes in the school play and peeing his pants onstage when everyone booed him?"

"No, the one where he gender swaps *Fleabag* to make it about his sexual awakening in London."

"Oh no . . . not *Dickbag*."

"*Dickbag*," she confirms solemnly.

"It was really good to be fair," I say on a shrug.

"Yeah, I'm sad I missed it; in the article the critic gave it four stars."

My shoulders deflate. "But I'm glad nobody here saw that. You are a genius, thank you."

"No worries. I know you're under a lot of pressure right now and didn't want to stress you out with another thing to do."

I shower her with appreciation, feeling quite sheepish that I didn't think of covering those tracks myself.

When I hang up the call, I immediately search Spencer's name, then Wyst. The feeling of relief is laced with something I can't quite put into words. Something cold and sharp digging into my side. I've locked the safe and forgotten the code. Spencer is now all over my Wyst. An infestation that I invited in. I know better than most, once something is out there, once it's been smeared everywhere, it's near impossible to scrub it clean. But now the story has been rewritten. Wyst was launched and created by Spencer Cole.

Maybe it's a weight taken off my shoulders that my life is no longer attached to this thing that has felt like a phantom limb for years. But what am I without Wyst? Just a girl who had a horrible thing happen to her, and she did nothing about it. She created a company, a concept, the bare bones of a thing, and could do nothing with it until someone more talented and better suited came along. Someone who everyone always loved more, listened to more, commanded the attention of a room like she never could. But I put Spencer here. I asked him to do this. How can I complain about him for doing a good job?

"SPENCER!" THE BOOMING voice of Dominic Odericco penetrates me to my core as we enter the sparse backstage area. It's not the bustling hub it was during Round One. As the competition becomes more serious, the company teams aren't meant to be back here during Round Two. I'm purely here to give Spencer a final talking-to before finding my seat. When we realized there was no chance of us getting away with our *Freaky Friday* plan this time, I wasn't too aghast, since he doesn't seem to want to follow my lead anyway. My pulse ratchets up when Spencer immediately paces toward Dominic.

"Hey, how are ya?" Spencer is so laid-back, whereas my shoulders are up to my ears.

Spencer turns his body in line with mine, leaning in to introduce me. "This is my assistant, Violet."

The urge to impress Dominic curdles inside me, the desire to sideswipe Spencer and declare, "I'm actually the brains behind this operation." But I think about what Oliver said at the pool: Do I want Wyst to succeed? Or do I want credit for it succeeding?

I smile and lean forward to shake his hand, my palm just touching Dominic's when Spencer continues, "She was just about to get me a coffee. Can she get you anything?"

I blink, trying to keep the shock off my face. Blood stains my cheeks as I meet Dominic's piercing emotionless gaze.

"I'm good, thank you. My team is already on it." He shoots me a tight smile.

Swallowing my pride like a gumball, I return the smile.

"I'd love a latte before we start." Spencer gestures with his eyes in the direction of the door, clearly trying his best to be polite while also telling me to fuck off. When I match his forced smile, I pivot on my heel in a robotic fashion and, once out of sight, stomp over to the coffee bar.

The metal cylinder is letting out a steady flow of steam. I squeeze in between the other assistants to make Spencer the worst coffee he's ever tasted.

Five pumps of Irish cream–flavored syrup, check. I know he hates that after we stole a bottle of Baileys from the fridge at Christmas when we were fourteen and drank the entire thing in our bedroom. Spencer proceeded to throw up at the dinner table, all over his roast dinner.

Almond milk, he pretends to like it around his artiste friends but has an unusual disdain for the stuff so check.

Three sachets of artificial sweetener just to take it over the edge, check.

When I return, he's still standing close and chatting away like old chums with Dominic, lifting on the balls of his feet to say something into Dominic's ear. It's the first time I've seen the usually stoic man smile in real life. He looks at the floor as he laughs; his teeth are perfect, straight, and white without looking like veneers. What would Spencer have said to get him to laugh like that?

I hand the coffee over to my *hilarious* boss and watch as he takes a sip, trying to hide his obvious revulsion for the drink. I smile politely, "Will there be anything else, *sir*?"

"No, that's all. Thank you," he replies, his voice thicker than usual. He hands the cup back to me, the coffee spilling a patch onto my shirt.

I leave the backstage area once the main lights start to dim; now that the competition has heated up it's "essential personnel only." The auditorium is packed, with even more people attending than the first round. Meandering down through the aisle, I finally spot an empty seat right at the back, the rest of the row in shadow. As I get closer, I catch sight of Oliver sitting in the seat next to it.

I step forward, then hesitate. Turning around and then back to him as I look for any other seats at the back. Turning back, I find Oliver staring right at me, a bemused look on his face.

"Stop being weird and sit down," he says quietly with a furrowed brow, holding his hand out to the empty seat. He glances at my outfit as I sit.

"I spilled coffee on my shirt," I lie, cracking open my water bottle and taking a swig only for something to do with my hands.

"Seems like that's a habit of yours," he says, not looking away. His jaw is shadowed by the dimming auditorium lights. I watch his throat bob as his lips curve an imperceptible amount.

After a few seconds, Oliver's scent reaches me. The peppery smell magnetizes me toward him, a feeling I actively have to fight.

Focus on Spencer.

I read my brother the riot act this morning as we were getting ready, including a list of things he specifically wasn't allowed to say, plus a revised, more realistic version of his outrageous Round One pitch. My anxiety is as high as it was then. I trust that Spencer is going to do a good job; he can speak eloquently and command the stage, but ultimately I have no control of him. That fear combined with sitting next to Oliver's magnetic presence makes my brain feel like it's on a spit roast rotating over a campfire.

"Seems like these things only happen when you're around," I parrot, roll my eyes, and sink into the chair. Our arms brush, causing a thrill to jolt up my back. I take a sip of my normal cup, trying to reduce the heat swirling in my stomach.

He relaxes into his chair. "Awww, that's sweet. You get distracted and clumsy around me; it's understandable to lose executive functions when you're turned on."

I cough on my coffee, the spluttering drawing the attention of several people around us.

He pats me on the back as I lean forward, glancing around at the eyeballs on us. "She's fine, just excited to see Dominic."

A few people roll their eyes, shifting back to regain their comfortable position in their fold-down seats.

Oliver's pats become slow circular strokes as my breathing levels out. Tracing his palm around until I lean back, the theater seat bouncing with the force. The final lights go down and the crowd begins to murmur.

"You okay?" he asks, his face shadowed.

"I'm fine," I say, my cheeks flaming hot from the combination of limited airflow and embarrassment among my TechRumble peers.

Applause erupts as Dominic steps his Prada lace-ups onto

the stage. "Welcome to TechRumble Round Two. It's fantastic to see so many familiar faces from Rome."

I came to the conclusion that Spencer is better speaking on his own terms, instead of parroting my language.

I glance around at the crowd. They are so in awe of Dominic. Hard and stoic like the Zeus of tech bros. My eye cuts to Oliver, who isn't really paying attention, leaning his chin on his palm as his elbow rests on the armrest between us. He must be so used to seeing this kind of spectacle.

"Of course, not everyone has made it this far. Starting with two hundred contenders, please give yourselves a round of applause for making it to the final fifty."

How intense should I look right now? Obviously, the level of nervousness I actually feel isn't appropriate. No assistant would look like their entire life depends on the outcome of this panel talk. Mirroring Oliver's relaxed position I try to stop my foot from frantically tapping against the floor.

His breath brushes my neck as he leans over and whispers, "By the way, I've secured the ten minutes with Dominic."

"Really?" I turn to him wide-eyed, our faces so close it's like we're back in my room again.

"I'm a man of my word. You scratch my back, I scratch yours."

"Remind me to scratch your back more often," I say before I can think. Thankfully the dimmed auditorium lights shroud me in partial darkness, covering my warm face.

"Well, you have a very nice back, so the pleasure was all mine."

We hold each other's gaze for an unfriendly amount of time, until finally he breaks.

"So after the mixer thing tomorrow I have the night off. Maybe we could go get a drink or . . . dinner?"

My head immediately nods, not breaking eye contact. I do want to spend time with him. But then, I blink. And the butterflies in my chest start disintegrating into dust. I picture going for dinner with him, having a great time, and maybe getting to relive that night in Rome with the ending we both wanted. But what happens after that? After the competition ends? I say, *Hey, by the way, my name isn't Violet; it's Jess, and I'm actually the CEO of that start-up I'm pretending to work for. The start-up that's competing in a competition judged by your boss slash cousin.* That's insane. It's not sensible; it's not safe to continue something that can never go anywhere, even if I desperately want to feel his hands all over me again. To get to know him outside of the confines of TechRumble.

I open my mouth, close it, then open it again on a nervous laugh. "Ummm, actually, I don't think it's a good idea. At least not during TechRumble."

"Okay, right. Yeah, sure." He glances toward the exit over my shoulder and then back to me.

"I'm sorry, I—" I sit back, damping my urge to move forward and kiss the embarrassed look off his face.

"No, please don't apologize. It's totally fine."

"Maybe if we—" My words are interrupted by blasting music followed by the rapturous sound of shouting, whooping, and clapping echoes around the auditorium. This feels like if the *Hunger Games* was introduced in the *Wolf of Wall Street.*

Oliver licks his lips and swallows as he sits back in his chair. I flick through the brochure from my seat to see the group Spencer will be paired with for the panel talk. A language app that aids learning through images rather than words, a gaming system for "online athletes" that uses a VR mouthpiece, and a new age social media platform, which allows you to "at" someone directly on any page of the internet instead of sending a link. A fairly decent bunch, and I get why we are in with this group. It's our best shot of making it to the next round. It's creative, not the fintech, SaaS management, cybersecurity, or AI-based categories Spencer would fall short against. He will understand all three of his competitors and what they do, better the devil you know. I'm hoping all their founders are complete nerds; that's one thing you can rely on in the start-up industry. Perversely, Spencer has the advantage of not caring *too much*. If I was up there, I'd be so stressed out I'd probably end up mincing my words and self-sabotaging. Spencer's lack of investment gives him an easy air compared to everyone else, and hopefully for the judges that will translate into confidence onstage.

The contestants step out to much less applause than Dominic. They all look so stressed apart from Spencer, who *waves* to the crowd like he's a comedian on a late-night show. His laid-back demeanor makes it look like he doesn't even need the money. Maybe this is what all companies should do, hire a charismatic front man who can talk about the company without a true passion for it. Move hubris out of the way and appoint a spokesperson for everything. Who knows how much further Wyst would be right now if I'd done this sooner?

CHAPTER 18

Business Account (WYST) BALANCE: £2,782.43
Personal Account BALANCE: -£1,857.10

From the coverage online it seems like we made it out of the panel talk relatively unscathed." Cecily's voice blasts from my headphones as I sit tucked into a corner in the hotel lobby.

I drag my thumb down the social media notifications, watching for any indication of doubt. Any sign that someone had seen the live feed or been here in person and realized Spencer had no idea what he was talking about.

"Okay," I breathe and sink into a red medieval-style armchair in the lobby. "No drama. That's good."

"Ummm, minor drama . . . there might be a problem with Dr. Bernie."

My eyebrows raise. "What happened?"

"Well, do you want the good news or the bad news?" she asks.

"Ideally, I want no news."

"Well, *FemTech Monthly* is reporting that she's considering a strategic partnership with a different brand."

My eyes widen. "What?" My voice echoes across the marble, causing a few people wandering into the conference room nearby to shoot daggers in my direction. "Who?" I say quietly into the receiver.

"It's a period pants start-up."

"Fuck," I say.

"Yeah," she agrees.

"Why is she wavering? Can you talk to her people?" My hands start to sweat against the back of my phone.

"Because of the money, most likely. They have funding, and for every pair sold they donate a pair to a homeless person."

"But that doesn't even make sense. If someone doesn't have easy access to washing facilities, surely that's a health and hygiene issue?"

I can hear Cecily's blazer shift as she shrugs. "Periods are hot right now; she's going with the crowd."

"I guess. Is there any way to get her back on our side?"

"The positive press coverage will help for sure, but I think we're going to need a contingency plan if she notices that Spencer is onstage, not you."

"I know," I admit. "Do you think she'd still go for it if she thinks Spencer is in charge?"

"I'll put some feelers out this afternoon," she says before clicking off the line.

I sit in silence, staring at the wall. If we lose Dr. Bernie we can kiss this expansion into media goodbye. Running a hand over my face, I pace back into the hall for the next "voluntary" activity on the TechRumble calendar.

The chairs are arranged in two long parallel lines, each seat facing its opposite. The crowd is formed into different social pockets, nervous companies gathered together like puppies huddling for warmth.

Dominic Odericco steps up onto the stage as the crowd hushes. "Thank you, everyone, for coming and making time in your busy schedules. I appreciate and take note of all who have attended these voluntary events in addition to the competition events."

"Okay, so they definitely are not voluntary then," I whisper to Spencer out of the corner of my mouth.

The only thing I would be doing instead of this is inhaling tiny packets of complimentary nuts and wine on the sofa bed in Spencer's room. This came with a free lunch, thank god.

Dominic continues, "A benefit of TechRumble is meeting fellow industry experts, entrepreneurs, and innovators to make professional connections and build a strong network. Whether you are a founder, CEO, coder, or marketer, your business has been personally selected by me and my panel to compete in Round Two. Some of you will be selected to join us in Vienna next month. This means everyone in this room is already in the top 10 percent of the current start-up ecosystem."

The crowds murmurs excitedly. In front of me, a man whispers to his colleague, "We should put that in the next user update."

He's right; if we don't get to the next round, Wyst can use this as a jumping-off point. I need to get a grip and appreciate that this is something to be happy about, not something I just need to hold on tight and get through. No matter whether we make it, it will force the investors who rejected Wyst to rethink their decisions. For a moment, my tight chest loosens, opening up enough room for a featherlight feeling of hope to slither through.

"My hope for this networking session is you all leave with valuable connections. With just three minutes to introduce yourselves to each person sat opposite you, you can maximize the new connections you make during your time at TechRumble."

Spencer nods along enthusiastically, admiring Dominic from afar. "Very efficient."

"All right, Steve Jobs, that's only 1.5 minutes per person. We need to make sure we use the time effectively."

Spencer rolls his shoulders; he was born for this. He whispers back to me, "It's not my fault you're a grower not a shower."

My arms break into goose bumps when I catch sight of Oliver across the room. He's watching Odericco's speech from the back of the crowd while holding a laptop like a clipboard. He's taller than most of the people around him, but something I can't put my finger on makes him stand out beyond that. The way he holds himself, like he's so comfortable being here he's almost bored, clashing against the feeling that he isn't meant to be here at all. After a few seconds, his eyes flick to mine, like he sensed me watching him. My immediate instinct is to look elsewhere, but I force my gaze back to his, feeling the heat rise in my cheeks as he subtly tilts his head, his face morphing from outrageously bored into an amused smirk. Did he get hotter overnight?

We shuffle over to our randomly allocated seats. I am in one of the seats that remains stationary throughout the next hour, whereas Spencer will be out of earshot moving along the row of chairs.

After three or four of the same conversation with identical men in their late twenties promising to change the world with their new food delivery, scooter rental, nutrition guide, or laundry service app, I look down the long conga line of people in suits. Counting their heads to calculate how many minutes I have left, I pause on Oliver, leisurely running my eyes over every inch of his face as he politely listens to his partner. He asked me out. That hot man asked me out and I wanted to say yes. It feels like a triumph in itself that I even wanted to pursue something with him. I haven't felt that butterfly-in-stomach sensation for so long. Finally experiencing that again but Oliver being the one person I can't act on it with leaves a bittersweet taste in my mouth.

Taking a quick look at the people down the line, I snag on a familiar one. Blood drains from my cheeks and my eyes can't look away from the face of the man who ruined my life, Malcolm Steward.

For the next few minutes, I am almost in a comatose state, the numbness on my skin and panic in my ribs like raging water thrashing against a concrete dam. What happens when we get face-to-face? Maybe he won't recognize me. My name is different here. I've changed my hair. I look older and I'm not dressed like a people-pleasing junior financial analyst anymore, but if the roles were reversed, I could spot him in a crowd of a thousand. In some morbid way I'd almost be offended if he didn't recognize me. *Does my face haunt your days and nights like yours does mine?*

The timer goes off with a bloodcurdling ring, and the line of bodies move across the chairs.

"Hello again," a voice that sounds like Oliver's says.

"Hi," my mouth says in return.

The butterflies I had expected to feel when Oliver sat in front of me have turned into vampire bats, draining the blood from my cheeks.

"How are you?" he asks.

"Good, you?" I reply in a monotone voice, glancing at Malcolm again. Has he seen me? I deliberately changed everything about myself since we last saw each other in that meeting with the head of HR. When the terms of the agreement were made. Now I wish I'd filed a restraining order just to guarantee I'd never have to look at his face again. I just wanted it to be over as quickly as possible. I should have pushed for more. I would know what to do now. But maybe that's the curse—the only people who know how to act in extreme scenarios are the ones who have already been through them.

"Yeah, I'm good," Oliver says. I can feel his confused gaze on me.

"How are you?" I ask.

He lets out a nervous laugh. "Still as good as I was five seconds ago."

"Good." I force my eyes back to him and show a tight smile.

We sit in silence for a few more seconds. I guess you would call it an awkward silence, but for me, it comes loud and fast. Like a roaring, metal grinding in my ears as I contemplate the man now only a few seats down from me.

Oliver's fingers entwine on his lap as he shifts in his seat. I study him, watch his lips touch and part as he struggles to find something to say, but my brain can't think of anything other than the name of the man sitting six seats away. Can I just get up and leave? Dominic is standing to the side, and like he said, he is noting everyone's presence. I'm not the CEO in his eyes, but I still represent Wyst. Getting up and leaving in the middle of this event is a no-go.

The bell rings again as he gets shuffled along. I barely notice as Oliver moves to the next seat, still staring at me. My eyes can't even focus on the next person. A couple of people come and go, staring into my glassy eyes and telling me about their initiative to make online transactions simpler for freelancers and amazing technology that helps cancer patients during chemotherapy. My body is frozen solid like a rabbit playing dead in the woods, hoping the fox will pass me by without noticing. Every ring of the three-minute timer triggers a wave of nausea to rise to the surface. Every three minutes Malcolm is getting closer.

"You okay?" Spencer shuffles onto the seat in front of me, a brief respite when I don't have to pretend to keep it together.

My voice shakes as I try to subtly deliver this vital information. "Malcolm's here," I mouth.

His brow knits. "What?"

I close my eyes for a second at the idea of having to explain out loud. "Malcolm, from Graystone. He's here."

Spencer's face goes white. "Why the fuck is he here?"

"I don't know. I don't know if he's seen me." I grip the edges of the chair.

"Do you want to leave? I thought he got fired?"

"We can't leave; everyone will see. It will look odd and it could damage our chances of making it to the next round after all our hard work."

Spencer looks to either side of us, straining his neck to see the executives managing the event chatting among themselves in the corner of the room.

"Making it to the next round doesn't matter, Jess. We can leave right now; just say the word and we'll go . . . Or I can deck him if you'd prefer." Spencer shoots me a tight smile.

"No. I can stay. I just can't have him recognize me. He'll see my name tag is wrong." I rub my face with my hands, wishing I'd used the severance money to get a full face transplant instead.

Spencer considers, scanning my face before nodding. "Okay. You're going to switch with me."

My brain must not be fully functioning because I just stare at him, trying to process what he wants me to do.

"When the bell goes off, switch seats with me. I'll stay put and you keep moving," he says slower, enunciating each word. "Just follow my lead, okay?"

I nod silently; he reaches forward to touch my knee for re-assurance but hesitates. I'm meant to be his assistant, not his sister. He can see I need comfort, but any unnecessary touching would look inappropriate and unprofessional. After what feels like an eternity, the bell rings. As we both jolt upright, Spencer pulls a pile of brochures and papers from his folder and lets go; they slap against the ground, and I instinctually go to help him pick them up. He steps behind me, slapping my leg to move. If you were watching us closely, we'd look insane, but everyone here is so enthralled by who they are meeting next they don't notice when I sit down on the next seat over from Spencer's and Spencer sits in mine.

Letting out a long breath, I glance at the person now in front of me, a woman about my age with a dark brown slick bob. I instantly relax, recognizing her as one of the assistants from the hotel pool.

"Hey!" Her face warms as she also recognizes me. "Violet, right?"

"Yeah." I smile, my eyes squinting as I try to remember her name. "Sorry, is it Kat?"

"Kit," she confirms as we shake hands. "You've seen me in my underwear. I think we can go by nicknames now." Her infectious laugh puts me even more at ease.

My memory finally locks into place. "Did you end up getting kicked out of the hotel that night?"

"No." She laughs. "Luckily one of the guys we were with is the assistant to the governor of Rome so he managed to negotiate a slap on the wrist instead of a full banning. What would all the big-wig investors do in his city without their precious personal assistants, hey?"

"Society would crumble." I nod solemnly, my pulse finally regulating.

"Exactly." She smiles.

"Sorry. I don't think I got a chance to ask, which company do you work for?"

She smooths her dark hair to briefly reveal an electric-blue strip underneath. "Well, I'm an 'assistant's assistant' at the moment." She holds her fingers up in quotes, rolling her eyes at the ridiculousness of her job title. "At a cybersecurity company. I applied for an intermediate coding job, but they offered me this instead. It's boring but it pays the bills. I'd much prefer working somewhere like Wyst." She points to my name tag with my fake name, fake job title, and real company typed in Impact font. "What's that like?"

"Oh, it's great." I launch into pitch mode, giving her the rehearsed spiel with personalized elements to suit a cool coder. This is a verbal safe space. Unlike Spencer, talking to hundreds or even thousands of people at once isn't my strong suit. But one-on-one conversations, connecting with other people on a human scale, is where I can thrive.

We talk back and forth for our remaining time; then I move to the next seat along. I relax into my chair, knowing I'm out of Malcolm's eye line now with several people separating us.

After the final bell rings, we're meant to stay and swap details with people we connected with, but I trust Spencer has this in hand. Under the cover of the mingling crowd, I flee toward the side entrance, glancing over my shoulder to make sure no one has noticed me leaving. I turn around, my chest seizing as a large bony body bashes into me.

"Hey, watch—" The man's voice goes silent.

"Sorry," I say at the same time, keeping my head down and pushing past to the exit. But as I go to move, a hand on my arm stops me. My whole body tenses as I cut a side glance up.

"Jess," Malcolm says. Not asks.

With a single look from his piercing eyes, everything comes flooding back. Everything he did, everything he said, everything that happened to me. The fear, the shame, the disgust— they crawl under my skin, wrenching fingers around my lungs and gripping tight. I want to punch him, scratch his eyes out so he can never look at me again, but then he'd definitely know it's me.

"No, sorry. You must be thinking of someone else," I answer his nonquestion with a shaky voice, my mouth so dry the words pour out like sand.

I shift, pull my tingling arm from his lanced fingers, and push the bar to open the door into the cold air. Heat rises up my throat as I shut the door behind me and run until I reach the end of the street. I heard the door latch about ten seconds after me and pray he didn't see which way I disappeared. Or maybe he was just coming to get a second look, to confirm his suspicion. Either way, Malcolm cannot definitively know that I, Jess Leigh Cole, am here. Him knowing my real identity could ruin everything. A wave of heat pushes into me as I turn a corner and vomit into the bushes.

CHAPTER 19

Business Account (WYST) BALANCE: £2,321.63
Personal Account BALANCE: -£1,857.10
Recent transactions:
Microsoft Office annual business fee: £460.80

The last evening in Paris is celebrated with a contestants' mixer party on the exclusive rooftop of the hotel; the bar is jarringly modern compared to all the other surroundings. The hotel is three hundred years old, so why does the bar have multicolored strobes lighting up the walls? Maybe I'm being a snob. But maybe it's catering to the tech crowd who crave modernity and forward thinking, who need the next best thing to feel like they are living life in the most efficient way possible, therefore maximizing their prowess over everyone else in the room.

When Spencer and I got back to our hotel after the speed networking, I asked him to look Malcolm up online. He's working as a tech and business journalist for a small-fry online magazine based in London. Just seeing his author profile on the website made me feel like I was going to throw up lunch all over again. At least I can relax knowing journalists aren't invited to this part of the event, and we're getting on the last train back to London tonight. Once the results of Round Two come out later tonight, we will no doubt be voted out of the competition and this will all be over. I'll never have to see him again.

"How many people in this bar do you think have blood boys?" Spencer leans in to ask.

I scrunch my face. "Blood boys?"

"You know, where they infuse their blood with a younger, healthier person's blood as a way to slow down their aging."

I side-eye my brother. "Ew, where did you hear that?"

He shrugs. "Twitter. But the main reason they want to live longer is to conquer more businesses. It's weird because the people that live the longest are Mediterranean great-grandmothers who have eaten tomatoes, focaccia bread, and wine their whole lives."

My stomach growls at his words, having survived the afternoon hiding out in the hotel room on nothing but complimentary biscotti and espresso.

"So the things they want to live longer for are the things that are killing them faster?" I offer.

"Yeah, like you'd live longer if you just took that money and chilled the fuck out, ya know?"

My mind drifts to an image of me living in a beach hut; sand in crevasses at all times, sunburn, sea-salt crunchy hair. I shudder, a nightmare. But on second thought, a beach bar with no responsibilities does sound good right now.

As we step into the throng, Spencer converts to CEO mode, immediately abandoning me for his new friends. This is just like when we started secondary school. We'd always been in the same friend group, but he'd insisted that we have our "own friends" now that we were in Big School. Of course, whenever I had friends over, he would charm them, declaring them as his own once he'd socially conquered them. He would have sleepovers and I was not invited.

He bounds over and is greeted by his new besties. All founders and CEOs. They are acting like they are friends now, but I don't think he fully understands how each one of them would throw him into traffic for a shot at placing in the top three. To him, this is just a fun experience he can look back on fondly, but for them, TechRumble is a battle royal in Armani suiting.

Left to my own devices, I beeline toward the open bar. After ordering a Negroni, I lean against the cold edge and scan the crowd. A sea of gray, navy, and black with pops of tie color, but never too loud because that would be obnoxious. My eyes snag on Dominic, a commanding presence with so many eyes on him. Studying his face among the average businessmen truly makes me understand how Spencer was describing him. This man looks like a movie star. So unbelievably unattainable based on his face and stature alone. But combined with his wealth and unique brand of magnetic yet stoic charisma, I can see why every single person's body language subtly gravitates toward him. I know the feeling of everyone knowing who you are when you walk in the room. But my version doesn't stem from awe and adoration; it was from a sickly mix of judgment, anger, and pity. Maybe going through that experience makes you acutely aware of when people are staring at you. Which is how my skin buzzes when I catch sight of Oliver looking straight at me from a group of Odericco assistants. His demeanor shifts, tensing at the sight of me. He tilts his head, furrowing his brow into a question.

"What?" I mouth, taking a sip of my drink to avoid looking awkward and uncomfortable under his scrutinizing gaze.

As he wades over to me, I can't stop my mind flashing to how he looked in the hotel room, the last time we were alone. His thumb brushing against my open mouth. He glides through the crowded floor with ease, a tiger swimming through lily pads as people ebb and flow to give him purchase. People glance at him, some a second glance, probably due to his access to Dominic Odericco. To many, he's the gatekeeper and access granter. To me, he's the person my brain is telling me to stay away from, but my body refuses to leave. My feet remain glued to the floor until he's towering over me at the bar, his scent lingering against my lips as I take another defiant sip of my drink.

"I thought you'd finally decided on disliking me." His lips curve as he scans my face with bright twinkling eyes.

I crinkle my nose. "What are you talking about? I—" I stop as the memory hits me. "Oh my god, I completely ignored you this morning. I'm so sorry."

He blushes ever so slightly, giving me a confused look. "Were you blowing me off because I asked you out?"

I place my drink on the bar and shake my head. "No. Well, yes. Maybe. Not really."

He huffs a laugh. "Well, I'm glad that's cleared up. I just thought you weren't interested in me."

My chin tilts to meet him. "I haven't fully committed to the plan of not being interested. It's just . . . complicated."

"Then this is me generously giving you the opportunity to explain yourself." He lifts a brow and crosses his arms. His thick hair flops to the side as he leans against the bar. There's a cheekiness to his demeanor, but I can feel the undercurrent of nerves passing through him.

I guffaw. "I have nothing to explain. I think I've made myself very clear already." Heat crawls up my spine.

He scoffs a laugh, running a hand over his light stubble. "Are you serious?"

I know for a fact that I haven't made myself even slightly clear. I'm confusing myself with my own actions. My focus should purely be on this competition, but my attention continues to be dragged in the opposite direction, toward the big red arrow saying "hot, charming American wants to take you out."

Am I acting just like Spencer? Playing pretend, living vicariously through a character I've made up. Violet isn't meant to be any different than Jess except in name, but only when I saw Malcolm did I realize I've felt so much lighter playacting as Violet. The past felt detached, rather than etched into my bones.

Maybe Oliver would like Jess as much as Violet, but I can't take that risk. Can I? Every man who has entered my life doesn't stay long enough to garner a second date. But being forced into these situations with Oliver has allowed him to get under my skin, even if he doesn't realize he's doing it.

He raises his hand and orders a drink from the bartender. "You've said you were only interested in being friends, and yet whenever we're in a room together, you can't take your eyes off me."

My cheeks flare. So much for subtlety. I guess I'm not as covert as I thought.

"Yes, I can." A feeble attempt at rebuttal considering I can't currently unlock my eyes from his.

Oliver thanks the bartender as a matching Negroni in a frosted glass is placed in front of him. He takes a long sip, then begins to cartoonishly count on his fingers. "You kissed me in a hot tub; we had an *amazing* time in the shower. In your room, you looked like you wanted me to kiss you, but then you say you would *never* want to go for dinner with me, then you start making the . . . what did you call them?" He taps his soft lip with a finger. "'The ooey-gooey eyes'? Then you give me ooey-gooey eyes from across the room at the speed networking thing this morning, but by the time we were face-to-face, you acted like I didn't exist."

My lips purse. Fuck, I am throwing him for a serious loop here. If the gender roles were reversed, this would be a toxic red flag nightmare.

He tilts his head. "So forgive me if I'm confused, but you haven't exactly made yourself clear. If you want to be friends, that's fine. I'll happily be your friend. But that's not how you look at friends, Violet."

The fake name hits me like a truck, a big fat reminder as to why I've been acting like this.

I go to take his arm. "I'm just—" My elbow smacks against my drink, knocking it clean over and leaking red liquid across the bar top. The crowd looks over at the sound of smashing glass, a few resounding "wheeeeeeys" coming from the British contingency in the room. Negroni creeps over the edge and begins to drip on the floor, causing both Oliver and I to jump back. I glance at the crowd, feeling the heat rising in me completely dissipate into cold embarrassment.

"Fuck, sorry," I say to the bartender as I take napkins and try to soak up the booze, cutting my hand on a tiny shard of glass in the process. "Ow."

Oliver steps toward me, taking my hand and assessing it. He pulls a small shard out of my palm, blood oozing out of the cut. He takes a black napkin and presses it against my skin, using his thumb to put pressure on and wrapping his fingers around the other side of my hand.

"It's okay. I got it," the bartender says with a weak smile, obviously annoyed to have to stop serving for a couple of minutes to clean up my mess. The crowd waiting for drinks aren't the most patient of clientele.

"Sorry," I repeat, internally cringing that this keeps happening in front of Oliver.

My eyes dart back to the crowd to check if anyone is still looking at this display of fondness between the two of us. My first glance brings a sense of calm that nobody really cares what is going on at the bar. That is, until a sharp jolt of pain runs up my neck, goose bumps rising all over my body. I glance again, eyes locking on Malcolm's. He's in the crowd, inconspicuous, blending in with everyone else apart from the bright blue eyes that are fixed onto mine.

People say in these moments your blood runs cold. But mine goes hot, like someone is holding a lighter to my arteries. Why is he here? Did he come here, uninvited, just to check his theory? A journalist just following a hunch? The pure hatred radiating from him goes straight to my stomach, lancing me so hard I have to check a shard of glass didn't penetrate me there. I thought maybe I'd gotten away with it at the speed networking event, but now the look of satisfied recognition curling around his mouth tells me he's finally certain.

Malcolm knows Violet is Jess. Malcolm knows Spencer is not a CEO. Malcolm knows Jess is a liar and a fraud.

My heart barrels over itself, beating so hard it covers the sound of the mingling crowd. My fingers grip the edge of the bar, sweat instantly pouring from my palms. My breathing hitches, coming out in broken inhales and shaky exhales. My hands begin to shake, my vision blurring and knees turning to jelly.

I can't be here. I have to get out of here.

I glance back at Malcolm's position in the crowd; he is talking to a man I don't know, but his eyes won't get off me. Like bugs crawling under my clothes. I swallow down the stinging in the back of my throat, begging my breathing to slow. He could be telling that man about me right now. Malcolm doesn't know the full extent of what's going on, but he knows Spencer is an actor and my real name. Even at the surface level, it's enough to get us kicked out of TechRumble. Enough to make me a laughingstock again, enough to tarnish Wyst's reputation, enough to bury me and everything I've worked for in a grave of shame and online gossip.

"You're shaking," Oliver says, squeezing my palm. "Are you bad with blood?"

I clamp my eyes shut for a second, trying to assess which course of action will cause the least damage.

Finally, I pick the lesser of two evils, giving Oliver a small piece of the truth. "You said I seemed distracted earlier?"

"Yeah." He blinks, waiting with bated breath.

I swallow, my mouth dry. "Right before you sat down in front of me, I found out my ex is at the conference."

He blinks, brows knitting. "I'm guessing that didn't end well?"

"No, it ended really fucking badly." My voice cracks.

He studies me. I'm vibrating, glancing around the party making sure Malcolm isn't anywhere nearby. Fuck, I have no idea where to go. I don't even have a room key.

I turn back to Oliver, his eyes following me to the man staring daggers at me through the crowd. "Can you take me somewhere that isn't here?" My voice is squeaky as I look up at him.

He straightens. "Of course, want me to tell your boss?"

Scanning the crowd to locate Spencer, I find him talking animatedly to Dominic, who looks genuinely enthralled. At least he's making use of those ten minutes Oliver secured.

"No, I don't want to interrupt them. Are you allowed to leave?" My eyes are watery as I glance up at Oliver's taut jaw.

"I'm here as an errand boy, and getting you out of here is more important right now." He squeezes my arm. "Let's go."

Leading me out of the thickly crowded room, Oliver puts a protective arm around my waist. "This okay?" His weight around me feels like a buoy stopping me from drowning.

"Yeah," I breathe. I don't know whether the feeling of electricity is the stress of seeing Malcolm again or Oliver's skin on mine. It's confusing, but my stunted heartbeat evens out as we burst out of the room into the empty hotel lobby and head straight out the front door.

CHAPTER 20

Business Account (WYST) BALANCE: £2,321.63
Personal Account BALANCE: -£1,857.10

We walk for fifteen minutes up the cobbled streets, early evening twilight blooming across the town up ahead, past little shops selling patisserie, textiles, and cooking equipment all closed up for the night.

"Are you hungry?" he says, our feet clicking against the gravelled pathway.

"Famished." I nod.

Eventually, once the panic has melted into something more malleable, I realize this is the town I was meant to run to the other day when we make it to the main square. A huge ageing fountain marked with festoon lights and the swelling sound of classical music coming from the nearby restaurants.

We wander past a few until we reach a quiet little bistro with enough tables and chairs to fit maybe thirty people. Some of the tables are filled, a group of friends laughing over a carafe of wine, a family eating quietly as one child plays on an iPad and the other smears ketchup on the tablecloth, a couple deep in conversation, their faces flickering in the candlelight. Oliver hops ahead to open the door for me.

Once we're sitting, I examine his face for an answer before finally asking the question as we're led to a table by a smiling older man with a gray beard. "Why are you being so nice to me?"

"That feels like a loaded question." Oliver shifts to get comfortable in the wooden chair before leaning his forearms on the table. His face softens as it's cast in candlelight.

I rephrase. "Why, after everything I've done? Kissing you, rejecting you, nearly kissing you again, rejecting you again—"

He holds a hand out with a sheepish smile. "All right, you're just rubbing salt in the wound now," he says, looking down at the table.

"Sorry. And I'm sorry for being a bitch to you."

"You haven't been. You've been . . ." He pauses to think. "A puzzle to solve. An enigma on legs."

"An enigma?" I shrug as the waiter appears. "Suppose I've been called worse."

He leans over and speaks to the waiter in French.

I smile at him, and he rolls his eyes before waving his hands around lazily. "Fromage, coq l'orange, vin rouge. I can go on."

Letting out a cathartic laugh, I join in. "Macaron, pain au chocolat . . ."

"Wow, you too? See, we have so much in common." His eyes glow a bright amber in the candlelight before he sits back and sighs. "I guess I just see something in your eyes that reminds me of myself. When I was going through a bad time." His mouth twists as he contemplates his next words. "Now I think I know *who* caused the bad time?" It's phrased more as a question than an assumption.

I wring my fingers under the table. "If I looked like I was having a bad time, it was probably the shrimp canapés?" I let out an emotionless laugh, hoping to lighten the mood, to avoid telling him the truth I so desperately want him to hear.

"You looked like you were grieving."

My eyes snag on his as I glance up, holding my breath. A bullet of truth hitting me in the chest. Nobody else has ever phrased it that way, but I guess I was grieving. It feels selfish to call it that, knowing other people have been through much worse than me. But I am grieving. Grieving the old me. The fun, carefree version of myself before my life went to shit. Before the pressure to reclaim a life someone else took from me over-rode the need to enjoy it.

The waiter reappears with a matching carafe of red wine to the group of friends across the room.

I clear my throat. "What makes you think that?"

He looks down at the table, his fingernail scraping at the wood grain as he considers what to say next. "My dad died last year, dropped dead at his desk from a heart attack. I saw the same thing in you that I've been feeling for what feels like forever."

For a second I'm taken aback, endeared by the thought that he'd be willing to be this vulnerable with me, to crack open the vault for someone he barely knows to peek in. I lean forward, placing my hand over his. "I'm so sorry. Were you two close?"

"Kind of, in the way that you see an adult version of them and they see a kid version of you." He hesitates for a second. "He wanted me to be an investment banker or something in finance; we had a lot of disagreements about that."

"He wanted you to be the next Dominic Odericco?" I tease, pulling a small smile from his somber face.

He nods. "But I wanted to be a chef. I always enjoyed and wanted to pursue cooking but got pretty good grades at school, so my dad *heavily* encouraged me to get a business degree. A lot of people in my family are in the field, so he thought it would be the best thing for me. Longevity, a career with a path already laid out, I would know how much I was making in five, ten, fifteen years."

I tilt my head, studying his face. "So no offense but . . . why are you an assistant?"

He laughs, pouring the wine for me and then himself. His gaze flicks up from his glass in a way that makes my blood fizz. "Do you want the short story or the real one?"

"Hang on." Holding a finger up, I take a sip of the wine, swilling it in my mouth for a second before swallowing. "Okay, real."

He looks me up and down. "Were you waiting to see if I ordered shitty wine?" He mimes stabbing himself in the heart. As our glasses hit the table, the waiter appears again with two giant plates of food.

"I was seeing if I needed to order something stronger if we're about to get into the weeds. Real story please." I offer up my glass to clink with his, relieved to not have Malcolm at the forefront of my mind for the first time today.

He lifts his glass to mine, not taking his molten eyes off me as the *ping* of the glasses echoes off the stone walls.

"My dad was a claims manager for this big insurance firm in the U.S. for, like, forty years. Before the funeral, I went to his office to collect his things from his desk." He sighs before continuing. "But they'd already cleared everything, and someone else had put their things up. Family pictures, trinkets, their favorite mug. My dad's stuff was dumped in a box left in a storage cupboard with an 'our condolences' card on top of it, gathering dust, next to the spare pens and printer paper. He gave that firm forty years of his life, and they'd replaced him in a week. The entire time I'd been alive, he'd gone to that same office every morning. His whole career, everything he'd worked for, his entire life summed up in a fucking cardboard box and a life insurance check."

He takes a breath and runs a hand through his dark hair. "So when my mom insisted I take half the money, I used it to buy a plane ticket and enroll in a culinary school in London. I needed a fresh start, and what better way than to pursue something I'd always wanted to do. Every meal you make touches a different person; you can tell a story through food. When I die, I don't want my legacy to be a box and a check."

My brow furrows. "So why are you at TechRumble instead of some Michelin-starred restaurant?"

I watch his throat bob as he takes a large swig of the wine. "For the first couple of weeks of the course, I had this almost manic level of motivation. I was excited by the idea of becoming this incredible chef and meeting people whose dreams aligned with mine. But once the initial adrenaline wore off, I spiraled. I hadn't processed anything that had happened with my dad. My work got sloppy, sometimes I wasn't able to get out of bed for days, and I began missing classes, getting behind. At the end of the first year, they told me not to come back for the second. I was devastated, confused, and angry, but I didn't want to go back home. That felt like the ultimate failure. So I reached out to Dominic and asked if I could crash at his place for a few weeks while I figured things out."

He shifts, scratching the back of his neck. "Then once the student visa department got wind that I had been kicked out of school, I needed a job to stay in the country. That's when Dom offered me a full-time assistant role."

"You never really chose to be where you are now? It just happened to you."

"I guess, but it was more trying to make the best of a bad situation—turns out you can't outrun depression." His face briefly cringes. "I'm good now. Well, settled."

My mouth twists into a sympathetic, closed-mouth smile. "If cooking is what you love and you have the money saved up, why don't you do that now?"

"Scared, I guess. Of failing again. Even if I don't enjoy this job, at least it's safe."

"If I had that money, I would go for it." I take a breath, saying it to myself as well as him, "If you fail, you fail."

His jaw tenses. "If I fail, I'm going to end up right back here and be just like my dad."

My hand lays across his, fingers squeezing. "I'm sure your dad's legacy is more than what you imagine; his work probably affected more people than you know."

Oliver tries to avoid rolling his eyes as I continue. "A claims manager makes sure people *get* their money, right? What if someone's house burns down? Your dad making sure they got the money meant they could rebuild their lives."

His gaze softens, a dimple appearing on one side of his mouth. "Is that what you're doing? Rebuilding after the house burns down?"

I remove my hand from his and run my finger up the stem of the glass. "That's one way to put it."

He doesn't ask a follow-up question, just leaves the space open for me to share if I want to. I consider Cecily's words of encouragement, Dr. Bernie's advice onstage, and whether I'm already in too deep with my feelings for Oliver.

Maybe I should pull back and continue to hide this part of myself from him. But if I wanted to do that, why am I here? I've been saying I don't want to know him, that I don't want him to know me. But I want to tell him what happened to me.

"He, my ex, took photos of me. When we were being . . . intimate." I clear the words from my throat. "And he sent it to a group chat with his work friends. My colleagues."

Oliver's brows turn inward. "Fuck, what a piece of shit."

"The photos didn't have my face in them, but we were newly exclusive, so who else would it have been? Once they inevitably spread, people knew it was me. Malcolm was in some of them too, but people didn't care that it was him; the photos were *of me*. I came into work, and everyone was staring and whispering. I don't know how I knew what happened, but I just knew."

I take a fortifying gulp of wine. "There were only a few other women in the office. One of them said she had heard rumors of what was being circulated. When I asked Malcolm about it, he didn't deny it.

"I never saw Malcolm as my person, like the love of my life or anything—we'd only been exclusive for a few months, but to have someone you trusted do that to you . . . it was like it was his plan the entire time we were together, when he was pursuing me . . ." I trail off, unable to express the feeling. "Afterward, my entire world imploded. Work, friends, family, how others saw me, how I saw myself . . ."

"Jesus, I can't ever imagine wanting to do that to someone," Oliver muses, staring at my hand.

I shrug, almost numb to it. "Those kinds of companies are always pitting the highest-performing juniors against each other . . . I was doing better than him, receiving more praise from our mentors, getting invited to more high-level meetings. One of the few women in your office outperforming you isn't a good look in those kinds of circles. Especially your own girl-friend."

Oliver looks disgusted. "So instead of trying harder, he did . . . that."

My voice wobbles as I nod solemnly. "In hindsight, I think he wanted it to wreck me."

"Isn't revenge porn illegal in the UK? Did you press charges?"

I nod my confirmation. "Since 2015. But because Malcolm was not only my boyfriend but also my colleague, instead of immediately going to the police, I went to HR and reported it." I shake my head. "I should have gone to the police, but our director convinced me to not press charges. I guess Graystone didn't want a public scandal. They'd already been in hot water for their manager wage gap and their appalling lack of diverse hiring. The last thing they wanted was one of the few women who they let in being photographed without her consent, and the press getting wind of it." I wipe an escaping tear from my cheek. "They told me if I went to the police, the chances of prosecution would be minimal, so they offered me a deal in-stead. They told me they would get rid of Malcolm if I agreed to an NDA, if I didn't *make a scene*.'" I finger quote, remember-ing the exact way the head of HR said the words. "Malcolm was put on temporary leave while they decided what to do with him; the deliberation period was longer than he and I were even together. After it was all over, I stayed at Graystone for a while, but I knew everyone there was judging me, had seen underneath my clothes, and measured me by what they saw. Every side-eye when I entered a room, every off comment from a male colleague. I knew they would never respect me again. I couldn't handle it. Every person I spoke to, all I could think was 'Have they seen it?' I couldn't concentrate, couldn't perform to the standard I was before because every time anyone looked at me, it felt like that day all over again. I couldn't get through a day without a panic attack. So eventually, I left."

In the moment, I decide against telling Oliver that my director noticed I was spiraling and bought my silence with an offer of garden leave and a generous severance package. The money I used to create Wyst. Instead, I bend the truth. "That's why I work for Wyst. If I had access to information on exactly what to do in that situation, I would have gone to the police instead, pressed charges."

Instead of accepting a bribe that's drying up before my eyes.

Oliver's jaw ticks as he studies my face. "And I'm guessing you had no idea he was going to be here at TechRumble?"

"No. I blocked him on every social media platform. Turns out he's a business journalist now." I shrug. "If you can't do it, write about other people doing it, I guess."

He leans forward, placing his hand on mine like I did his. "I'm so sorry you went through that."

I don't correct him. I don't tell him that I'm *still* going through that. I've spent so much time thinking about Malcolm it feels like we were so much more than just a fledgling relationship. When we both agreed to the deal Graystone presented, we signed a contract together. Forever bound by ink and paper. A marriage of convenience—I don't press charges; he deletes the images and requests everyone he sent them to delete them. But I would be naive to think that would be the end of it. Once an image is out there, it's never completely gone.

I sit back, blowing out a breath. "Sorry, that was a lot. Maybe it's all the competition in the air; we didn't need to have a trauma-off." I laugh, wiping at my lash line before another tear escapes.

He keeps his hand wrapped around mine, running a comforting thumb over my palm. "The experiences are part of us. They shaped who we are, for better or for worse. But yeah, I think we deserve a stronger drink."

After another glass of wine, we ease into lighter topics—likes and dislikes, favorite books, and movies. Mine: *Legally Blonde*. His: *Ratatouille*, obviously. I admit I missed out on all pasta and gelato in Rome, much to his dismay.

"At the risk of sounding like a stalker, I couldn't find a trace of you anywhere online after Rome."

"I don't have social media, not anymore." I don't mention that I use the safety blanket of the Wyst accounts to get my fix of dopamine.

He nods with a look of understanding. "If I had your number, I would have called you when I was in London."

I place an olive in my mouth with a small smile, relieved to not be talking about Malcolm anymore. "You're assuming I would have picked up."

His eyes twinkle as he pulls his phone out of his pocket and types "Violet Leigh" into his contacts before handing me the phone. To register for the conference entry lanyards, I also had to come up with a fake last name. Clearly, I wasn't feeling particularly inspired the night I filled in the form, using my middle name as the fake surname. My eyes sting against the name illuminated in LED light, a new pang of guilt hitting me from a different angle with each digit I type in.

I delete the fake name, unable to stomach it after the almost truth I just unveiled. I type in a new contact name and my phone number before handing it back to him, our fingers lingering against each other's.

"'Enigma on legs'?" he recites with a smirk.

"Feels more accurate." I shrug.

He calls my phone, giving me his phone number.

"What should I save you as?"

He stretches nonchalantly. "'Handsome Multilingual Charming American' has a good ring to it."

I type out "Olly Olly Olly, Oi Oi Oi" and show it to him.

He looks aghast, scraping his chair against the stone floor. "Well, I was going to pay for dinner, but now I think you can treat me. For the good of transatlantic relations."

I blink as he stands and starts walking to the door. "Fine, only because I like to pay my getaway drivers a fair wage."

As I hand the waiter a small wad of euro notes, he points at Oliver and says in broken English, "No, no. Your husband, he already pay." I blush, say my thanks, and follow Oliver out the front door.

NEITHER OF US want to go back to the real world just yet, so we move on to a dark bar with wine on tap, red and black fabric-lined walls softening the edges. Not quite seedy with a capital *S* but definitely on the verge. Somewhere you'd expect a showgirl to start dancing on your table at any second, but it's calm, the calmest I've felt for weeks.

Our hands tangle tentatively under the table as we relax on an oxblood chesterfield sofa, sending a thrill down my spine like a lightning strike down a tree. The glow from tiny tea candles emblazons the bar with warm dappled light, like the whole room is on fire and everyone is totally okay with it. My blood feels hot as I study Oliver's contrasted face, the furrow of his brow even stronger in the shadows. I cross my legs, my dress inching up my thighs just a fraction. He smells like black pepper and dark chocolate, two foods I've never thought of putting together and now am craving nothing but.

There is no point in the past hour where we haven't been touching. Our shins, leaning against one another under the table in the restaurant, our arms, as he offered the crook of his elbow for me to dangle off over the cobblestone streets, his thumb tracing over my palm like he's reading my fortune. His hand engulfs mine as we stumble back to the hotel in a giddy, tipsy, flirty cloud. Despite the chill in the air and the light misting of rain, taxi after taxi drives by unhailed as we try to draw out every drop of the night, our thirst for each other unquenchable.

It's only when I can see our eventual destination in the distance that I remember we're staying at the same hotel. The weight of expectation guts me. It's not that I don't like sex anymore—my bedside table drawer is a testament to that fact. But maybe sharing that part of my past has changed things between us. I've made it not as fun for him anymore. It's heavier now. I remind myself Oliver is so unlike Malcolm. We are not in competition with each other; he has no motive to do something like that to me. Malcolm did it because he was scared and jealous; he was a misogynist asshole who aimed to embarrass, shame, and degrade me in front of my peers to get ahead. Oliver believes I am an assistant, and he doesn't want to be one. He doesn't even know my real name. The thought of telling him the whole truth occupies my mind, but I would be a hypocrite to Spencer. I pick at the thought like a scab. What good is a name when everything else is true? My attraction is true, my aching center a testament to the need to be near him.

The hotel lights shine in the distance, the soft glow washing over Oliver's face. My phone starts to buzz in my pocket but I ignore it. It buzzes again with a text from Spencer:

Where are you? Call me x

I didn't give it a second thought before I let Oliver whisk me away into the night without telling anyone where I was going.

"We should probably head back . . ." I start to say, my whole body protesting the sentiment.

"Probably." He grips my hand tighter for a second, then slowly unfurls his fingers from mine, the cold immediately turning my hands numb.

"Before anyone sees," I clarify.

"Sees what?" He smiles devilishly, then glances left down an ancient-looking street, with carved wood apartment doors and Parisian iron streetlights twinkling in the fractured air. He holds his arms out as he pivots on a heel, gesturing around him. "Sees me walking down this aggressively French street?"

"What are you doing?" I whisper-shout, curling my arms around myself to try and replicate his body heat.

"Sees me hiding from the rain in this beautiful doorway?" he whisper-shouts down the street. "Wow, you should really come see this."

I laugh, glancing a final time at the hotel lights before following his route, my heeled boot footsteps considerably louder than his. Trying to step lightly feels like a bomb going off with each tap of the sole against the stone. Or maybe that's my heartbeat.

"This is a normal doorway." I scoff, holding my hand out to a red door with peeling paint.

He takes my hand and pulls me out of the rain under the cover. He steps back, leaving me on the raised concrete step, holding up his thumbs and forefingers into a square to create a makeshift frame. "Now, it's a beautiful doorway."

I roll my eyes but can't help laughing. "Oh my god, that was the cheesiest line I've ever heard."

He shrugs. "When in France."

I tilt my head to him. "I think you mean, 'When in Rome.'"

He matches my tilt, stepping forward. "There was something I wanted to do in Rome and still want to do in France." We're the same height, face-to-face so I can admire him in more detail.

"And what's that?" I smirk, heart racing as I lean in closer.

His eyes sparkle. "Say good night."

"Good night," I say.

"Good night," he says.

"Good night," I say.

He kisses me.

It's soft at first, as delicate as the rain falling onto our cheeks.

Immediately evaporating once landed, it could practically be nothing. It's barely raining, you would say if you saw it. We're barely kissing. Lips brushing like morning dew brushes the grass.

I place my cold hand against his face, feeling the bristly stubble. His hand snakes into my open coat around my warm waist, and I melt into him. My blood turns molten as the kiss deepens, and I feel his heart hammering as hard as mine. His smell invades my senses, and I curl my cold fingers around his wool lapel, needing him as close as possible. He presses me back gently until I'm against the door, and the peeling paint crinkles as it grazes against the fabric of my coat. He pushes up the step to meet me, eyes glazed and towering over me once again. My lips are swollen as he presses a thumb against them, tracing them like he did to my cut palm in the bar. I pull him in, biting his bottom lip. His lips thin as they smile between my teeth. When I let go, he trails his mouth down my jaw to my neck, turning my legs to jelly.

"You taste amazing," he whispers, kissing the soft spot between my collarbone.

I let out a half laugh, half groan. "Michelin starred?"

"A different tire brand needs to make a whole new level of grading for you." He squeezes my waist. "What do I have to do to get you back to my room?" he says, practically begging.

"I'm getting on a train home in three hours." I moan, hating every word spilling out.

"Fuck." He rests his forehead against mine. "I forgot about the train, officially my least favorite mode of transport."

We hold one another in silence, both basking in each other's presence for a few seconds longer. The question is on the tip of my tongue: *Can I see you in London?* But I don't verbalize it.

"Want me to walk you back to your room?" he asks, before adding, "No strings attached."

I imagine bumping into Malcolm with Oliver in tow. What would happen if he said something in front of Oliver? It would just take a sentence for this whole operation to blow up in my face. And even if it didn't, he would notice I'm sharing my room with my fake boss. "No, it's okay. I'm a big girl."

Oliver sighs. "We should probably say good night, for real this time."

We kiss again, urgently. If we are trying to get this attraction out of our systems, this is making it a lot worse. Like wanting to finish every bite of dessert despite being uncomfortably full, and Oliver is crème brûlée. With a groan, our lips eventually tear apart, and he steps down, holding his hand out for me to drop down beside him. We walk in silence to the end of the street; the moment we get within eyeshot of the hotel, things have to return to professional.

But I don't want to stop. I never wanted to do anything less.

"Good night," I say.

He gives me a chaste peck on my hand and passes me his umbrella, somehow the gentlemanly gesture of all things making me blush.

He looks at me like he's already committed the evening to long-term memory. Our hot, heavy breath mingles in front of us. His glassy eyes bright under the streetlights. "A *very* good night."

I feel his gaze on me as I walk the remaining few minutes until I'm back to the hotel's front door, periodically turning around to see him walking a few yards behind like a comforting specter. Close enough to keep me safe but far enough away to not raise questions. By the time I make it through the sliding doors and into the elevator, Oliver has disappeared. He didn't follow me through the front. Thanks to working with Dominic, he must know all the staff side entrances like the back of his hand.

Glancing at my reflection in my dark phone screen, I look like I've been making out. My lips plump and naturally pink, my pupils dilated, and hair frizzy from his hands running through it in the rain. As the elevator hums toward my floor, I scan through several additional missed calls and texts I've received from Spencer and Cecily.

Spencer: OMG

Spencer: What the actual fuck

Cecily: JESS!!!!!

Cecily: Answer your bloody phone!

My stomach drops, my thumb slicing over the barrage of messages to get to whatever has gone wrong. Did Malcolm do something? Did he expose us? Maybe he went straight to Dominic after he saw me leave the party?

As the elevator dings open at my floor, I freeze. Hands shaking, I finally reach the source of the texts.

Spencer: WE'RE GOING TO VIENNA BABY!

CHAPTER 21

Business Account (WYST) BALANCE: £2,158.68
Personal Account BALANCE: -£1,857.10
Recent transactions:
Car rental fee: £162.95

Instead of working on our Eurostar back to London, I spend the majority of that time in a daze with Spencer lightly snoring on my shoulder. At passport control, I sheepishly asked what he was up to tonight, in the hopes of avoiding my final destination, but he's meeting friends for drinks and to discuss a new show. I played it off, too embarrassed to acknowledge that I was so desperate for someone to talk to about the last twelve hours. A turgid pavement greets me as we step out of St. Pancras. Spencer waves goodbye, rolling his suitcase down to the underground. I pull up Citymapper on my phone and for a moment forget I gave up my flat. A plan that felt much more sensible when sleeping on the sofa in the conference room was still a week away.

Waiting for the bus outside the station, a cold wind bites at my cheeks as I watch a young couple quietly chatting and giggling under the lamplight, holding each other for warmth in their own little world. My mind drifts to kissing Oliver, how quiet the street was compared to the roaring of London traffic. He's still in Paris but I can't help but feel him here.

You can have him or the truth, not both.

Flicking on the light switch in the office brings everything into focus in one fluorescent, squinting glow. I stare at the four identical desks, only distinguished by the individual knick-knacks and photos identifiable to the three of us who occupy this space full-time. Spencer has a few things but not for decoration. An empty notebook, a Burt's Bees lip balm, and an Owala water bottle were left behind while running in for a few days, cashing the check, then hauling out in the direction of his latest project. In a way, his life seems quite nice. Not having to rely on yourself for a paycheck, instead floating in and out of jobs, not letting anything affect you because you're not truly responsible for anyone or anything other than yourself.

I head into the meeting room to hunt through my moving boxes for some fresh underwear. At least I had the foresight to wash almost all my clothes before spending an entire night folding them into neatly organized boxes. Sometimes being type A is a good thing. My finger presses the dimmer switch, and I scan the room with a downturned mouth. Maybe the building's cleaner has moved them? I deliberately labeled them things like "merchandise" and "printer paper" in thick black Sharpie pen so to not arouse any suspicion that this is my new place of residence. My feet pad around the table, leaving my carry-on suitcase by the door. No boxes anywhere. With panic rising, I check one more time. I'm tired. My brain probably just didn't register them. Finally, my eyes land on a neon-pink Post-it note stuck to the middle of the conference table.

Call me if you ever want to see your boxes again.

C x

The rising panic is immediately subdued and replaced by confusion.

"Why do you have my stuff?" I ask down the receiver.

"I needed a bargaining chip," Cecily says. I can hear an oven fan whirring in the background.

"And what are your demands?" I say, a smile creeping across my face.

"My only demand is that you get in the Uber that will be pulling up in . . ." I hear a series of taps against the phone. ". . . six minutes."

"So you're holding my clean underwear hostage and now you're actively kidnapping me?"

"Yes . . . but in a friend way," she clarifies, the sound of a popping cork punctuating her statement. "We're celebrating Paris, and the other bottle of champagne is chilling in the fridge for you."

"You don't have to do this," I say, the guilt rising up my throat.

"Too late, Isaac is on his way in a Fiat Punto. Au revoir!" She hangs up before I can protest further.

Thirty minutes later I'm on the outskirts of central London, staring at the exterior of a fancy town house. Ivy runs the length of the thin five-story building, making the city home feel like you're stepping into a countryside manor. I've never been to Cecily's parents' place, but by the looks of things, my dirty jeans and T-shirt with a mystery stain are probably not guest appropriate. Before I have a chance to pull back the wrought iron lion-shaped knocker, the door swings open.

My eyes sting as I embrace Cecily, the scent of roasted chicken wafting through the entryway. "Smells amazing."

She smiles and takes my suitcase before shouting over her shoulder, "Please hold all praise until *after* you've tried my cooking."

I laugh as I follow her through the quiet black-and-white tiled entryway into the midnight-blue kitchen lit by antique sconces. "Where are your parents?"

She shrugs. "Oh, they are never here. I think they are in the Maldives at the moment. Maybe Bora-Bora."

Cecily has the kind of parents who are so rich they don't specifically have job titles. They serve on various boards of businesses and organizations in an advisory capacity and spend their days throwing events and charity auctions. You can't really blame them for preferring to advise from a luxury cabana next to the topaz-blue ocean and white-sand beach. Cecily once suggested we ask her family for money as a way to fund Wyst, but they much preferred the idea of her getting into the family business of galas and balls.

Cecily has everything but a present family. She's an only child. In her words, her mum was very much a "one and done" kind of mother. Providing an heir to the family fortune, she put her life of fundraisers and meetings on pause to raise Cecily in good standing and taste until she was eighteen, then carried on with her life as though her daughter didn't exist. I'm sure a lot of people would kill for Cecily's life, but now, viewing it from the inside, it seems incredibly lonely. I find Spencer irritating at the best of times but I can't imagine what it would have been like to grow up in a world of adults, without any siblings and cousins and barely any friends to grow up with.

She blinks away an emotion I can't quite place as she hands me a glass of fizzing champagne and clinks our glasses together. "And anyway, it's good they're out of the house because I want to hear *all* the filthy things you got up to in Paris."

Before dinner, she brings me up to a room on the fourth floor with varying shades of cream, green, and oak. The wooden sleigh bed takes up the majority of the room, with a sage-green accent chair in the corner matching the curling vine print wallpaper in the en suite bathroom.

The bedside table has a tray stacked with essentials you'd find at a five-star hotel: fancy shampoo and conditioner, lavender pillow spray, moisturizer, toothbrush, toothpaste, and hairbrush.

"I'll just be here for the night," I say, a nervous laugh escaping my mouth as I realize I'm probably being a massive inconvenience.

She makes a "pfft" sound and waves away the notion. "You can't launch a successful business while sleeping on a lumpy sofa. Stay as long as you need."

"Thank you for this, for everything." My throat tightens as I pull her into a tight hug before collapsing onto the soft bed.

She flicks her hair cartoonishly. "Now, freshen up and be downstairs in twenty minutes for the worst roast of your life."

I laugh, balancing the base of my glass on my stomach. "Just keep the drinks coming, and I probably won't notice."

After a deceptively delicious dinner, we lounge in Cecily's

bedroom with bowls of tart apple pie and creamy custard. Subtle pops of blue, yellow, and pink add a youthful edge to Cecily's room's Georgian-style moldings and old furniture. I lean on a pillow decorated with multicolored velvet bows against the iron bars of her bed frame.

"I can't believe you didn't miss your train." Cecily's astonished face makes me smile.

I roll on my back, lock my fingers over my full belly and stare at the ceiling. "Oh trust me, I wanted to, but I think in the end it was best we didn't have a repeat of the night in Rome." As the words leave my mouth, I know in my heart they're not true. This time felt different, like something more. And something more is incredibly dangerous.

"I don't think I should see him again," I affirm to myself and Cecily.

Her mouth hangs agape. "What? Why?"

"It's too risky." I take a nonchalant sip of my wine, as though this thought hasn't been emotionally, physically, and mentally plaguing me for weeks.

"But that's why it's so hot!" She throws a pillow at me. A puff of fresh linen and vanilla hits my nostrils. "How often do people get to have a scandalous affair where *neither* of the parties are committing adultery?"

"Yeah, I'm just committing *identity fraud*," I remind her, whispering as though the whole building is bugged. From what I've heard, Cecily's family has every inch of this place under observation. More for monitoring the movements of their only heir rather than necessarily for her safety. "I'm lying to a guy I really like about who I am; it's not fair. I either need to stop things from going any further or tell him the truth. But then if I tell him, it makes him an accomplice and that puts his job at risk. Even if he hates his job, I don't want to be the cause of him losing it. Morally, I have to break things off, even if I don't want to."

She scrunches her face and holds a palm out. "Does it even count as a crime if you aren't technically stealing anyone's identity?"

I raise my eyebrows before taking a much bigger swig of wine. "I don't know about in the eyes of the law, but in the eyes of Odericco Investments, yes."

Cecily lays back on the bed, considering. "Hmmm, nope, sorry. I think the hidden identity thing makes it much, much hotter."

My mind briefly slips back to last night, his hand grazing my thigh, bunching the fabric of my skirt in his fist. Barely able to contain himself from lifting me up, hooking my legs around his hips, and having me against the old door in the rain.

I swallow the feeling. "He doesn't even know my real name; there's no explaining that without everything else. It would be impossible to have any kind of normal relationship with him. I couldn't hide the truth from him forever. No matter which way you swing it, eventually it would go wrong." I nod to myself. "Better now than when we're both too invested."

Cecily's shoulders deflate as she sighs. "Yeah, you're right. When are you going to tell him?"

"Maybe after the ball? That's the final event in Vienna." I internally swoon at the idea of being with him at a black-tie ball but shove the idea back down.

Cecily blinks, shaking her head. "Hang on a second. Did you just say a ball? In Vienna?"

I run a hand through my hair. "Yeah, it's where they're announcing the winners. We can't afford the tickets, but I got word that every other finalist company will be in attendance. I need to find a dress for it and everything. Do you have time to come with me to H&M or something? I think there's a sale on at the moment."

Cecily jumps up from the bed, expertly avoiding spilling her glass all over the white patterned sheets. "Are you serious? Why didn't you tell me it was a ball?"

My eyebrows fuse together. "What's so special about it?"

She ignores my question and paces back and forth in front of the bed, pressing her fingers against her temple. "Where *exactly* is the ball?"

I pull up the event on my phone, scanning through the information. "A place called Music—with a *k*—vary-in?" I squint at the invite, a red PDF with gold and silver sparkles dancing around the page.

Cecily drags her eyes to the ceiling and rubs her face. "Fucking hell, we don't have much time." She sprints out of the room, leaving me seriously confused on the bed.

"It's not for another two weeks! Just come to the shops with me tomorrow and we'll find something!" I shout, hearing her running from room to room like Coyote preparing for Road Runner. I brace myself as I hear her stomping back down the hallway before bouncing into the bedroom, out of breath with a black dress bag in hand.

"You need to wear this." She unzips the bag in one liquid movement and holds out a deep royal-purple silk gown with off-the-shoulder straps and a fitted skirt. "And you'll need gloves, white ones ideally. I think we have some in the attic. And jewels, I'll text my mum to see if she'll let me borrow one of her diamond chokers out of the safe."

My eyebrows raise in surprise, taking in the glossy fabric. "This dress is gorgeous, but why do I need to do all this?"

She throws her hands out. "Because you are going to ball season in Vienna. Ever heard of the Viennese waltz?"

I purse my lips, holding a hand out. "As in the dance they do on *Strictly*?"

She closes her eyes for a second, taking a long breath. "As in the dance that originated at these balls because they are *such* a big deal. And you, my sweet but idiotic friend, are going to the Philharmonic Ball at Musikverein. That's, like, *the* ball to end all balls. I mean literally, it's the last one of the season!"

My eyes widen. "No wonder our tickets cost more than our entire hotel stay."

She nods, planning out something in her head. "Odericco Investments are going to be watching you and Spencer like hawks. You have to look and act the part."

The alcohol in my stomach sours into vinegar. "Well, maybe I shouldn't go. Just leave Spencer to it?"

She throws her arm out. "I have no doubt Spencer will flourish in this environment. But don't waste the money you've already spent. This is your moment—you're going."

"I guess I can be . . . formal," I say, knowing the last formal event I went to was my sixth-form prom.

"Will the tall drink of water formerly known as Lover Boy be there?" She shoots me a teasing smile.

My heart skips a beat, imagining us both dressed up in

finery, dancing the night away like we're in a Disney movie. *Cinderella* is my only reference for a formal ball. Maybe I can have one last night?

I shrug. "I'd imagine so; he's been at every other TechRumble event. I can't imagine he'd miss the final evening."

She holds out the dress bag to me to try on like my Fairy Godmother. "Then you should *definitely* wear this."

CHAPTER 22

Business Account (WYST) BALANCE: £2,158.68
Personal Account BALANCE: -£1,862.90
Recent transactions:
Transport for London: £5.80

Thirty minutes into our practice session, Spencer wrings his fingers as he stands in jeans and a fern-green wrinkled shirt in front of a bright projector screen. We've spent the day fielding any issues ahead of the beta launch, which feels both exciting and anxiety inducing. Sign-ups have skyrocketed since we got through to the final round of TechRumble, and we've been singled out in social media coverage as one of the few companies focusing on women.

"What are the growth projections for the next twenty-four months?" Cecily asks as we sit across from Spencer at the conference room table.

"Ummm, good?" he replies with a smile.

I drop my pen on the table and rub my eyes. "Spence . . ."

"What? You don't want me to be positive?"

I look up through my fingers. "Did you read through *any* part of the script I sent you?"

His lips form a straight line. "I've had some other things on my mind."

"What could possibly be more important than this?" I say, feeling immediately guilty as the question leaves my mouth.

He shifts from one leg to the other. "I've got an audition."

"Oh. That's great!" I say.

Sensing my hesitancy, he clarifies, "No, like a *big* audition. For a new TV show pilot with BBC America."

"Oh my god! That's amazing!" I jump up, throwing my arms around him. But I don't feel the usual reciprocation. We pull apart, but I keep hold of his arms, studying his face. "What's wrong?"

He looks sheepishly down at the floor, scuffing an old ink stain on the gray carpet with his shoe. "The audition is on the eighteenth."

My chest tightens and I can already feel the back of my eyes prickling.

"The eighteenth of . . . March?" Cecily asks, double-checking the itinerary for the Vienna trip. Her face drops as she confirms her suspicion.

"Okaaaay . . ." I say to both of them, drawing out the word so I have some extra seconds to think. "This is manageable. Have you asked if they can push it to another date?"

"The casting director is based in LA and only in London for the day." Spencer's shoulders sink, his face cringing. "I can't miss this opportunity, Jess. The director is a huge deal."

I shoot him a tight smile. "It's okay. I get it and I'd never ask you to do that." My heart pounds hard against my chest; this is fine. It's all fine.

Before I have a chance to go into full damage control mode,

Spencer continues, "It's at 10 a.m., and I'll probably be done by like 10:45 . . . so maybe I could jump on a flight straight after?" His eyebrows raise high in anticipation.

I draw out the schedule in my head. If Spencer left immediately after his audition, he would have to get there two hours before a flight, the flight is two hours long, then an hour to get to the hotel. So if we have the final round before 3 p.m., we're fucked.

"We've been scheduled last for the other two rounds . . ." I mutter. "But we won't know until the day before what time slot we have."

"What about Dominic's assistant, the guy from the plane?" He blinks.

I huff a laugh. "Oliver?" I can't believe the last thing I told Spencer about him was on the plane back from Rome.

"Wait, do you not know?" Cecily blurts out.

"I know they hooked up in Rome?" Spencer replies.

Closing my eyes I sigh and admit, "Something happened in Paris too."

Spencer blinks at me, dumbfounded. "What happened to 'he's a conflict of interest'?"

"We just kissed!" My tone comes out like a teenager getting caught with a boy in the chemistry lab.

Spencer's demeanor shifts. "Text him right now and find out when we're scheduled"

I don't want to. But I've inadvertently asked Spencer to put his life on hold to help me regain mine; the least I can do is compromise on his audition.

"Yeah," Cecily agrees, a sly smile appearing. "You should text him."

Reaching out to Oliver feels like the exact thing I shouldn't be doing right now, but any man in my position would leverage their contacts to get ahead.

Guilt rises in my throat, but I remind myself that this is nothing confidential. I'm not asking him to give me a printout of all the questions Spencer is going to be asked during the hour from hell.

"How do I even start this conversation?" Even with my reluctance, a small tingle runs over my body at the idea of texting him.

"*Hey, you up?*' usually works for me," Spencer suggests with a shrug.

"This isn't a booty call. It's 11 a.m. on a Tuesday—of course he's up!" I reply, typing, deleting, then retyping several embarrassing openers.

"Just be casual," Cecily says. "Like no big deal, super chill." She leans back in her chair, reveling in my discomfort.

"As Jess is famously known to be," Spencer adds. Pacha laughs in the corner from behind his computer.

We contemplate for a few seconds, until I glance to the corner of the room at an object leaning against my desk. "I have his umbrella?" I say as more of a question than a statement.

"That's . . . something." Cecily taps her finger against her lip.

"How about a playful threat?" I suggest. "The umbrella in exchange for information."

"I don't hate it," Cecily says, suggesting she doesn't love it either.

I pinch my lips together. At least that way it wouldn't feel like I'm trying to leverage sex for knowledge.

"*If you want to see your umbrella again, you must tell me what time Wyst's one-to-one is scheduled,*" I say as I type it out.

We all nod and shrug in agreement and I press Send. A reply comes back within seconds.

And if I don't?

Electricity prickles at my fingertips.

You'll be receiving the duck head handle in a box via post in the next twenty-four hours.

Please, he's like family to me.

I smirk, loving that he is as lame as I am.

Tell me the time then. I type out the words, punctuating the message with an umbrella and a knife emoji.

I will only upon safe return of the umbrella.

That could take days in the post!

Then you better bring it in person tonight.

A thrill shoots through me. I wasn't planning on doing anything tonight because we won't get out of here until around 9 p.m.

I show Cecily the text, and she jumps up and down on the spot.

"Can you find out what his big three are while you're there? I want to do his charts."

"You aren't doing his charts. I told you, that's too invasive for new people."

"Oh, so you *care* about his feelings now?" She gives me a teasing look as Spencer and Pacha turn their heads.

"No . . ." I feel my cheeks burn as they all stare at me. "There's just no way to ask for someone's exact birth location and time without seeming like you're invested in them."

"But what if his sign isn't compatible with your Scorpio sun?" Cecily asks, deadly serious.

Pacha snorts a laugh. "Then he'll have to buy some sunscreen."

"JUST GO. STOP thinking about everything so bloody hard and just go!" Cecily pulls me up by my armpits from the meeting room chair. We've been here for hours, practicing every possible question Spencer could be asked.

> Still want that umbrella?

Desperately.

I glance at the time in the corner of the screen.

> It's not too late? Won't Dominic be mad if I make you wait up?

Dominic is in control of many aspects of my life but I put my foot down when it comes to my bedtime.

My mouth contorts into a smirk, feeling the urge to say something flirty back. As I'm typing, an address pops up on the screen. I bite my lip and despite my better judgment copy and paste the address into Citymapper.

> I'll be there in an hour, just finishing up.

For the next thirty minutes, I'm barely cohesive. Listening to Spencer practice his questions over and over again. Hashing out the minute details Pacha insists they will ask about and the multiyear marketing strategy Cecily refuses to let him leave without having fully memorized.

As we start to gather up our things, my nerves begin to kick in. What if this is a bad idea? This is a cut-and-dried reconnaissance mission. Seeing him during the event we are both independently attending is one thing, but actively choosing to see him in London, on the home turf, with the flimsy excuse of returning an umbrella, something we both know not to be of any importance, is risky.

You can just drop it off, get the info, then go. It's not a big deal if you don't make it a big deal.

Solidifying my resolve, I repeat the sentiment to myself on the bus ride over and the long elevator ride up to the eighth floor of an extremely fancy high-rise apartment building. Padding through the sconce-lit hallway, I smile politely and nod at a redhead and sandy blond couple leaving their apartment hand in hand.

When Oliver opens the door, I'm greeted with glinting hazel eyes, a shy smile, and a warm glow. His body briefly darkens the doorway before he steps aside and gestures for me to come in.

"I can't stay long," I immediately announce, my fingers interlocking at my stomach. I look around the room, the black, white, and brown sharp-edged apartment a stark contrast to how I'd imagined Oliver's home. It's also way above an assistant's pay grade. "Do you actually live here?"

He scratches the back of his head. "Yeah, but technically this is Dominic's place."

My eyes widen. "Excuse me?" I glance around the room from the doorway, my heart starting to pound out of rhythm.

Oliver shakes his head with a laugh, holding his hands up. "Don't worry, he's in New York for a few days. It's just me and his cat right now." He gestures into the unoccupied front room.

Once again, I scan the room from the doorway with a skeptical look on my face.

"Warren Buffett likes to keep to herself," he says with a smirk.

My eyebrow lifts. "Dominic Odericco named his female cat Warren Buffett?"

"I thought you would be more progressive than that." He tilts his chin, teasing me.

I shoot him a dirty look. "I meant why *that* particular billionaire?" I'm not shocked by the cat itself. Dominic does in fact give off Big Cat Energy.

"You'd have to ask him." He steps in closer. "Can I take your coat?" His T-shirt pleats in the middle as he holds out his hand, the light blue cotton wrapping around his full bicep.

I cross my arms, lifting my chin to meet him. "I can't stay," I reiterate, mostly to myself.

"And why's that?" His face furrows ever so slightly, the lamplight deepening his brow and emphasizing the end-of-day stubble scattered across his jaw. The urge to run my fingers over it, to feel the prickles against my skin is undeniable.

I tilt my head, running a hand through my hair as I lean against the doorframe. "It's been a long day."

His gaze follows my fingers, then drops back to me. "All the more reason to relax and have a drink with me." He smiles, coaxing a matching one from my lips.

I sniff the air. "I also don't want to keep you from your dinner." My mouth waters at the smell, rosemary maybe? Something earthy and savory that I can't quite place but smells amazing.

"Have you eaten tonight?" he says, sliding one hand into the pocket of his jeans.

I huff a laugh. "If by 'eaten,' you mean inhaled a fruity protein bar I found in the back of the office cupboard, then yes."

He rolls his eyes. "Just get in here." He takes my free hand, like he knows I need to be alleviated of the burden of choice, culpable innocence in the face of late-night mistakes. My fingers tingle in his as he guides me through the doorway into the warmly lit apartment.

My shoes click on the herringbone wood flooring as I ease off my coat, place it on the black coatrack, and follow Oliver into the kitchen. The building feels brand-new, but the mid-century-style interior, arching windows, and the giant ficus in the corner make the apartment feel warm, moody, and lived in. "This is not how I was imagining Dominic's apartment."

He tilts his head. "What were you imagining?"

"The Fortress of Solitude." I nod.

"That's over there." He points to what I imagine is Dominic's bedroom.

"And where's yours?" I ask, the seemingly innocent question burning my cheeks.

He smirks, nodding his chin down the hallway. "The *much* smaller one down there."

"Awww, I hope you don't have square footage envy." I pout.

"How does that old saying go? It's not how big your bedroom is, it's how you use it." His eyes glint mischievously.

I blush, letting out a nervous laugh.

Sensing my awkwardness, he changes the subject, gesturing around the kitchen. "But this is mostly my domain."

"So you are the cat sitter and his personal chef?" I glance over the kitchen counters, which have an air of organized chaos, clean but cluttered. Tupperware containers and chopping boards stacked neatly like Legos.

"You'd be shocked and appalled by the amount of takeout consumed in this household." My mind jumps to the image of Oliver and Dominic hanging out, watching TV, and eating Chinese food out of the plastic tubs.

"So what's the special occasion?" I ask, gesturing to the bubbling pot on the stovetop.

His gaze runs over the busy countertops before reaching me. "An emergency hostage negotiation. I thought you might be hostile, so I wanted to get on your good side."

I look down at my leggings, oversized sweater, and boots. "I'm not dressed for dinner, if that's what you're suggesting."

He purses his lips, taking the opportunity to scan up and down my body. "I think you look perfect for truffle and rosemary pasta."

I stare at a bloodred pasta maker on the kitchen counter

with fresh flour sprinkled over its machinery. "You *handmade* pasta?"

He shrugs, crossing his arms over his broad chest. "You said you didn't get to eat any pasta in Rome. I'm only an eighth Italian, but I think it's pretty good."

My knees weaken. "You're kidding? How long did this take you?"

His small smattering of freckles becomes more pronounced as his cheeks redden. "I'd rather not say. I need to retain a small amount of my dignity."

"And you made me ice cream?" I can't help but sound like an awestruck little girl when I see the freshly cleaned machine on another counter; there's no way to make that question sound like it came from the mouth of a high-functioning adult.

He leans against the counter. "Well, I didn't know what kind you'd like, so I made three. Miso vanilla gelato, sea salt chocolate ice cream, and strawberry sorbet."

My heart palpitates; nothing has ever been as sexy as that sentence.

I look at him as though he's crazy, but my chest is swelling. Nobody has ever done something so nice for me with no expectation that I would even show up to receive it.

I gravitate toward him, overlapping my fingers with his on the countertop. "Thank you. I can't believe you did this, especially when you didn't know if I'd even show up."

His palm flips upward, rubbing his thumb against my fingers, turning them into live wires. "I thought worst-case scenario if I didn't get to see you at least I could eat my feelings."

I glance briefly at his lips, then swallow. "A solid plan B."

"So will you stay for dinner?" He looks slightly nervous as he asks, but his hand confidently glides around my wrist and runs the length of my arm.

"You've presented a very strong argument." I follow his movement, holding onto his forearm as we inch closer together.

He studies my face, tucking my hair behind my ear before cupping the side of my jaw. I lean into the warm touch.

A wooden spoon hits the stovetop with a clang as the saucepan starts to bubble over. "Fuck," he says, dropping his hands and lurching toward the oven dials, taking the bubbling pappardelle off the heat.

I laugh, grabbing the kitchen roll and throwing it to him. He catches it with one hand, which is way more attractive than it should be.

We talk and eat at the kitchen counter. Well, I eat and drink at the counter and try not to moan in pleasure at the delicious pasta. Oliver stands with a towel thrown over his shoulder, taking big bites from his plate as he puts the finishing touches on dessert and makes us orange Negroni spritzes. It's sexy, seeing him in his element. At one point, I feed him from my fork while he stirs a bowl of sorbet until it freezes over ice. I try not to focus my attention on how his biceps tense or his lips as he runs his tongue over them. He tries not to focus on my finger as I lick a spot of pasta sauce from it. Okay, maybe I did that one on purpose.

Despite his protests, I help him clean the kitchen: wiping down surfaces, loading bowls and plates into the very high-tech dishwasher, and trying not to watch how his shoulders flex when he lifts pots and pans into the sink.

We meander into the living room for dessert; he's adorably

nervous as I try each ice cream and deliberate the merits of each as though I'm a judge on *MasterChef*. In reality, the only way to improve upon his recipe is if I could eat it off him instead.

"I think that was the greatest meal I've ever had." I sigh, leaning back into the sofa as my leg grazes his.

He laughs, rolling his eyes. "Don't flatter me. I can do a lot better than that if you gave me the chance."

I ignore the fluttering feeling in my stomach at the almost ask out; the moment holds for a dangerously long time until heat washes over me. Warren Buffet chooses to be the ultimate wing-woman and appears with the cutest little mew I've ever heard.

She saunters up to Oliver and brushes her face against his legs. Her fluffy tail curls around his calf like she's claiming him, her purr intensifying as her mouth opens. Like she knows I was moments away from wrapping myself around him.

"I think it's dinnertime," he says to both of us. "Gimme one minute."

He strokes a palm along her back as he lifts himself off the sofa, and she jovially pads after him. I can't help a smile creeping across my face when I hear him talking to her in the kitchen.

"Were you just having a conversation with Warren Buffett?" I suck in my cheeks, trying not to laugh.

When he reenters the room, he holds his hands out incredulously. "I had to explain to her what I made."

"Oh my god, did you make *her* dinner too?"

He runs a hand over his face, reclaiming the seat next to me. "Okay I will admit something if you promise to never tell another soul."

The sofa dips slightly, and I let it draw me closer to him as I mimic crossing my heart.

He tugs at his shirt sleeve. "Dominic insists she needs to be on a special diet, which has to be freshly prepared twice a day."

I cough out a laugh. "Is she one of the weird designer-breed cats or something?"

"No, she's from a shelter. They found her on her own in a trash can as a kitten."

My chest twinges at the idea of her as a sad little kitten—how lucky she was to be found.

I clear my throat. "And what's on the menu tonight?"

"Chicken liver." His mouth tightens into a straight line.

"Gross. I think what you made me was better." Not that it's a competition, but I'm oddly envious of her getting to see him every day.

He holds out a hand. "Hey, don't knock my cat cooking. I'm pretty sure my cooking is the best thing she's ever tasted."

"Lucky girl, having you tend to her every night." The two words leave me in a way I didn't intend, making me blush.

He huffs a laugh, shyly looking down at his drink.

I try to change the subject. "And what's the best thing *you've* ever tasted?" I take a sip of my Negroni, the acidity dancing across my tongue a stark contrast to the velvety ice cream.

He opens his mouth on a silent laugh, then closes it, tilting his head my way with a devilish look. "There is one thing, but I haven't tried it yet."

"Why not?" I say, running the edge of the glass with my finger.

He shifts his weighted gaze back to the tumbler in his lap. "Bad timing." He smiles behind the glass before taking a sip, letting the crest of the orange liquid linger on his mouth.

I take in a deep breath. "And if you had all the time in the world?"

He cuts a look to my lips. "You really wanna know?"

I swallow, nodding as my nerves crackle.

His shoulders shift as he moves toward me in a slow, smooth motion, taking the drink out of my hand and placing it on the coffee table with a clink. His gaze explores my face, hazel eyes flicking up from my lips. "It still wouldn't be enough."

My paper-thin resolve to keep things professional completely disintegrates as I let him guide me up onto his lap. He runs a hand through my hair, pushing it back from my face and lightly cupping the back of my neck, sending a jolt of electricity down my spine. My final ounce of common sense crumbles. I lean in, grazing my lips across his, savoring the moment before pressing my mouth to his, tasting the sugary strawberry and bitter aniseed on his tongue. My palms stretch over his shoulders while he drags down my torso before smoothing over the edge of my leggings. Every soft touch leaves a fiery path of want in its wake. My head lolls as I straddle him, my whole body heavy, becoming acutely aware of every inch of me he isn't touching.

His fingers run to the underside of my thigh, making me shiver. His hand returns up the center of my back, and I groan with disappointment, making him laugh against my neck. Before I can protest further, his fingers dip under the seam of my leggings.

"I haven't stopped thinking about you since Paris," he says onto my lips as we press farther into the sofa, his body sinking lower so my shins rest on either side and I'm straddling him. I can feel just how much he's thought about me pressing against his jeans. I place my palm against him, stroking his length over the fabric until I successfully draw a hissing moan out of him.

He cups me, dragging a finger down my center, before bringing it back up and licking it like sorbet. My cheeks burn at the sordid sight, but I can't help the throbbing, languidly rubbing my thighs against him in hopes of some sort of release.

Despite the beta launch, he has always been there at the forefront of my mind. The way he looked at me when I was trying on Jocelyn's clothes; the way he dropped everything to leave the mixer party with me, no questions asked; the way it took all his strength to say good night in Paris. I've never had that, someone so into you they have to peel themselves away like a sticker from an apple.

He presses in again, and I rock against his hand, taking in sporadic breaths as the pressure from his fingers coaxes my center. The sensation feels so good it makes me want to laugh. How has it never been this good? How have I spent twenty-seven years not knowing it could be this amazing?

The pressure builds, heavier and heavier, until I feel like I'm going to melt onto the floor and through the cracks of the floorboards. I grip his hair, maneuvering his mouth back to mine to muffle my moans of pleasure as he takes me close to the edge.

His warm lips run against my ear. "You feel so good against me. Fuck, Violet."

Stunting those final waves of pleasure, my eyes flash open. The high-pitched guilt in my stomach overpowers the low throb between my legs.

Like a false start, I pull back. "Wait."

His eyes flash defeat for a second, then soften, his hand sliding out of my leggings, grip loosening on my hips. "Everything okay?"

My vision darts around the room, clocking where my boots, jacket, and bag are strewn across the floor. I can't do this to him. "I'm sorry, I just—"

He takes my chin in his hand, pulling my focus back to him. "You don't have to apologize for anything." I force a smile despite my shame and he gently kisses it away. My lips melt into his, and we ease into each other once again, before I pull away placing my hands on his warm chest.

"I need to talk to you about something." It blurts out of my mouth before my brain has time to catch up.

His voice is hoarse as he says, "Sure."

Okay, I need to not be touching him. My head is spinning, trying to claw its way out of the lust-induced fog. I can't think with his . . . *him* pressed against me like this. This is a delicate situation. I need to get my mind straight, to do this in the right way. What do I even want to tell him? That this can't go any further? Or the truth? They likely both have the same outcome between the two of us. My body wants to cling on to him and fight what's coming.

Suddenly, the reason I'm here pops into my head. "What time is Spencer's one-to-one in Vienna?"

Oliver's heavy eyes blink, trying to recall through a matching mind fog. "He's the last one of the day, at four."

"Okay, good. Good." I nod mindlessly, tucking my tousled hair behind my ear. I step off his lap and start to gather up my things. "Can I use your bathroom?"

"Sure, it's down the hallway. Third door along." His lips are slightly swollen and pink, his brow furrowed as he leans forward, elbows balancing on his thighs and brushing his hands together.

I methodically count the doors as I walk past a dark study and a neat gray bedroom before reaching the black-and-white bathroom.

Maybe you don't have to end this. Maybe you can just tell him. It will be fine. You like him, maybe really like him. He likes you; this isn't the weirdest thing to ever happen. It's practically a misunderstanding.

I wash my hands and run the wet fingers through my hair, pressing the cold palms against my face and closing my eyes. Taking a deep breath, I quietly click open the door. As I'm walking back down the hallway, my eyes snag on a photograph. A picture of Oliver and Dominic with family—they're maybe ten years younger but it's clearly them. My worries soften as I stare at the boy who has yet to go through the trauma of his father's sudden passing. He looks more free here. Less burdened by the weight of familial expectation.

My heartbeat slows as I scan the other faces in the photograph, trying to figure out which are his parents, when my phone buzzes.

Text message from unknown sender:

Did you think I wouldn't recognize you? I know what you're doing, Jess.

Followed by a picture of me, mid-sentence, talking to Oliver at the Paris hotel bar as he tends to my cut palm.

I drop the phone, jolting as it smashes against the floor, clattering across the wood.

"Are you all right?" Oliver's voice bounces as he leans against the hallway wall with crossed arms, studying me as I pick up the phone. I can feel the broken screen against my fingers as I shove it into my pocket like I've just stolen his prized possession.

"Yeah, I—er, I just remembered I have to get back to the office. I forgot something important." I hide my shaking hands as I stride past him into the living room, picking up my boots and sliding them on while avoiding eye contact.

"Hey, are you sure you're okay?" He holds me still; a look of genuine concern laces his confusion, his heavy brow shadowed in the lamplight. "You look like you've seen a ghost."

"Yeah, everything's fine. I'm just really busy right now so I think"—I clear the shakiness from my throat—"I think we should probably cool things off for a bit; coming here was a mistake."

His jaw ticks as he studies my face. "If you need time, that's okay. I wasn't expecting anything from you coming here; we can just hang out and talk." He lets out a nervous laugh, glancing at the ceiling, then back to me. "Maybe I was being stupid, but I thought this could, y'know, be something we could explore outside of the competition?"

"It could," I say. Oliver relaxes at my words, taking my hands, but I draw my fingers slowly from his, the hurt permeating my chest like rotting fruit. "That's why I can't be here right now."

"Violet?" he calls after me as I run out the door, slamming it shut behind me.

CHAPTER 23

Business Account (WYST) BALANCE: £1,062.68
Personal Account BALANCE: -£1,880.30
Recent transactions:
Office rent: £1,096.00
Transport for London: £17.40

Three days later my head is starting to loll at my desk when I finally call it a night. I've been putting the final touches on the Vienna presentation, and a small light of hope is cracking through my chest. There are only ten companies left. A 33 percent chance of placing in the top three doesn't seem like much, but compared to the 0 percent chance I thought we had, it feels almost like a real possibility.

I change into my leggings, sneakers, and a running top, hoping to get in a half-hour run to clear my head before traveling back to Cecily's house. I head out the door and shout good night to Pacha. He doesn't hear me as he's locked in for one of his ill-advised all-nighters. When he started working at Wyst, I questioned his bizarre working hours. Sometimes working twenty-four hours straight on the days he doesn't have his two girls, to solve a problem that's bothering him, then not showing up for two days. I'm used to it now, knowing not to question the method when the work he does is invaluable.

To be fair, I don't exactly scream work-life balance. When I get back to Cecily's tonight, I need to finish running through the bug report Pacha sent me. Checking the small fixes he's made to get the new access-only forums ready for their beta launch. We plan to host guest AMAs from health professionals, career advisers, and relationship coaches. As well as providing a free community hub for users to connect with others going through similar experiences. I'm so excited about this launch that I'd do a million all-nighters to make sure it goes off without a hitch. And once it's live in a couple of days, Spencer can demonstrate it in real time to the judges during the Vienna Round Three one-to-one.

The moment I step out onto the small set of concrete stairs outside the office, the cold night air hits my face. Fresh air cuts through my thoughts as I stretch my calves on the steps.

A voice from the shadowed street makes my heart stop. "Oh, look, it's Jess Cole, or do you just go by Violet now?"

I freeze, my body going completely numb and heavy. Eventually, I squeak out, "What are you doing here?" My voice is quiet and strained.

Malcolm steps into the lamplight, scanning me with an upturned scowl. Our first true mutual acknowledgment since that day in the conference room three years ago. The feeling hits me like a freight train, the terror and loneliness as I walked into a room full of lawyers completely alone. Realizing I was unprepared, that nobody had told me what to expect. Graystone had its legal counsel and so did Malcolm. I had no one because in my mind I didn't need it for something so obviously cut-and-dried. An obvious case of guilt and innocence.

Malcolm's meager voice permeates the air, dragging me back to the present. "I wanted to come offer my personal congratulations. I saw Wyst is doing *so well* at TechRumble." He shoots me a mocking look before lifting his chin up at the white office building . . . "So I thought I'd come see the operation for myself. I've watched all sorts of people coming and going from the office, but I've yet to see the new CEO come out. Your brother, Spencer, right?"

The heat in my throat gutters, all the blood draining from my face as I try to appear unaffected by his insinuations. Has he been here all day?

When I don't respond, he spits out an emotionless laugh, squinting his eyes. "You know, I swear you'd said he was an actor?"

My chest begins to heave and his eyes crease in disdain. My vision blurs at the edges.

"You're not meant to be talking to me," I say, reminding him of the no-contact clause in the nondisclosure agreement we signed. I wrap my arms around myself, struggling to hold his gaze without nausea creeping up my throat.

As he steps closer to the bottom of the steps, my fight-or-flight instinct starts to signal alarm bells. Thumping against my temples to warn me that he is trying to block my path. I notice his previously light blond hair is dirty and unwashed, darkening at the roots. The clean-cut face I remember is now littered with patchy brown stubble. His boyish, lighthearted, happy-go-lucky appearance that originally drew me in has all but disappeared. Replaced by a weathered and gaunt figure holding a look of disgust like it's a weapon. It's someone I no longer recognize but perhaps the real him: the true dark soul underneath the pristine layer of privilege and entitlement. The facade that I inadvertently broke down, a mask I dragged off his face as he was pushing me to the ground.

"I know, but it's my job now to follow a good story." His voice drips in sarcasm. "And this smells just like one." He sneers, his sharp blue eyes sending a shiver up my spine. My whole body wants to run at him, scratch at him to reveal the monster underneath, but my brain knows the less I do the better. For all I know he could be recording this conversation.

You just need to get out of here and run to the nearest Tube station.

I hate that he's seen me naked, maybe as much as I hate him being the reason others have too. That I can never again have 100 percent autonomy over my own body. By taking those pictures, he stole a part of me I'll never get back.

Finally, blood returns to my jellied legs and I begin to move down the steps. Walk away from whatever this is, making sure the set of keys in my hand wielded in a spiky manner is ready if he tries anything. He doesn't move, his hand remaining casually in his coat pocket like he's just a stranger asking me for the time. He watches like he knows every inch of me. I cut a disgusted look as I take more steps down to the street and pace away. Thankfully, he doesn't follow me; my lungs let go of a long breath until I hear him speak again. This time, his voice booming.

"And when I saw you at TechRumble with someone else's name tag on, I thought that was . . . odd." He says it loud enough for me to hear him from several meters away. He pulls a hand out of his pocket and gestures around. "Does anyone else know about your fraudulent behavior?" He projects his voice even louder; the few pedestrians walking around us flick their eyes up from their phones, craning to view the street drama unfolding.

With a renewed sense of morbid amazement, I stomp back toward Malcolm, pulling on his coat sleeve into the alley next to the office. A risky move but worth it to stop passersby from recording or trying to intervene. Now I'm closer to him, I can smell alcohol on his breath; his nose is red and his eyes are glassy. I shudder, imagining him sitting in the park across the road, drinking on one of the iron benches where my team has lunch on sunny afternoons, watching us through the windows.

"What do you want, Malcolm? Why are you here?"

He lets out a harsh laugh, outraged that I wouldn't already know. "I want to know why you're going by the name Violet at TechRumble and who you're trying to fuck over this time. Is it Dominic Odericco?"

My voice shakes. "I don't know what you're talking about. I've never tried to fuck over anyone."

His eyes crease into slivers. "I saw you leave with his assistant. Are you shagging him? How long until you turn on him and come for *his* career? Or is he in on it with you? Rigging the competition?"

I don't say a word. The idea of Oliver getting dragged into this makes my skin crawl. His livelihood being put at risk because I wasn't strong or brave enough to leave him alone.

"You don't even regret it, do you?" Bits of spit shoot out of his mouth onto my cheeks, making me want to gag. "You think you could change your hair, your clothes, your name, and I wouldn't recognize the girl who ruined my life."

I scoff, hiding my shaking hands in my pockets and attempting to steel my body from doing the same. "I ruined *your* life?" My pulse bangs against my temples like a baseball bat.

"You destroyed everything! You stupid fucking girls don't realize what these accusations do to men! You created this false narrative when all I did was take a photo of *both of us* having a good time. I didn't even show your face. I didn't tell anyone your name? You said it was fine!"

"I said it was fine that *you* had them, even though you didn't ask if you could take them. I didn't say you could share them with the whole fucking office."

"Well, you should have told me to delete them if you cared that much, instead of calling for my head on a spike!" He looks genuinely upset. Confused that I would do this to *him*. What kinds of internet rabbit holes must he be down to conjure up this victimized mindset instead of going to therapy? I couldn't afford therapy; my parents wouldn't help me and practically blamed me for what happened. They didn't want me to "dwell" on it. They had to break the news that their daughter was leaving her big-girl grad job; god forbid they would have to say their daughter was being treated for PTSD. Maybe they didn't know how to describe it. I certainly didn't, and Graystone used it to their advantage. Because I was barred by the terms of the NDA, I couldn't even apply for free counseling or get an official restraining order.

Instead, I scoured the internet for reliable resources. Once I eventually found them, among the sea of forums, articles, and opinion pieces that put the onus on the victims, I couldn't help but think how a teenager would react to seeing this. I like to think I am a resilient person, and even I came close to doing something stupid. Think how many people we could help if we created something to make it easier to get support.

You were the victim. You still are the victim. This is not your fault.

"No one would hire me afterward," Malcolm continues, his face getting pinker by the second. "I had to get a fucking unpaid internship, use my trust fund to survive. Do you know how shameful it is to be a twenty-five-year-old intern?" he spits.

"You have no idea what shame is." My bones turn into lead pipes held together by PVA glue. "If you did, you wouldn't be here."

When you've been publicly shamed, people around you react in one of two ways: They avert their eyes or they can't stop staring. Both make you feel less than human. Somehow both make you feel like a carcass, like your immovable body is being pecked at by crows until there's nothing left. Your only legacy, your entire existence, eroded and consumed and decayed until it's whittled down to that One Thing. When I went back to work, everyone knew I was the reason Malcolm was fired. Unfortunately for me, he was friends with *everyone*. When we started casually dating, I was brought into that sphere of attraction. He was the one hosting parties and encouraging people out for drinks. I gained some social clout just from hanging around him. For better or worse, he was a magnetic force. Everyone else was shrapnel that dropped to the ground the moment he disappeared. They blamed me for the mess. The men in the office said it was my fault, that I consented to the photos and therefore it wasn't a crime, that I was lying, that I was a selfish bitch for encouraging his expulsion.

My head is a bowling ball rolling across the edge of the gutter. "You committed a crime, Malcolm." Bile creeps up my throat; this conversation is one I could've never imagined having.

Before I have a chance to react, he gets up closer and points a bitten-down finger in my face. "I am not the criminal here—you are, *Jess*." He spits my name like a curse.

"I don't know what you're talking about," I repeat, knowing damn well denying it is only going to anger him further. My learned instinct to calm down the angry man alone with me. I risk looking away from him for a second, glancing down both ends of the street for someone, anyone who can help me get away from him.

"There's no point denying it. I'm a journalist now . . ." He raises his eyebrows, as though I'm supposed to be impressed by this news. "Do you think for a second that I would let you get away with this? Rigging the competition, tricking the public into supporting your company like you tricked everyone into thinking I was some sort of . . . predator?" For a second, a flash of real hurt appears on his face, before switching back into anger and outrage.

I swallow. I want to get this over with; there's no way he's really here to "do the right thing." "So what do you want? Money? Why are you here?"

He scoffs, shaking his head like I've made a hilarious joke. "Please, I've looked into Wyst's financials. You don't have any fucking money."

I blink away the embarrassment and cross my arms again. "Then what?"

He lets out a breath. "I want you to tell everyone you were wrong. I want you to release a statement saying the truth, that it was a made-up, false accusation and you are sorry for all the pain you've caused."

My stomach lurches like a fist has just slammed into my gut. "What? Why?"

He paces in front of me. "Because right now I should be in a plush corner office suite with a hot secretary and a Nespresso machine. Not in a newspaper's unlit basement. I want my career to get back on track. I want to not be a social pariah anymore."

I almost laugh. "No way. After everything you put me through. Why the fuck would I do that?"

He lowers his chin, a dark look in his eyes. "Because if you don't, I'm going to expose your company for the sham that it is and tell everyone about the grift you're pulling at TechRumble. Why would anyone trust a so-called feminist business again when they find out the CEO is pretending to be a man."

He steps in closer, so close I can tell it's whiskey he's been drinking. My body freezes. I can barely breathe. He's not much taller than me, but he's bigger. Bulkier. I realize it was a mistake to pull him out of public view on the main street. I grip my keys tighter.

Malcolm studies my face. "Or . . . I could make it good for you; we could do it together. Get your side of the story. You coming to the man you wronged for the exclusive would *almost* make up for all the damage you've done. You come clean about everything . . ." He puts a finger to his chin, thinking out loud. "But then, on the other hand, exposing you myself would be much more satisfying. Maybe this is a pattern of a misandrist compulsive liar who abuses her gender to get ahead. *'What will she lie about next?'*"

"So either way, you're going to dredge everything back up and call me a liar?" My voice breaks as I try not to let a terrified tear escape. "You're going to breach the NDA?"

A scenario flashes before my eyes: everyone at TechRumble hearing about this, seeing the photos, just like that day at the office. This time an entire auditorium full of spectators to my downfall. My legs begin to furiously shake.

"I think I'll see how you do in the final round." He shrugs, pursing his lips in thought. "The further Wyst gets, the bigger my story gets." We both briefly glance to the end of the road, hearing noises of a group of people begin to echo around the corner.

He steps in again, not quite touching me, but the bile rises in my throat like he is. His wretched mouth whispers near my ear, "Good luck in Vienna, *Violet.*"

He turns away, stalking down the street at a quickening pace. Leaving my body cold against the February air. My whole body starts to shake as I watch him walking like he's just leaving work and heading home. My fingers cling to the stone wall behind me; my chest pounds, breathing heavily until he rounds the corner. I wait a few more seconds before letting the bile claw up my throat. Heat overwhelms my chest as I vomit onto the drain embedded in the street, one hand still clinging to the wall. My hair hangs over my face, but I can hear the footsteps of a group of people on the other side of the street. The male sniggering makes another wave of nausea hit me.

"She's had a few too many!" one of the men shouts, his partner bashing him in the chest with her handbag and tutting.

"You all right, love?" Her heels click as she steps across the road.

I can't speak so instead I nod and try to calm my breathing. I wipe my hair back over my ear and take the tissue she offers me, willing the retching feeling pulsing in my stomach and throat to stop.

My lips twist into a polite smile, my vision blurred around the edges. Eventually, I squeak out a thanks and nod at her.

The woman studies me, realizing I'm not drunk, perhaps recognizing the signs of an experience so many women go through. "Are you okay? Do you live nearby?"

Instead of explaining fully, I just say, "There," and point to the Wyst office building. It has an old town house facade, so she isn't fazed. Eventually, my fingers release from the wall, the muscles pulled taut and frozen in place. Pain shoots through my hand as I stretch out the muscles. As my body starts to straighten, the woman loops my arm and walks me over to the door, the rest of her group straggling behind.

My shaking hands grapple with my keys, the adrenaline of what just happened and what could have happened if this group of blissfully ignorant, unknowing vigilantes hadn't stumbled upon the same street Malcolm had cornered me in.

The woman's partner, seeing me struggling and taking the situation more seriously now, takes my keys. "Let me do that," he says softly.

Once again, a tight smile forms on my face as I try and retain a modicum of grace. I blink, the blurriness not leaving my line of sight. Black dots start to appear like floating specks of dust in my vision.

The woman studies me for a final time, her eyebrows forming a concerned line in the middle of her forehead. She squeezes my arm. "Whatever it is, things will be better after a good sleep."

"Thanks," I say again, stepping through the threshold. I click the automatic lock behind me, double-checking it's shut before climbing the three flights of creaking stairs up to the office, where I sit down at my desk, make eye contact with a confused-looking Pacha, and finally let the tears come.

CHAPTER 24

Business Account (WYST) BALANCE: £1,062.68
Personal Account BALANCE: -£1,915.30
Recent transactions:
Welwyn Garden Florist: £35.00

Spencer and I arrive with frizzy hair and crumpled clothes in our parent's town. It's just enough outside of London to warrant two trains and a fifteen-minute walk uphill, as both Mum and Dad are too busy to pick us up from the station. It's been a week since Malcolm showed up at the office, and I still feel on edge. After Pacha drove me back to Cecily's house, I could hear them talking downstairs as I drifted into a fitful sleep.

The last thing I need right now is to get an inevitable lecture from my parents, but it's Mum's birthday, so this dinner feels unavoidable.

"Weird, one of them can usually pick me up," Spencer says as our suitcases rattle against the cobblestones.

I don't tell him they don't make the effort for me. Back in university, I didn't complain when they didn't pick me up once when I was coming home, and it's been that way ever since.

Spencer must have kicked off about it, so therefore, he must be picked up.

"I don't think I'm ready for this," I admit.

Spencer throws a reassuring arm around my shoulders. "You need to just, you know, make-friendly. Ask questions, compliment the food, and smile."

"Asking her how crochet club is going isn't going to undo years of mutual resentment," I say under my breath.

He grunts, forcing his suitcase over a rock. "Well, I need you to do something soon. Your stink is starting to rub off on me. Did you know Mum said I *might not* make the subject line on this month's family newsletter?"

I mock a shocked expression. Even if he got cut, Spencer will no doubt still maintain a starring role in the body of the email for just existing.

The air becomes crisp as dark clouds begin to circle above us. "I think you need to just go in with a positive mindset," Spencer advises. "Ya know, it might help you to not see everything as doom and gloom for once?"

I avoid his suggestion. "Maybe you could help me out. Like when they ask you about work, you could mention how well Wyst is doing," I say, every three words punctuated with a breath as the incline steepens.

"But . . . it *isn't* doing well." A bead of sweat drips down the side of his face. "That's why you needed my help."

I give him a cutting side-eye. "I didn't *need* your help. I could have just as easily hired an actor to play the CEO."

"No, you couldn't; you're broke," he jibes.

"And you're not?" I raise an eyebrow under my beanie hat. "You jumped at the idea."

"Touché," he relents.

I throw my free hand out dramatically. "Face it, we're as destitute as each other. Twins to the bitter end."

We round the corner, creaking the wooden gate open to traverse the garden path to the front door. Un-bloomed pink rosebuds wind in tendrils pinned by metal hooks up the cream and brown bricks, flirting with the edge of the white windows.

We don't bother knocking, just bust through the door as Spencer shouts our arrival. The house has that distinct family smell. The scent of home fills my lungs like a ghost returning to its body.

"We're in here!" Mum shouts in a singsong tone from the kitchen at the back.

It's not lost on me that the house is littered with photographs of Spencer. The ones that feature me are the ones that also include my brother. The one single photograph of me is a portrait from my christening, a bald head and white robe with a lacy collar and pudgy little fingers. It's faded with the sun, a white streak bleached from the past twenty-seven years of morning rays.

Mum is frantically stirring a wooden Christmas spoon in an aged Le Creuset saucepan while Dad is reading the newspaper with intense focus. We kiss cheeks hello with both of them. Mum seems annoyed about something, not fully meeting my eyes as we exchange pleasantries and I hand her an overcompensatingly large bouquet of flowers. This isn't new behavior. She never acknowledges it when something is wrong. As though part of the penance for upsetting her is to delve deep into yourself and offer up reasons why she would be disappointed in you. I used to play along, listing the various things I'd done wrong in the past few months like some sort of fucked-up family confessional. Somehow, despite not actually being Catholic, our entire family dynamic is fueled by Catholic guilt.

After thirty minutes of awkward chat about annoying neighbors and distant relatives and two glasses of wine, we sit down for a nice dinner of beef bourguignon. The sound of clinking cutlery on plates, clearing of throats, and chewing teeth fill the air, nobody making a sincere attempt at conversation. A school friend once observed that the Coles don't ask each other questions. We simply make statements at one another in quick succession and call it a conversation.

"Good beef, Mum. Is this a new recipe?" Spencer says, cutting a giant piece of carrot in half, his knife scraping against the plate.

She beams. "Yes, it is! Thank you for noticing, Spenny,"

"Yeah, really good," I agree, nodding frantically.

"Darling, please don't speak with your mouth full."

"So how is work?" Dad asks, looking specifically at Spencer.

Spencer doesn't reply until he catches our parents staring directly at him.

"Oh, yeah. Everything's great." He purses his lips before taking another sip of wine.

"Any new parts coming up we can know about?" Mum wiggles her eyebrows. The way Spencer has spoken about secrecy in the entertainment industry has made them believe a one-line part on *Holby City* is as on lockdown as a Marvel movie. "Or are you still helping Jess?" She briefly glances at me, then my plate, then back to Spencer with an uplift of her eyebrows.

Spencer's shoulders raise to his earlobes. "Well . . . yes, I am, but not for much longer."

My gut sinks to new depths as my muscles tense ready for impact. It's an internal dread, which you gain a sixth sense of over time. My throat goes dry, and I try to moisten it with a too-large glug of wine.

"What did I say about taking up all his time?" Mum tuts in my direction.

I clear my throat and take another long sip of wine before answering. "It's actually going quite well and—" I get cut off before I can finish my sentence.

"For you. But Spencer is putting his career on hold to keep your business afloat," Dad chimes in. His face is stoic, but his fingers are gripping his knife and fork so tightly his knuckles are turning from pink to white.

My eyes jump back and forth between Mum and Dad before cutting to Spencer. He's looking down at his plate, pushing a piece of beef around, leaving red-brown smears on the floral-patterned china. Unwilling to come to my defense. Is he seriously not going to correct them?

"And what *career* is that exactly?" I roll my eyes, popping a potato into my mouth. "Sorry I can't provide you with five seconds of screen time at the cinema."

Out of the corner of my eye, I clock Spencer wincing.

"Sorry," I say, instantly regretting my words.

Mum scoffs, refilling her glass. The red wine sloshes up the sides, leaving light streaks as she brings the glass to her thin lips.

Usually, I would just keep my mouth shut and my head down, just get through the forced family time with as little friction as possible. But the situation with Malcolm has been replaying in my head for days now, the regret that's been searing through my blood ever since that night. I didn't stand up for myself then, and I can't let that happen again. Especially not with the people who are meant to support and love me no matter what, in the place that I'm supposed to be the safest in the world. Anger, bitterness, and jealousy rise up my throat. I know some people aren't born with the privileges of safety, support, and love at home. I understand I'm lucky compared to other people. But Spencer has received the kindness, forgiveness, and understanding I've craved, causing an insatiable need in my bones, a hunger I've never been able to subdue.

My cutlery clatters onto the china as my chair scrapes against the floorboards. I'm a bomb that's about to go off, and I need to get out of here as swiftly as possible.

"Spence, can we go please?" My voice shakes as I ask. I pick up my plate and storm into the kitchen.

Spencer doesn't respond, just stares at his plate as Mum gets up from the table to follow me.

"There's no need to take Spenny with you—in fact, I think that's the whole problem."

"Sorry for dragging your precious baby down to my level," I spit over my shoulder.

Mum's voice softens. "You know, you could get back on track. Ask for your job back and just move on without all that . . ." She waves her hand around as she tries to think of the word. ". . . drama like last time."

"Drama?" I repeat, my mouth wide in disgust. "It wasn't 'drama,' Mum."

The memory of Malcolm's whiskey breath as he threatened me reappears in my nostrils.

She sighs as she continues to ignore me. "And maybe you're

right; maybe we did put too much attention on Spencer, so now you feel the need to lash out for attention."

My voice breaks, tears stinging my eyes, and my plate clatters into the sink. "You think I went through that on purpose?"

They've never said it outright, but I could tell. I could feel the disappointment radiating off them like an odor every time they saw me.

My father's face is red as he stomps into the kitchen, clearly having heard our argument echo through the house. "Your penchant for making poor decisions was the first step toward it being your fault. Then make a big song and dance about it all, trying to get that boy fired, ruining his prospects too and bringing more attention onto yourself for no reason."

The words slam into my bones like he shot them out of a gun; jagged shrapnel marking home in my body.

The thought was already lodged in my brain, a snake slowly wringing its way around the soft tissue, tightening when I wasn't watching it. But the way I shattered, buckling under the fractures, was a long time coming.

My shoulders cave inward. "Dad . . ." My chest cracks open under the armor.

I look at my mother, and she stares at the floor. Not fully agreeing with his harsh assessment but not disagreeing either. Probably her attempt to stay neutral, but it feels like a double negative.

"You were on track to do well. You could have made something of yourself. I just don't want you dragging your brother into your mess too. You walk around acting like you have the weight of the world on your shoulders."

I take a shuddering breath. "Maybe I do act like that, and

I'm sorry. But my world collapsed in an instant. I'm just trying to pick it back up again before it crushes me." My voice
wobbles. "I just wish you both would help me do that."

My dad interrupts, "I think we've done the best considering
you—"

"Stop." The room goes silent as my brother stands in the
kitchen doorway. "Just stop."

To my surprise, my parents do stop. Like well-trained dogs,
they pause in place and turn to Spencer.

He swallows. "None of what happened is Jess's fault. We're
doing well. With my help, we are going to go all the way. You'll
see how great of a job she is doing when we win the prize money.
When we come home with a million pounds' investment."

My stomach drops. I know Spencer is trying to be supportive, but my eyes widen, begging him to stop divulging the
details of TechRumble. To not get their hopes up for this to
actually be something.

For a second, I panic, my whole body tensing at my parents'
reaction to Spencer's admission. But then I soften; maybe with
Spencer's support, I don't need to care about what they think
of me.

Before I have a chance to explain, Spencer continues, "Jess
is the smartest, hardest-working, greatest person I know. I'm
sorry you can't see her the way you see me, because you're missing out. If you want to start acting like real parents, we'll be in
Vienna."

He holds his hand out to me as we leave without saying another word.

CHAPTER 25

Business Account (WYST) BALANCE: -£4,403.78
Personal Account BALANCE: -£1,915.30
Recent transactions:
London to Vienna flights: £298.00
Vienna hotel: £549.46
Staff salaries: £4,619.00

The hotel in Vienna is practically bursting at the seams. Competitors, reporters, businessmen, investors, anyone wanting a sniff of the Odericco Investments prize money. My mind is full of the past week; the best, then worst days in a long time swirl around in my stomach like oil and honey. The joys of our beta launch going off without a hitch and spending time with Oliver outside of the competition are marred by Malcolm's threats, my ravaged bank account, and my family's disappointments.

I've been in a frozen state, avoiding all of the above. My head needs to be in this. Once the final round of the competition is over, I can deal with everything else in my life. For now, placing in the top three is the only thing that matters. This final round will make or break everything.

I caught the later flight with Spencer, wanting the time to prep him on the plane and to avoid being in the same building as Malcolm for as long as possible. We check in with the blond curly-haired receptionist before heading through the main lobby. Spencer and I throw our bags onto our matching single beds. I smooth down the static baby hairs in my middle parting as Spencer steps into the bathroom to get changed into his navy suit.

"You ready?" I say as he emerges.

"Are you?" he says, looking me up and down.

"What?" I ask.

"You're still in your flight clothes."

"Oh." I pick out the clothes at the top of my suitcase and click the bathroom door shut.

Spencer lifts one of the complimentary biscuits on the minibar to his mouth. "I feel like out of the two of us, I should be the one who looks like they're about to vomit."

"Right, sorry," I say, before rubbing my eyes. "Just overwhelmed."

We make our way back down to the lobby and catch a shuttle bus across town to the Sofitel Hotel. Ideally, we would have been staying in the main hotel, but at this point I'm so low on cash, I'd need to sell my kidney to even get a pullout sofa bed at that five-star establishment.

We sit in silence as men bellow around us, trying to play off their obvious nerves as excitement and confidence. We're all about to change our lives, our businesses, our futures. At least I'm honest about it by looking sick to my stomach.

Pulling up to the hotel, we file into the main entrance and follow signs into a suite of conference rooms. Spencer and I still don't talk as we shuffle forward in the line until we get to the front of the Odericco-branded sign-in desk.

"Oh, hey," a disembodied voice says. The spark of familiarity shoots up my spine, lifting my chin from my long list of emails to meet soft hazel eyes. They twinkle at me with a mixture of embarrassment, confusion, and excitement. My mind instantly jumps back to me running out of his apartment still flustered from his hands on me.

"Hey," I manage to get out before completely collapsing inward.

"Spencer Cole, Wyst," Oliver says, straightening his posture while he taps at a tablet to sign us in. "And Violet Leigh." He smiles at me, and with his blue Odericco-branded pen, he points to a beige door to our right. "Additional personnel can wait in there."

"Is that where you also keep the emotional support animals?" I joke, but my tone comes out . . . off.

"It's just refreshments and free wi-fi." He shrugs nonchalantly, his light blue shirt hugging his chest. The navy fleur-de-lis-printed tie slices through his torso, framing his lean body.

"Right, thanks," I mumble, taking my name tag and complimentary lanyard. Briefly looking back to see Oliver's focus already honed in on signing in the next contestant.

THE CLOCK TICKS away as I bite down every one of my nails into scratchy stubs; our slot was meant to be thirty minutes, but it's been nearly forty-five. I guess that could only be a good thing, right? No, they've figured Spencer is not the CEO and he's currently being tied to a chair and interrogated. Eventually, I give in and burst out of the waiting room for some air.

"Hey, is everything okay?" Oliver's chair scrapes as he stands up from his position behind the desk.

My eyes scrunch shut. "Shit, sorry. I didn't know you were still here." With Spencer being the last appointment of the day, I assumed Oliver would have been dismissed by now.

He shifts his weight. "There was a start-up whose one-to-one didn't go so well; they were trying to get in for a do-over. I'm hanging around just in case."

"Right," I say, running a hand through my hair. "I hope you get paid extra for that."

"What are *you* still doing here?" he asks, an eyebrow raised as he slides a hand into his pocket, using the other to lean against the desk.

"I guess it felt weird just dropping Spencer off and leaving. I'm just . . . nervous." I cross my arms. "For Spencer," I clarify, almost forgetting that he doesn't know the full truth. My stomach knots. Now I'm back in his calming orbit, every fiber of my being wants to tell him everything.

His shoulders loosen at my words, but his jaw remains tense. "I wanted to call you after . . ." He trails off.

"Why didn't you?" I ask, before I answer my own question, nodding. "Because I ran out of your home like a crazy person."

He lets out a nervous laugh. "It's okay. You were busy, and you said before you even arrived that you couldn't stay. I'm sorry if I moved things too fast or—"

A pang of guilt hits me. "No, it wasn't you at all." I squeeze my forearm between my fingers. The idea that this has been weighing on him for the past couple of weeks adding another layer of shame. "I just have a lot on my plate right now."

"You seemed like you needed some space," he echoes, scratching the back of his head. His hazel eyes glint with concern under the fluorescent lighting.

"I did. Not from *you*. Just from . . . life." I'm blinking furiously, trying to keep everything down.

We're two bubbles, holding our edges together as tight as we can. If we bump into each other, we might burst, or maybe we'll attach, fusing our edges into one.

My breath holds as he comes out from behind the desk in one fluid movement. He's unsure, measuring my response to each step before taking another. He's so unbelievably aware of me. He can read me; even if he doesn't know where the emotions are coming from, he seems to get what they mean. The overwhelm, the madness of guilt and shame, jealousy and anticipation, bitterness and anxiety. They curl around us like vines, pulling us closer because we both feel them but in different ways. The way he looked when he confided in me about his father is the way he looks now as he studies me.

"You can trust me," he says.

My eyebrow twitches involuntarily. "With what?" I avoid his sincere gaze, staring at the dark green bobbled carpet tiles.

He slides his hands into his pockets as he gives me a polite if not slightly exasperated smile and leans against the wall. "With whatever you've got going on. With anything. I don't know why, I just guess I need you to know that."

For a moment I contemplate telling him what happened with Malcolm, about my parents, about Spencer, but telling Oliver would be opening Pandora's box. Adding so much more chaos to the web of lies I've been weaving for weeks.

I stare at him and shift the conversation. "Are you going to the ball tonight?"

His smile widens. "If you'll be there, I wouldn't dare miss it."

My cheek reddens as he strokes his lips across it and leaves the softest trace of a kiss. His deep, peppery scent lingers like my want for him.

CHAPTER 26

Business Account (WYST) BALANCE: -£4,986.78
Personal Account BALANCE: -£1,915.30
Recent transactions:
Vienna ball tickets: £583.00

Flashing cameras blur my vision as Spencer and I step out of the taxi to the dramatic stone staircase leading up to the theater's grand entrance. My white gloves hide my face as event photographers try to get pictures of the hottest new tech founders before they hit the big time. Glancing around at the other guests gliding up the stone stairs to the main entrance I can't help but feel self-conscious. This is Cecily's dress, and her mother's jewelry; Spencer's tuxedo is rented; and we are still every bit of a fraud as when we started; but I'm more self-assured than I was at the start of this competition.

Even if we don't make it to the top three tonight, we are TechRumble finalists. We made it, and I have no doubt we will find some sort of investment from this experience, whether it's in this building or not. I straighten my shoulders and head in.

The warmth of the candles and three hundred people hits my cold bare shoulders. I watch as the other ladies part with their designer coats and unveil their glamorous dresses like haute couture flashers. I fiddle with my white gloves, pulling them back up my arms until they sit taut at my elbows. I feel like a kid playing dress-up in my purple silk gown, but it's the anticipation of seeing Oliver that's making me truly nervous. My hands tremble as I take a glass of champagne from a tray and say thank you to the waiter who smiles back politely and nods. Maybe he can sense that I scrounged the business accounts for ticket money like a hand down the back of the sofa, that I'm sipping on a glass of two-hundred-pound-a-bottle champagne with less money to my name.

We step toward the main hall, and I try to play it cool, like I frequent places like this all the time. But in reality, this is the most beautiful room I've ever seen. The walls are lined with gilded gesso and ten sparkling chandeliers hang from fresco ceilings. Red and purple lights shine up the walls at intervals and there are so many pillar candles it must be a fire safety violation, casting everyone in a flattering moody glow.

"Jesus Christ," Spencer says under his breath. "I looked it up before we left; apparently this is one of the more casual balls of the season."

My eyes pop out of their sockets. "Where are the others? At the fucking palace?"

He glances at me briefly, eyebrows up in awe. "Yes."

I whistle. "At least we didn't have to spring for tickets to *that* one."

Spencer sips on his champagne as he scans the crowd, shoulders rolled back and head high like he's actually comfortable in his sharp tuxedo. That's the skill of an actor, being able to seamlessly slip into any role you need to play, any position you need to hold to get ahead. You figure out who people want you to be and become it.

I turn my head to him, pitching my voice low so no passersby can overhear. "Before we go in, I want to thank you for doing all this for me." My eyes begin to burn, but I take a breath and pull it back. "Even though you've created a lot more work for me." I let out a cathartic laugh. "You don't know how grateful I am."

He studies my face. "We're a team." His mouth moves into a sly smile. "And for the record, I would have done it without all the fancy hotels."

"Are you serious?"

He pokes his elbow into my side, talking out of the side of his mouth. "Come on, Jess, you're the CEO of a TechRumble finalist company; you've gotta get better at negotiating." He downs his glass of champagne in one swift movement before grabbing another from a passing tray.

I roll my eyes with a laugh. "Trust me, I'm never doing anything like this *ever* again."

"Sure, you keep telling yourself that. But I know you, and I think you secretly love a high-risk, high-reward move. Taking risks is what life is all about . . ." He trails off, a glint in his eyes as they drag up to a theater box on the second-floor balcony.

My mouth goes dry as I follow his gaze and catch sight of Dominic Odericco. The ceiling fresco frames him like a god. Renaissance angels and clouds surrounding him in heaven as he presides over his mortal subjects. My nerves kick up into high gear as I realize Oliver must already be here too.

Like he can sense it, Dominic's eyes flick to Spencer.

The sense of authority makes me shiver. "Wow, what did you do to piss him off?"

Spencer laughs and shakes his head. "Oh, that's not his pissed-off face." He says it so casually I don't know how to respond.

"Did you ever in a million years think we'd end up here?" Spencer muses, his attention remaining fixed on Dominic.

"I thought the graduation disco was the peak of luxury." My bright pink eyeshadow to match my A-line poofy pink dress with platform heels still gives me shivers every time I see the photo.

As we step arm in arm farther into the building, my eyes widen at the full orchestra placed on a tiered stage; the rhythmic tune of violins and cellos echoing across the walls makes it feel like I'm stepping back in time. Waves of black tuxedos interlaced with fine silk, velvet, and tulle flow around us as we take in our surroundings.

We pick up cheese and fig canapés before an Italian man approaches Spencer and drags him away to meet his new founder friends. A twinge of something that feels like jealousy briefly etches on my chest, but I'm coming to terms with the fact that if they knew the truth, I wouldn't be accepted into the Vienna Boys Club with open arms anyway. And there is no point in wasting energy desiring something that will never love you back.

When we get home, the first thing we need to do is put together a plan for how to transition Spencer out of the CEO position and me in. But whenever I think about stepping back into the role, my gut twists. It wouldn't be like it was before.

All the extra eyes on Wyst have been fantastic for the future of the company; we've received more press and online traction than I ever thought possible. But when I imagine going back to the place I was in three months ago, being all consumed by the work, having no work-life balance, no room for anything or anyone else in my life, anxiety fizzes in my blood like the edges of crashing waves.

While Spencer holds court with his adoring fans, I head to the bar to get a stronger drink. I need to feel like I've gained that ticket money back somehow, and the open bar feels like the best place to start. The fresh Negroni stings against my tongue as I take my first sip. The bar spans the length of the hall, with waiters rushing to get everyone's order as fast as possible.

The swell of music begins and the crowd descends onto the dance floor, men in tails and their dates following along like multicolored ducklings. Stunning women with twinkling jewels and fabulous dresses spin and twirl around their partners. The colors blend under the soft lights on the dance floor like the aurora borealis.

I lean against the bar and glance left at the dispersing crowd to find a pair of hazel eyes already on me. A pang of longing hits me. His dark hair looks shorter than normal, in a slicked-back formal style instead of its usual undone effortlessness. His tuxedo fits him perfectly, the black-and-white contrast pulling all the attention to his tall form and broad shoulders. My core aches and I swallow as every other person in the room melts away. I wanted to slow my feelings down, but I think I'm done for. I want to approach first, to run into him and kiss away the apprehension on his face. To spend the night in his arms. He's surrounded by people I recognize to be major players at Odericco Investments, but at this point, I don't care. All eyes are on Spencer tonight, not me. The competition is nearly finished; the decisions have likely already been made. I hold my breath and cross the floor toward Oliver. It's time. I want him to know the truth because I want him to know me, to tear down the barrier even if it means risking how I think he feels about me.

"Hi," he says, a slight furrow on his brow.

"Hi," I breathe out, finally feeling something close to relaxed.

"You look . . ." He studies my dress, swallows, then glances at the managers around him. "A word I can't say in front of colleagues." His smile leaves goose bumps all over my body.

"So do you," I say, giving him a shy but knowing smile.

We stare at each other for a few quiet moments, chests breathing deep, before I can't take the heat of his gaze. I look away before his eyes consume me completely.

"How are you feeling?" he asks, studying my face.

My lips do their best attempt at a reassuring smile as I swallow my pride. "Can we talk somewhere alone? Before the winners are announced?" I have to tell him.

He looks down, then flicks his hazel eyes up to me. "I have to do something first, but I can meet you in ten minutes. Dom should be finished using the study now. Wait for me upstairs and we'll talk in there."

"Isn't it VIPs only upstairs?" I ask, gesturing to a sign that says exactly that.

He winks at me. "I'll make sure you're on the list."

I swallow and nod, heart palpitating as I watch him walk back to his colleagues. Glancing up to the gods of the theater, the red swags hanging in scalloped edges over the sides of the boxes. "Okay, see you there."

Is it right to tell him here? After tonight, I might never see him again. I will get this done and he can hate me and we can go home to our separate lives. A clean break.

I've taken only a couple of steps toward the stairs before a hand lands on my arm.

"That was a quick ten min—" My whole body freezes as my eyes cut to the last person I want to see right now. Malcolm, in a full tuxedo with tails, grins at me, his yellowing teeth on show.

"Good evening, *Violet*." The way he says the word shows his intent immediately.

The blood drains from my cheeks as I violently shake my head. "No, you can't be here."

His clammy fingers grip my wrist. "I'm a journalist. I can be wherever I deem a good story to be." He looks me up and down, getting his fill of every curve of my frozen body. "Nice dress, shall we dance?" He pulls me in the direction of the crowd.

"Fuck you," I spit, forcing myself to follow without making a scene. One wrong move and this could all be over. I glance at Oliver, his eyebrows forming a subtle line in the middle as he watches Malcolm lead me to the dance floor, my arms stiff by my sides. I open my mouth to say something, but nothing comes out. I urge my face to explain the entire situation to him, but how am I meant to start summarizing what's happening? My heart pounds like a jackhammer as we enter the throng of couples, blending into the sea of men and women enjoying the music. Malcolm flicks me around until I'm facing him. A dress with a fitted skirt and stiletto heels is now a regretful decision because I can't bolt away or knee him in the balls as his hand slithers down me and rests on my lower back. He takes my other hand in his and begins to lead me in a dance. My eyes are jumping from face to face, trying to find Spencer in the crowd for help and avoiding looking straight into Malcolm's jet-blue vacant stare. Bile runs up my throat as I try not to think about the last time he had his hands on me, how just like now, he took a moment of intimacy and turned it into a weapon of humiliation.

His mouth moves to my ear, leaving a permanent imprint on my skin. "Smile, Jess, or I will go to the front of the stage and announce everything you've done through the fucking speakers."

My eyes sting as I draw a weak smile across my face. "Did you come all the way here just to drop your article?"

He grins, pushing his hand on my back so my body presses into him. Dancing cheek to cheek with him makes the champagne in my stomach turn sour. Sensing me trying to pull away, his stubble claws at my face as he tightens his grip.

"Funny you should mention my article. Since I last saw you, I've been doing some thinking. I was misguided when we last spoke." He pulls away from me, a wide cheery smile on his face for everyone else in the crowd. "Spin."

My eyebrows furrow at the word, not realizing it's an instruction as he twists me around, forcing me to twirl so fast I stumble and nearly fall over my feet. My eyes scan the crowd as I turn, looking up to find Oliver now on the upstairs balcony focusing on me. The moment is gone too quickly to try and translate the look on his face. And how could I even begin to explain this situation in a single glance? How do you explain that yes, this is the man I confided in you about, the man who did that to me; we haven't reconciled; yes, he is the reason I left you, but only because I'm hiding my true identity from you and he knows the truth.

My stomach twists as I'm brought back to Malcolm, gripping his shoulder to stop myself from falling. "You've finally come to your senses and realized blackmail is illegal?"

He laughs like I've just said something terribly charming and plants a kiss on my cheek. Dread fills my chest at what Oliver is seeing right now. If he recognizes Malcolm from the mixer party in Paris, we must look like two former lovers finally reconciling.

"If we're talking about *who* is doing *what* illegal things, Jess, I think you're in the lead."

I don't reply, instead closing my eyes to stop the tears from falling and pray for this dance to be over.

"Smile," he instructs. "This is good news for you. I'm delaying my exposé."

My chest halts, waiting for the other shoe to drop. I want nothing more than to pry myself from his grip and run in the opposite direction, but I ask with a weak smile on my face, "Why?"

He gives me a soft smile, running a hand up my arm. "Because I think you are going to win."

"What?" Coming from literally anyone else in the entire world, the words would fill me with hope and warmth, but as they slip from Malcolm's mouth, they ring like an air raid siren in my head.

"Well." He huffs in a laugh. "Maybe not *first* place, but there's a formula to competitions like these. I've researched the paths of previous winners and watched Spencer over the past few months. He's doing everything right. And with the market being in serious need of *women's companies*," he drawls in a mocking tone, "Odericco came under fire last year for not having enough female entrants; they would be stupid not to choose Wyst for the top three finalists for the good press alone."

A swirl of emotions run through me like a truck. Nausea brought forth by shock, happiness, and intense sadness. I swallow them all back like a triple shot. "So what's it to you whether I win or lose? Are you waiting until I win to make your story as big a spectacle as possible?"

His lips thin. "As nice as a viral story would be, that's not why I'm here. Sure, if I'm wrong and you don't make the final three, I'll just press Publish and ruin your company and your reputation like you deserve." His fingers tighten, crushing the muscles in my palm and making my torso crease into him. He leans in to whisper like a secret love confession, "But if you do place in the top three tonight . . . you're going to give me half of Wyst."

I can't help the gasp that releases from my lungs; his demand would be laughable if I didn't know he was being deadly serious.

My head shakes violently. "No, no, I would never do that." My body goes into shock; my knees start to buckle but his grip holds me up. Tears begin to escape and run down my cheeks as he pulls me back into him. Through my blurred vision, I glance around for Spencer, Oliver, anyone who could help me.

He smiles and shrugs nonchalantly, completely unfazed by my response. "Or I suppose you could choose not to, and I'll publish the article on Monday."

My voice shakes uncontrollably. "If anyone finds out, I could go to *jail*, Malcolm." It quickly dawns on me that's what I said I wanted for him in the meeting with Graystone. I said I wanted him to be charged for sending the photos to everyone and for taking them without my consent, but Graystone convinced me not to.

"You deserve worse." Before I can protest, he flicks my foot with his and dips me; the crowd moves out of the way, oohing and aahing as they watch the graceful couple showing off their dancing skills. My back muscles lance as he holds me down in the position, his chapped lips brushing against mine as he whispers, "You deserve to rot in the ground for what you did to me, you fucking bitch." He smiles as his breath enters my mouth. He pulls me back up, my eyes so glassy I can hardly make out the hordes of people clapping around us, enjoying the show.

My brain goes blank. This is enough. I'm done. As he pulls me back up, I slam my stiletto heel into his foot so hard I feel the stone floor reverberate through my knee. I wince, pulling myself from Malcolm's grip as he coils over in pain. I beeline for the side stairs, glancing at where Oliver was standing in the gods. My head spins around the room as I pull my dress up to my ankles and push through the crowd.

What the hell was I thinking coming here? Having my main character moment. Of course Malcolm would be here. I'm an idiot for thinking he wouldn't show his face. This was all a huge mistake; if I'd never sent that fucking email, none of this would have happened. I should have let it all die, let Wyst teeter off and splutter out in quiet dignity. Instead, I've risked Spencer, Cecily, and Pacha too. To try and save their jobs, I've risked sending them to jail. My breath shortens as I run past the VIP sign and straight up the stairs.

If we place in the top three tonight, Malcolm will blackmail us. If we lose, he will blow everything up. Cutting every opportunity we'll have from the competition for outside funding. After all this work, we'll be dead anyway.

Either way, I have to find Oliver. I have to end this before I cause any more damage.

CHAPTER 27

Business Account (WYST) BALANCE: -£4,986.78
Personal Account BALANCE: -£1,915.30

My heels click against the stone stairs as I run to find Oliver. Malcolm's offer, if you can even call it that, replays in my mind like a siren. Handing over half of Wyst to Malcolm is ridiculous; I'd rather burn the whole thing to the ground.

Multiple sets of footsteps echo up the stairs behind me. I freeze, fists ready at my sides to physically fight off Malcolm if I have to. But instead of the man I assumed would be hunting me down, two security guards appear at the end of the hall.

"Miss, can we see your pass, please?" one of the men says, holding his hand out to me.

I run to the next door, banging on it like my life depends on it. Oliver answers, still in his full tuxedo but his bow tie undone around his neck.

"Can I come in?" I ask, a relieved smile plastering my tearstained face; he doesn't smile back. At that moment, my stomach sinks, the weight of my mistakes threatening to push me through the floorboards. Everything I've done, everything he doesn't know I've done, has created this invisible chasm between us.

One of the men steps forward. "Miss, if you don't have a pass, you need to leave this area immediately."

My head swivels back around, shooting a pleading look at Oliver.

He studies me a final time, and with a bobbing throat, he says, "She's with me." He pulls a shiny black lanyard out of his jacket pocket with one hand, placing the other on my arm. It's not a comforting touch, just a formality he is reluctant to take part in.

The man looks at him and shakes his head. "I'm sorry, sir. There must have been a misunderstanding."

Oliver ushers me into the room, hand still gently gripped on my forearm. "No problem," he says to the two men. He still hasn't looked me in the eye but he leads me into the room. "Have a good evening."

"Good evening, sir," the men both say, voices overlapping each other.

Neither of us breathe as he shuts the door with a click. I watch as it disappears into the paneled wall, giving the illusion of a secret entryway. The smell of leather and old books hits my nostrils; I wish it was his peppery scent.

A gigantic curved oak desk with a green leather top sits in front of closed gold sash curtains at the other side of the room. Ornate clusters of settees and grand leather lounge chairs are scattered around the room. A wooden bar covers the corner with sparkling crystal decanters like diamonds atop a crown. Oliver said it was a study, but it feels more like an old-school smoking lounge. Gold sconce lights cast an orange glow over the never-ending shelves of books. The orchestra's music swells through the minute cracks around the door like ghosts howling a collective memory.

My heart rate slows when I finally lean against the door. A minor sense of relief that even though tonight has been a complete disaster, at least I'm not actively being held against my will or being thrown out of one of the fanciest venues in the city. Glancing down, my hands are still shaking as I turn the lock to make sure if Malcolm manages to follow me up here, he'll be caught by security before he can reach us.

"Here." Oliver takes a glass bottle of water from the bar, undoes the cap, and hands it to me. He goes to speak further but stops himself, relaxing his rising shoulders. "Drink that, then explain why you're up here."

My stomach clenches; he's pissed. I told him I wanted to talk, but no less than sixty seconds later, I was dancing with a man I'd told Oliver I never wanted to see again. I analyze the situation from his perspective; from the balcony above, all he could see was me talking, dancing, and smiling with the man who ruined my life like we were old friends. There is no way from up there Oliver would have been able to see my hands shaking or the tears glazing over my eyes. He wouldn't have been able to hear the harsh words being spat at me. My head pounds when I remember Malcolm's lips so close to mine as he dipped me on the dancefloor. Based on his reaction to me now, Oliver must have left the moment he saw the disgusting scene. If he's acting like this, he must not have witnessed me slamming down on Malcolm's shoe and legging it for the exit.

Then again, Oliver could be just as pissed about me running

away and ignoring him for two weeks, for being weird with him yesterday at the final round, or bashing his door down and making a scene with security. Maybe all of the above. Either way, I owe him an explanation for everything. And I deserve every consequence that comes next.

My throat bobs as I gulp down the water, using it as an opportunity to get my thoughts together. He doesn't say anything, just paces the room, hands in his pockets, waiting for me to begin.

"Thank you for staying," I say in between breaths.

His jaw ticks. "I'm here with Dominic. I can't leave until he does."

My chest sinks as I nod. "Right." I take another long swig of the bottle, wishing it was something stronger. "We need to talk about some stuff."

He spits out a laugh, opening a decanter of amber liquid and pouring it into a glass. "Yeah, no shit." He paces the floor, the ice in his glass clinking as he moves. "Let's just get this over with; you're back together with your ex?"

I almost spit out the water onto the parquet floorboards. "What? Why would you think that?"

"You practically sprinted out of the apartment the other week when things between us started getting . . ." He stops himself. "Then you act all aloof yesterday like you're hiding something from me. And then tonight, you're laughing and dancing with him at the ball. You let him kiss you. What the hell else am I meant to think?"

I replay the events of the past two weeks. To an outsider's view, it does look as simple as that. I *wish* it was as simple as that.

"Surely, you understand where I'm coming from here, why I'm confused as hell," Oliver adds, knocking back his drink and running a hand over his face. "I've spent the past two weeks running through the dinner at my place, wondering where I went wrong. What did I do to make you bolt like a spooked horse."

"You didn't do anything wrong." I swallow the fear before unleashing the truth. "Malcolm is blackmailing me."

He pauses his pacing, the dark frustration in his eyes turning into liquid rage.

"The photos?" he asks in a low, morbid tone.

I take a breath, not moving from the door. "No, it's . . . something else."

His anger briefly subsides as he takes a step forward, his expression softening ever so slightly. "What else can he do to you? What else is there? If he did something to you again, I swear I—" He runs a hand over his mouth. "Please just put me out of my misery. *Please* tell me I'm not a complete chump for falling for someone I know is keeping secrets from me."

I blink at his confession. He doesn't flinch. He either doesn't realize what he just said or is so confident in his feelings that this is going to hurt so much more.

My voice comes out low and weak. "It's something *I* did, not him."

Oliver's eyes creased, scanning my face for some sort of answer.

I close my eyes and take a deep breath. "I've wanted to tell you. It's why I had to leave that night before things went any further; it's why I—" My voice cracks and I stop, trying to regain my composure.

He steps forward, takes my hand, and holds my gaze. "I told you, you can trust me." He says it in a way that makes my heart shatter. Knowing in my bones that I can trust him, but after I say this, *he* will never trust *me* again.

My voice cracks as I attempt to explain. "Malcolm is blackmailing me because he knows the truth. The truth about me."

Oliver's face tenses, the pulse in his wrist jumping under my fingers.

I close my eyes, taking my final breath as a person in denial. "Spencer isn't my boss; he's my brother. He's an actor who stepped in to pretend to be the CEO and founder of Wyst."

He blinks, trying to absorb the information. "So where is the real CEO?"

"Right here." I realize I'm shaking, not just my hands but my entire body. Like the lies are poison leaking out of my pores. "Spencer is pretending to be me. Wyst is *my* company."

His face softens; whether it's shock, sympathy, or pity . . . I don't know which one is worse.

He steps forward, shaking his head, his brows forming a tight line. "Vi, I—"

I step back, holding my hand up. "I'm not finished. My name isn't Violet; it's Jess. Jess Cole."

He leans against the ornate desk, rubbing his face with his hands. I stand in silence with nothing more to say, everything I've been keeping a secret laid out in the chasm between us, hoping that maybe the truth will fill the space.

"Everything you told me about you, about—" He stops himself, swallowing the question. He gestures between us. "Was any of *this* true?" I know what he's trying to ask from the hurt in his eyes.

Everything you told me, everything we shared, every time I touched you.

I blink away the heat building behind my eyes. "It's the only thing I *haven't* been lying about."

He stares at his hands clasped in front of him. "Why?"

I wring my fingers, moving tentatively to lean next to him instead of awkwardly standing in the middle of the room. "Wyst was getting zero traction and I was running out of money." I shake my head, correcting myself. "I'm *hemorrhaging* money. It's simple A/B testing, really. The only variable I could see was that I'm a woman. So when I made a mistake on the application and they thought I was 'Mr. Cole,' I went along with it. My bills were piling up. I was desperate."

"So you got Spencer to take the call with me," he adds, his face shadowed by the lamplight.

I suck in my flaming cheeks. "Not exactly . . ."

He slowly turns to me, confused for a second before his eyes go wide. "That was *you*?" His mouth hangs agape, his head shaking. "How?"

"I got our tech guy to set up a voice changer app." I shrug, a tight, awkward half-smile plastered across my mouth.

Oliver stares into the abyss, his eyes' focus jumping between the portraits on the wall in front of us as he tries to recall the conversation.

Finally, he cuts a look back to me. "On the call . . . I heard a woman's voice halfway through." He tilts his head, dark eyes laser focused.

I lower my head. I can't look at him so lock in on the frayed edges of the Persian rug. "Yeah, the app broke."

He stares at me, expressionless and silent, for what feels like hours.

I patch the silence, my shoulders pulled tight and high like a slingshot. "I'm so sorry; everything happened so quickly and I panicked, I just—"

Oliver bursts out laughing.

CHAPTER 28

Business Account (WYST) BALANCE: -£5,002.77
Personal Account BALANCE: -£1,915.30
Recent transactions:
FemTech Monthly **magazine subscription: £15.99**

My head shoots up to confirm I'm not imagining it.

Despite everything I've said, Oliver is smiling. A wide, toothy, genuine smile, his eyes creased as he tries to contain his laughter. "You're completely insane." He puts his hand on mine and squeezes. "I mean, who does that?"

"Be that stupid?" I ask, feeling the tension around my body melt like butter.

His laughing slows. "No, believe in something so much that they risk everything to make it happen?"

I start laughing too, so hard the tears I've been holding back come out. I'm laughing at how ridiculous this all is, how far I've come, how I would have never thought I'd end up here.

"Hey, it's all right." He moves in front of me, pulling the pocket square from his jacket and using it to wipe the tears from my flushed cheeks. It's a gentlemanly gesture I didn't think happened outside of historical romance books.

I shake my head. "It was a mistake, but I don't regret it, because I got to meet you. But I'm scared you're going to meet the real me and change your mind. You like Violet, not Jess. Jess is boring and serious and not fun. I wanted to try something new, be someone new. Someone who doesn't have this demon on their back weighing them down all the time."

He takes my face in his hands, stroking his rough thumb across my cheek as he studies me, eyes soft and relaxed. He smiles. "My attraction to you is choiceless. If you let me, I'd have you with any name. Jess, Violet, fucking Gertrude, it's all the same to me. You are you." He smiles onto my lips. "But I could get used to Jess."

I let out a teary laugh and kiss him lightly, a long exhalation of relief coursing through me. We kiss again, soft but longer this time, slowly morphing into something more. Our tongues clash, and his arms wrap around my waist, lifting me onto the desk. We giggle as we both realize the skirt of my dress is so tight I have to sit sidesaddle to him.

His hand runs up the silk encasing my thighs in soft, caressing strokes until I can't take it. I slide the undone bow tie from his collar and unbutton halfway down his shirt. My dress is too long and there's too much fabric between us. My breath hitches as he reads my mind, wraps his arms around me, and starts to unzip my dress, the vibration pulling down my back as his fingers follow, smoothing over my bare skin until they hit the lace bra.

He drags me off the desk, lets my dress drop to the ground, and crouches on the floor to untangle my stilettos from the pooled fabric. With everything going on, I forgot about my gala-worthy underwear situation. Watching as his gaze travels back up my body, studying my matching stockings, black underwear, and bra with preternatural concentration, I cringe at the contrast between my immaculate lingerie and my messy hair and post-cry makeup, but he doesn't seem to care. His hands smooth over the backs of my calves, urging me back onto the desk as he parts them.

He snaps the edge of a stocking gently against my thigh. "These will make me forget *both* our names." Any resolve to get out of this situation intact drifts away.

After a swell of confidence, I ask, "What about these?" And move his hand to my underwear, his fingers running along the edge of the lace. My head droops to the side as he kisses the skin just below my navel.

"Name, location, year, everything. Nothing is as important as these." He laughs, warm breath tickling my skin as he moves back up my body until he reaches my lips.

I make light work of the rest of his shirt, my heart racing harder with every button until I can run my hands over the smattering of hair across his chest, perfectly framing his toned torso. I've seen his body before, but this feels like the first time. The first time we're being honest. The first time we're being completely ourselves. The first time we know this isn't going to be the only time.

I wrap my legs around him, my heels digging into his lower back and deepening the kiss. His hands smooth over my legs and up my waist, melting me to my core. His erection is hard between us, the muscles flexing and throbbing as my tongue glides over his.

"Sure you're okay with this?" I ask, already out of breath as he breaks to work his mouth over my neck.

He pulls back, furrowing his brow. "Why wouldn't I be? Got something else to confess?"

"You know everything now, but that makes you complicit." I hold his broad shoulders, more saying this to myself than him as the realization sinks in. "I've *made* you complicit. You should be running for the hills."

He strokes a finger over the fabric of my underwear. "That may be the sensible thing to do, but unfortunately evil masterminds with a penchant for reckless behavior turn me on."

My head comes to rest in the crook of his shoulder as I shudder from his touch. "Just for the record, none of it was on purpose."

"Well, *just for the record*," he mimics in a mocking British accent, "everything I've done with you is completely on purpose." As he deftly pulls the fabric to one side and slowly dips a finger inside me, watching as my mouth opens and chin lifts, he says, "I think you just couldn't resist my charms."

I laugh and moan at the same time, trying to stop my head from spinning. Trying to regain the high ground, I run my hand down his chest until I meet his straining trousers. I slip my hand in, watching as his dark eyes glaze over. I capture his mouth as it opens on a groan.

"Yeah, because I'm the one finding it *hard* to resist," I reply. He lowers me on the desk, his muscles taut as he hovers just above my body. He runs his mouth down my neck, breasts, and navel before straightening and checking his watch.

"Somewhere to be?" I ask, looking over my heaving chest.

He looks distressed. "Give me one second." He sits up onto his knees, legs on either side of my hips as he pulls his phone out of his trouser pockets and starts frantically typing. The lines below his hips taut as his cock strains painfully against the fabric.

My brow furrows. "What are you doing?"

"Handing over my duties for tonight to Dom's second assistant." He presses the Call button and lifts the phone to his ear.

"Are you allowed to do that?" I ask, looking up at him through heavy lashes.

"Hey, man," he says as I hear another deep voice down the receiver. "Yeah, everything's fine."

He smirks, giving me a mischievous look. "Can you take over for the rest of the night? There is an urgent matter I need to deal with." His dark eyes glide over my bra.

Electricity tingles through my body—am I the urgent matter? I sit upright, my mouth meeting his navel. His stomach muscles jerk as I run my tongue over the trail of hair leading under his waistline.

"The car should be here in ninety minutes. Just make sure he doesn't go AWOL this time; we don't need a repeat of Rome."

I look up at him sweetly, dragging his zipper down and kissing lower.

He closes his eyes for a second, sighing, then holds his hand over the receiver. "You're making this a lot harder than it needs to be," he says between his teeth.

"That's the plan," I say, rolling down his boxers until he springs out.

"Uh-huh," he says down the phone, his voice strained as my tongue runs up his length and across the tip before I close my mouth over him, rolling my tongue. "Yeah, it's scheduled for 2 p.m. tomorrow."

After a few seconds, Oliver drags his fingers through my hair and pulls my chin up to look at me as I take him in deeper.

He bites his bottom lip and lets out a long breath. "Sorry, man, this problem just won't solve itself. I'm probably going to be up all night working on it."

I stifle a laugh, my lips vibrating against him.

"Thanks, I owe you one."

My limbs feel weightless as he hangs up and throws his phone across the room onto an armchair. The subtle gesture, even knowing that I trust him, makes my heart somersault.

He lowers his chin to me. "You are going to pay for that."

I playfully push myself away from him. "On second thought, maybe this isn't a good idea. I should probably go back to my hotel for the night and—"

"Don't you dare." He takes me by the waist, drops me onto my feet, and kisses me, turning us backward toward the sprawling sofa.

I'm out of breath when I ask, "You're free for the whole night?"

"I'm officially off the clock until 9 a.m., so we have about eight hours until I'm obliged to do anything about this . . . situation." He brackets over me, lowering me onto the plush royal-blue cushions.

"Wow, that's great that you take your work-life balance so seriously," I tease. "So we have eight hours to do whatever we want?"

He smiles playfully. "That depends on what you want."

My fingers lace through his hair, pulling him closer to me. "I wanted to stay, in your apartment." I breathe out, "I wanted this."

"Me too. I should never have let you leave," he grits out.

"I'm glad you did," I say.

His brows furrows.

"I mean, I'm glad it didn't happen when you didn't know the truth." I clarify.

He smiles as he climbs up my body until his cock is nudging against me. "You wanted to make sure I was calling out the right name?"

I laugh. "Exactly."

"Well, *Jess*." He emphasizes the word like it's a curse. "Will you let me fuck you?"

"Please." I practically beg.

He slides against me, hard against my slickness. I feel the heat running up my body as he carefully enters me. I'm breathless at the feeling of him inside me. After a few more torturous moments, he pounds into me, hard and deep until my vision goes blurry. I can feel every inch of him as he slides his tip to my entrance, never quite leaving, teasing. My nails claw at his back.

He lifts us farther up the settee until I feel the wooden edges against my back. My hands wrap around the arm, trying to stop the wood from banging against the wall. My legs can't stay still, so he takes my knees, pinning one to his side and one over his broad shoulder.

"Is everyone still downstairs?" I say in between heavy breaths.

"Why? Looking for a better option than an assistant?" He pants, squeezing the flesh of my thigh.

"No." I laugh. "I just don't want you to get in trouble if anyone hears us."

He slows down, long draws through me, making me clench my legs around his waist. I sit up on my elbows, and he gets the hint immediately, pulling me up until I'm straddling him.

"That will only be a problem if you're planning on making a lot of noise."

"I think that's more up to you than me," I tease.

One hand pressing against my back, he uses the other to stroke my cheek before brushing a strand of my hair back. "You're perfect, Jess."

I swallow, struggling to find the right response as the air changes abruptly from frantic into something different as we hold each other, my arms draped across his shoulders. My fingers run through his hair as he moves lazily inside me.

He kisses me hard as his free hand glides between us, pressing light circles on me.

My throat constricts as he draws gasping breaths from me. I put my mouth over his shoulder, pressing my lips into his clavicle to try and muffle the sound of my moans.

"You just can't help it, can you?" he murmurs, running his hand through my hair and using it to gently pull my head back toward him. The featherlight touch contrasting with the deep thrusts takes my body over the edge. I let out a moan into his mouth, gripping his bottom lip with my teeth as I grind against him. The sensations collide in my center as it builds and builds until I see stars.

I ride the aftershock, shaking and twitching as his pounding increases speed and his moaning matches mine. We collapse in a heap of limbs, both spent from the emotional and physical toll of the past weeks. But after a few minutes of bittersweet silence, Oliver jumps up and runs over to grab his beeping phone.

Wide-eyed, he says, "Shit, they're announcing the winners."

"Oh my god." My mouth goes dry, like someone just took a leaf blower to my postorgasmic haze.

We attempt to wrangle my dress back on and run to a balcony. I would give anything to go down there, but I have no idea where Malcolm is. By the time I have a clear view, Dominic is pulling a piece of paper out of a gold-trimmed envelope.

"I don't like to mince words, but this company came out of nowhere and impressed me with their tenacity and go-to-market strategy. I see them achieving greatness."

"Wow, he really doesn't like to mince words," I say over my shoulder. Oliver looks just as nervous as I feel. He glances at me, and for a second I hope we don't place at all, because it makes his role in all this a whole lot stickier.

Dominic clears his throat, projecting into the microphone. "Third place and the prize funding of one hundred thousand dollars goes to . . . Wyst."

My heart swells before plummeting to the ground like a dodgy antigravity ride at the fair. Spencer excitedly bounds onto the stage to accept third place at TechRumble. We did it. I don't know what I wanted the outcome to be, but I know this feeling won't last for long. Spencer scans the crowd as he's handed an oversize novelty check for one hundred thousand dollars so large he can barely hold it on his own. He looks happy but confused, like he's scanning the crowd for . . . me. The "Radetzky March" begins to play the winners off stage, and the joyous crowd cheers and claps in time.

A hot tear runs down my face as I turn away. I'm a winner, but I still feel like I lost.

When we finally emerge from the study, the downstairs is almost completely cleared out. After the first and second places were announced—a cybersecurity company and a data storage

compression system—most of the companies left to either celebrate or commiserate. Spencer's also gone. Glassware clinks as
it's loaded into plastic crates by waitstaff dressed in aprons and
undone collars. A man in a traditional Viennese velvet frock
coat and white curled wig smokes a vape in the corner. Our
shoes echo against the floor as we make our way through the
empty ballroom.

Oliver places his suit jacket over my shoulders, the soft fabric
enveloping me. The jacket is so big I could wear it as a minidress.
He looks disheveled in the sexiest way possible as he rolls up his
sleeves, his fancy hair messed up, lips swollen, my new favorite
smattering of chest hair visible through the unbuttoned shirt.

He pulls out his phone and calls for a car as I take in my surroundings. The hall just filled with glittering gowns and sharp
suits, now hollowed out and echoes roaming free.

"Everything okay?" He steps back and snakes an arm around
me, placing a tender kiss on my cheek.

"Yeah, I just can't believe we actually did it. Wyst came
third; we have more than enough money to take us past the official launch." I don't say the rest, because Oliver already knows
what's about to happen.

My eyes begin to sting again, and I scramble to keep my
mind in the moment, instead of thinking about the coming
days. "And I'm sad the only time I got all dressed up to come
to a fancy event like this the only person I danced with was
Malcolm."

He smiles at me, an eyebrow cocked. "We have five minutes
until the car arrives?"

I swallow, gesturing at the stage. "The musicians have gone
home."

He clicks away at his phone, music swelling from the speaker, and places it inside his jacket pocket. The violin concerto begins to soar, vibrating lightly against my chest.

A wet laugh bursts out of me as I take his outstretched hand. Letting him pull me into a gentle sway.

A tear escapes me as I say, "Thank you for being . . . y'know. Okay with everything."

He pulls me tighter, more like a moving hug rather than a dance. "Thank you for telling me. I'm so sorry you went through that, that you're still going through it."

I rest my temple on his shoulder as we sway in silence.

Eventually, the song ends and he leans his chin down to me. "Do you want me to drop you back at your hotel?"

I cringe. "I'm sharing a room with Spencer."

He laughs into my temples. "All right, do you want to come to mine and eat room service in bed?"

"That's the most romantic thing anyone has ever said to me," I joke, but I might actually be serious.

He takes me by the hand, kissing it gently. "Let's get out of here."

CHAPTER 29

Business Account (WYST) BALANCE: -£5,002.77
Personal Account BALANCE: -£1,915.30

The rising sun trickles over us in slow, lazy rivulets. We've been awake for most of the night reintroducing ourselves to each other.

"When do you have to go?" he asks, running a hand up my bare chest until it reaches my neck.

"Never, if you keep doing that," I say, my eyes fluttering closed again.

He huffs a laugh, pulling me in toward him until my head rests on his side. I sink into him, reveling in a morning without the rolling wave of anxiety the moment my brain achieves consciousness.

"I have to go soon," I say into his chest. "I need to tell Dominic, then I have to tell everyone else." It's the only way to take control of what's happening, what Malcolm is threatening. Damage control before the damage is done. Well, not that I haven't already caused a lot to everyone around me. Making Spencer put on a high-stakes act, risking Pacha and Cecily's jobs, putting Oliver in a conflicting position without his knowledge. "Could you organize a meeting with him today?"

He runs a hand through my hair. "I think Dominic's already left; he was meant to fly back to London after the ball last night."

The sheets crumple as I sit up. "I thought you said he was staying at this hotel?"

"I said he has a *room* at this hotel," Oliver clarifies, "but Dom is like a vampire; he barely sleeps."

I nod. "That would explain the sexy brooding thing."

"And the bloodlust," Oliver adds, face deadpan.

"Booking a hotel room and not even sleeping in it is the level of success I aspire to." I stare up at the popcorn ceiling.

"He still has it until midday." He throws a mischievous smile in my direction. "Want to go up there and use the bathtub?" He kisses behind my ear, running his hand down my back in tiny circles.

I imagine saying yes, sinking further into Oliver's world. Lying my back against his bare chest in a sprawling bathtub filled with bubbles, his fingers exploring every inch of me. I groan, both out of being turned on and annoyed that the decision to leave just became a whole lot harder.

I tilt my chin toward him; the light reflects off the morning stubble lifting from his skin. "So very, very tempting, but Spencer and I have a flight to catch. And unlike Dominic, I can't afford to rebook. Maybe I could speak to him while he's in London?"

Oliver sits up on his elbows. "His schedule is kind of crazy over the next week. Receiving bad news at the moment is going to be stressful for him."

My stomach twists briefly when I remember the situation

I've put Oliver in. He knows everything; he could quite easily go to Dominic himself and expose the truth. He'd probably get a promotion for his honesty. Finally being honest with myself and the world is going to be my downfall. But at least this time it will be under my control.

I raise my eyebrows. "I'm kind of on a time crunch here. You remember, the blackmail of it all?"

He pinches the bridge of his nose and he sighs. "Fucking Malcolm. If he didn't exist, you could have just . . ." He trails off, looking sheepish.

I scoff, studying his face. "Were you about to say, 'I could have gotten away with it if it wasn't for those meddling kids'?"

He rubs the side of his jaw. "Maybe, I don't know." He shrugs and gives me a soft smile as the reality of this situation dawns on us in the daylight.

In a way, it's the best thing he could have said. His being unsure about what he would do in my situation makes me feel less like a criminal. Last night, everything seemed so dramatic, so at odds with everything I've ever wanted to do or be. But now, with the sun shining through, I know I have to do what I didn't with Malcolm the first time round. I didn't take control of my own decisions; I didn't do what needed to be done. Malcolm needs to be exposed for what he did and have a light shone against his darkness. Sure, I'm the collateral damage in this strategy, but maybe I deserve to be. I did this. I made Spencer pretend to be the founder of Wyst. At no point did I stop to consider the consequences. The photos Malcolm took were not my fault. But if I sit back and let other people have control of my life, I could never forgive myself. Even if finally destroying him might destroy me too.

I reluctantly drag myself away from Oliver, away from the warm king-sized bed and out into the chilled expanse of the hotel room. The window has condensation from the cold end of winter morning outside. We don't make the obligatory statements of intent, promises to make time and see each other.

We do this dance; a dressing rather than undressing one would usually expect with a make-out session this intense. He kisses up my thighs as I slide on my underwear, teases my nipples with his tongue as I button up a borrowed shirt. I use my tongue, gliding up his stomach as he slides on his trousers. By the time we are fully dressed, he's rock-hard and I'm utterly liquid.

"I should go," I say breathlessly over my shoulder. He somehow manages to help me step into shorts with one hand while running the other up the inside of my thigh. As I turn my back to him to leave, he keeps his hands on me like magnets. My palms push against the door, fingernails scraping across the grain as he brackets me. Clasping my jaw in his fingers, turning my chin over my shoulder to meet his mouth. Our tongues brush against each other's instead of talking. My fingers lace into his hair while his erection presses into me, turning my core completely molten.

"And I have a meeting in twenty minutes," he says into my mouth, curling a hand around my waist and into the front of my shorts, his peppery scent enveloping me like a blanket.

My voice comes out jagged. "I just need fifteen."

"How about ten?" he says with a smirk.

"Deal."

We know we shouldn't reverse the progress we've just made. My shorts are pulled back down in his fist as I grind against him. I undo the zipper and button of his trousers and rub him across my wet center in long languid strokes. His head drops to my shoulder, bumping his brow against the door.

"You are evil," he says, his voice vibrating onto my skin.

Twenty-five minutes later, I slip out of the room, giggling, as I watch Oliver, erection still pressing against his trousers, logging into his Zoom meeting and apologizing for his delayed arrival.

I wink at him before I shut the door, feeling weightless for the first time in years.

My mind is comfortably empty as I ride the humming elevator to the lobby, until the doors slide open and I lock eyes with my brother.

"Hey, where were you last night? I tried to find you. I can't believe we placed!" he says, squinting with a bewildered and panicked look on his face.

I rub my arm. "Yeah, amazing. Thanks for going up there."

He is still in his suit; did he stay out all night partying?

"Well, I didn't really have a choice. When Wyst was announced as third place, I had to go up there. I looked for you to pull you up onstage, but you and Oliver had disappeared." He looks me up and down. "I assumed you went back to his hotel . . . and looks like I was right. What was all that about not seeing him anymore?"

My heart palpitates for a few beats before the words burst out of me. "I told Oliver what we did."

Spencer lets out a gasping cough, taking my elbow and maneuvering me away from the crowd of tourists lining up at the check-in desk to a pair of purple armchairs in the corner. "Why the bloody hell would you do that?"

My lip quivers. "It was an emergency. Malcolm was there last night. He threatened me."

Spencer blinks, the outrage melting from his expression. "Fuck. What happened?"

"He told me if we placed, I have to sign over half the ownership of the company. If I don't do it, he will expose everything I've done. He's been watching us, Spence. He has a whole exposé written up and ready to go. He threatened me in London, trying to get me to be a part of his story, to say that I was lying about what he did to me as well. When I said no, he came to the ball and blackmailed me. He knows everything."

"He threatened you in London?! Why didn't you tell me?"

"I didn't want to throw you off before the final round, not that late in the game. I needed you focused." I nod, still trying to convince myself it was the right thing to do.

"Okay . . . so . . . what if we just give him half the money or something?" Spencer shakes his head, not quite believing the situation I've put us both in.

I spit out a humorless laugh. "As soon as it dries up, he'll want more and more. I don't have a choice . . . Malcolm is publishing his article on Monday, so Wyst's statement will go live tomorrow." I swallow a shaky breath. "But even if I did have a choice. It's the right thing to do. We can't keep lying like this to everyone."

"But we did it . . . The plan worked," Spencer says feebly.

I feel drunk, like my head is so woozy my neck can't hold it upright. I fold my cold fingers over one another in my lap, finally looking up at my brother.

"It's too late. I've already set it in motion by telling Oliver. I can't go back now."

Spencer's eyes turn from a soft garden green to an angry poison. "Are you serious?"

"It's time, Spence." I gesture around the lobby of the five-star hotel we can't afford to be in. "This has all gone too far. I have to tell Dominic before Oliver is obliged to. I'm doing the right thing," I conclude, mostly because I need to hear someone say it.

"Because it went so well the last time you did the right thing." He leans forward, lowering his voice. "This should be a joint decision between the both of us. Don't let that arsehole force your hand again."

We stare at each other, trying to telepathically come to the same conclusion as we always do. But the look in his eyes suggests he's just as confused as me. My own green eyes flare back at me.

He looks away. "I can't believe you would do this to me."

I scoff out a laugh. "What?"

"You weren't even going to consult me?" His eyebrows try to reach the ceiling.

"Why would I need to?" I blink at him. "Wyst is *my company*, Spence."

"Because you were the one who dragged me into this! You made me commit fraud for you! And that makes me a part of Wyst whether you like it or not. All I've been doing is working hard to make up for your mistake, to get *your company* out of a pit, and you don't even tell me when you've thrown everything I've done down the drain because what? You feel bad?" He lets out a long overdue breath.

For a second, all I can concentrate on is subduing my prickling eyes. "Because this whole thing is a farce. We're lying. And

Malcolm is going to expose us if I don't do it first. I don't have a choice." I rest my head in my trembling hands, trying to ignore the tourists side-eyeing us as they roll their suitcases past.

"Is this why you didn't tell me? So you could know for your own ego's sake if Wyst would place in the top three before you came clean?"

"I didn't tell you because *you* are not a real CEO; *you* are not the real founder. You just had to play your part, which you did brilliantly, so, thank you. You can go home now." I point to the door.

He rolls his eyes. "This is all you've cared about, and now you're throwing it away? You know you haven't even asked me how my audition went, the one I had to rush through to be here for *you*." He throws his jacket over his shoulder and turns.

I resist the urge to roll my eyes. "How was it?" I say after him.

"It was great! I fucking nailed it!" he shouts over his shoulder as he walks away, leaving me in Oliver's shirt and shorts and with my ballgown slung over my arm.

CHAPTER 30

Business Account (WYST) BALANCE: -£5,202.77
Personal Account BALANCE: -£2,005.57
Recent transactions:
Taxi fare: £90.27
Business account overdraft charge: £200.00
Adobe Creative Cloud subscription:
TRANSACTION FAILED

It's the first time back at the London office since Malcolm accosted me outside. Pacha has been checking in, threatening to actually murder Malcolm in a way that's oddly comforting. He envelops me in a bear hug, his Paco Rabanne cologne a familiar ease on my senses.

In an error of judgment, Wyst has misrepresented itself as a company while competing in TechRumble.

We cannot accept third place and will not accept the prize money.

We apologize to Odericco Investments, Dominic Odericco, and all our users.

Cecily scans the rest of the Word doc, cringing.

"You don't like it?" I ask, sipping my coffee and trying to fight my rising defenses. "It's just a draft."

She sucks her teeth. "It's too corporate. You need something less sterile."

"But it's a company statement?" I argue.

"Yes, but *this*"—she holds up the paper—"doesn't reflect the values of the company."

I purse my lips. "What do you think it should say?"

Her mouth turns into a soft smile. "I think if you want the users to understand what happened, it needs to come from you directly, not 'Wyst the Company,' and you need to tell the truth."

My stomach knots. "The whole truth?"

She nods. "And nothing but."

I take a long calming breath. "Okay, do you still have your camera?"

Several hours later I'm sitting in bed at Cecily's house. She's preloaded me with tissues, ice cream, and Peanut M&M's to numb the pain.

We uploaded the video to YouTube three hours ago, kept it unlisted, and sent it directly to Dominic with a separate letter stating our withdrawal from TechRumble. A courtesy ahead of the video going live tonight. We have yet to hear back from anyone at Odericco Investments, which is stressing me out more and more by the minute, but Cecily assures me they have seen it as it's been viewed twenty-six times and only two of those views were us.

The instant we sent the email, I wanted to call Oliver. To

ask for insight into Dominic's reaction, but also for comfort that this was the right decision. But he's not my boyfriend; we agreed we shouldn't put a label on things yet. It's not fair on either of us to put the pressure on right now, to define a relationship in the eye of the storm. Plus, the bad press it could bring to Dominic on top of everything else feels like I've stabbed him in the back with multiple different knives. *Hey, I made a mockery of your competition, committed fraud, and am falling for your cousin slash personal assistant* feels like too much news to deliver at once. Lying low seems like the right thing to do. Still, I can't help but miss Oliver's voice, his smell, his touch.

Cecily and I sit on the bed with gin and tonics in cotton pajamas as we stare at my glowing laptop screen. I fiddle with the scalloped edges of a throw pillow resting between my crossed legs.

"Are you sure you're ready for this?" she asks, squeezing my leg. "We can postpone the video if you want? Give you a few more days to process?"

"I'd love to." I sigh, hugging my knees close to my chest. "But Malcolm isn't exactly giving me a choice. If he wants to take this public, then so be it." This time I'm fighting fire with fire.

"True, it's only fair to give him what he wants after you shish kebabed his foot." She stifles a laugh and I follow suit.

As our laughter subsides, the heavy air returns.

"I might be about to blow everything up." I cut a glance to her equally solemn face. "We could be out of a job in a few minutes."

She looks at her watch. "It's actually going live in forty-eight seconds so maybe less," she says, having scheduled all the posts to go out on all social media platforms at the same horrendous time.

"Shit, shit, shit." I close my eyes and rock back and forth, the bed creaking under my weight.

"Ten seconds," she says as she grips my hand so tight it momentarily distracts from the pain about to come.

I tense for impact, as though I'm about to get blasted out of a rocket into the sun.

"It's live," Cecily says, refreshing all her open tabs to confirm. "Everywhere."

She refreshes the video, automatically causing my voice to ring out of the laptop speakers:

"Hello. My name is Jess Cole and I am the founder of Wyst.

"Effective immediately, I am stepping down from my role as CEO. I also feel like I owe you all an explanation . . ."

Bashing my finger violently against the keyboard, I mute the video before I throw up. I've already heard all this and don't need to torture myself further. After debating what extent of the truth should be revealed, I decided to come clean about everything. Even Malcolm. He was going to disrupt the terms of our NDA with his article anyway, and explaining to the world what a piece of shit he truly is might be the one silver lining in this whole mess.

Quiet fills in the short space between us as I lie back and throw a decorative pillow over my head. After a couple of minutes, I sit up, confused as to why the room hasn't turned into a battlefield. Why is there no one banging down my door like militant zombies looking for brains and internet justice? It's like it's not real. It's almost laughable; something that feels so huge in one arena has no impact on the air around you. No change to the clock still ticking away on the wall. The floor does not instantly begin to crumble and pull you down as far as you feel. Maybe it's a delayed reaction; a bulldozer is about to ram through the side of the house and crush us both.

"What's happening?" I ask, wincing at her silence.

"Not much to be honest." She refreshes again. "Oh, wait, never mind, it didn't refresh. The video now has a thousand views on YouTube, and we've lost a hundred followers on Instagram."

My limbs go numb at her words. I should be shocked by how quickly it's spread, but a scandal like this is just the kind of delicious news misogynist keyboard warriors love to devour. This is a five-course Michelin star meal in female stupidity. I nod my head and stick out my bottom lip in acceptance.

"But probably less damage than if this came from that dickweed," she consoles. "It was the best thing to do."

A tear escapes from the corner of my eye, but that's the only one I'll let out. There is a sick pleasure in the self-pity of it all, but the grief of lost work is superseded by the betrayal of my former self. How could I do that to her? Take all her pain and grief, her blood, sweat, and tears—just to throw in the towel.

"I just feel like I've let everyone down," I admit.

She pouts and pulls me into a hug. "You've put so much into Wyst. So much so it took you to some dark places. You created something good, but maybe now you can try and truly move on. Move forward."

I squeeze her tighter.

After a few moments of silence, the doorbell rings and Cecily leaps up, running out of the room.

"What was that?" I shout, clutching a pillow as the worst-case scenario runs through my mind like a bullet train. The press has already found me? The police are here because Dominic is pressing charges? Malcolm coming to get his revenge for a plan foiled?

"It's my present to you, for doing the right thing," she shouts back, eventually reappearing, her face too giddy for someone whose employment status is currently up in the air.

"Cec, you've done more than enough, I—" I stop my sentence as Oliver slips into the room, a sheepish but warm smile blistering his face.

"I'll be downstairs if you need anything, wearing large headphones." She wiggles her eyebrows at me before disappearing.

Oliver scans me with soft eyes from the doorway. "Can I come in?"

A smile barges its way through the anxiety on to my lips. "What are you doing here? Wait, how did you know where I was?"

He steps into the room, the floorboards creaking under his feet. "Funny story. Now I know your real name, it's much easier to track you down. And Cecily stole your phone and found my number." He cocks an eyebrow. "Apparently, I'm still in your phone as 'Olly Olly Olly, Oi Oi Oi'?"

My smile turns teasing. "I might need to change that . . . You shouldn't be here; it's a conflict of interest."

"I know, but I bake when I'm stressed and I didn't have anyone else to eat these with." He pulls a box of cookies out from behind his back. "I don't have to stay if you'd rather be alone. I just wanted to check you were okay."

My phone starts vibrating with text messages, social media notifications, and emails so violently it falls off the side table. I leave it on the floor, the rug muffling the buzzing sound.

"I'm kind of tired of feeling like I have to go through things alone," I admit, patting the empty side of the bed for him to join me.

"Are you okay?" he asks, sliding in next to me.

I sigh. "I'm okay. I'm relieved it's over, to not have to keep up with my own story, you know?"

He wraps an arm around me, pulling me into his chest, his chocolate and peppercorn smell enveloping me like a duvet. I still don't know what we are, but I'm glad he's here. I know what I want him to be; the words are practically bursting out of me.

I lift my chin to look up at his face. "How did Dominic take the news?" I pick off a piece of cookie and pop it into my mouth. Buttery, nutty, and sweet with a hint of sea salt.

He doesn't meet my eyes. "I'm not sure." His mouth twitches ever so slightly.

My eyebrows raise as I almost laugh. "Did it not come up at all?"

He bites his lip and studies the ceiling for a few seconds. "Not when I was quitting my job, no."

I sit up to face him, my hands remaining on his chest. "You did what?"

"I quit." He blinks at me.

"I'm sorry." I shake my head, trying to process. "When?"

"The moment I got back from Vienna." He nods, looking up to his right like he's recalling the conversation. The whites of his eyes are exposed before switching back to bright hazel, like snow melting to expose the bare forest trees.

My head is so full of questions, only the simplest ones seem to be able to squeeze out. "Why?"

"Well, it would have been even more awkward to do it over email," he teases. He's loving every second of this.

I drop the rest of the cookie, hold his shoulders, and shake. "You've got to give me a bit more information than that, seriously? What happened?"

He smiles. "Okay, okay. I didn't quit *because* of you. Not because of Wyst. I quit because you kinda inspired me too. I quit because I hate working there. Sure, the free snacks in the break room help, but oh my god, Jess, I hate being in corporate so much." He rubs his face. "Dom and I talked, and I told him I couldn't be his assistant anymore."

I hold a pillow for support. "And what did he say?" Ignoring the thrill of him using my real name so casually. Like he's spent the last two days apart practicing it.

Oliver leans back against the headboard, picking a cookie out of the box. "He actually offered me a promotion." He bites into the cookie with a smirk. "But I turned it down."

"Oh, how I would love to be related to a billionaire titan of business." I roll my eyes playfully.

"I told him I wanted to go back to culinary school. I want to give it another try." He nods, assuring himself it's the right decision.

"Have you told your mum?"

"Not yet, but I think you were right. I think Mom'll want what's best for me." He sighs. "I don't know if that's what my dad would want, but I'm going to start therapy sessions in a couple of weeks to try and work through that. I can't live my life for him anymore."

My parents flash in my mind, unable to comprehend why I wanted to leave Graystone and then why I wanted to start my own business at twenty-five years old. To risk the money. To be confident that, at the end of the day, your family will support you is a comfort I couldn't previously conceptualize. But finding that support in Cecily, Spencer, Pacha, and Oliver, maybe I could start to understand what that feels like.

My eyebrows meet in the middle. "How could me getting into this mess possibly inspire you?"

He smiles and tucks a loose strand of hair behind my ear. "Your passion, your drive, your relentless pursuit of your goals. You fired something up in me that made me rethink everything. I've just been living in this numb, thoughtless space for over a year. Ever since my dad died, I've just been floating through life, not really living. So I guess the cookies are also a thank-you present."

My eyes sting as I struggle to find the words. "I think that was all you."

He goes to speak, but I interrupt him. "Wait, that means you have absolutely no idea how Dominic reacted?"

He nods, lips in a tight smile. "No. I thought it would be less messy for you if I got out before things kicked off. As far as he knows, I found out the same time as everyone else."

My eyes zone out onto the white fluffy bedding, trying to process the last two days when I haven't begun to process the past few weeks.

He takes my chin in his hand, regaining my attention. "All I know is, you have had more of an effect on me than even I realized. You've made me rethink the little bubble I was living in. Feeling nothing, being nothing, achieving nothing. I owe you more than baked goods for that."

My fingers fiddle as I shake my head. "You don't owe me anything. I lied to you. I'm a coward."

He strokes my palm with his thumb. "You had this fucking awful thing happen to you, and it didn't stop you from taking a huge swing for something you care about. Jess, you're the bravest person I know."

The anxiety in my chest eases into something warmer, circling me and pulling me into its embrace.

He rests one leg over the other, grunting as he rearranges the pillows behind his back. "But if you *do* want to make it up to me, the culinary schools I'm applying to are all in London, so you'll have plenty of opportunities." He flashes me that winning smile.

I lean into him, our lips grazing each other's until his hand laces up my neck and through my hair, pulling me in closer. My hand lies on his, the other snaking around his taut waist, causing his stomach muscles to twitch under my touch. My phone continues to buzz incessantly from the floor. We sink into the bed, unwilling to stop until a knock thins the heavy air.

"Hey, Jess?" Cecily's voice is slightly muffled behind the wooden door.

"Uh-huh," I say, trying to dull my frustrated tone as Oliver releases my mouth and sends kisses down my neck.

"Did you happen to check your emails in the past ten minutes?" she asks.

"No, you told me not to," I reply, pressing on Oliver's chest to slow him down.

"Well, you probably should." She sounds tense. "Dominic has replied."

My muscles stiffen as I roll to the other side of the bed and pull up my laptop, still avoiding my phone like the plague. At least I can close all the open social media tabs and just focus on the email.

I scroll through thirty-six new emails since the video went live and find the one from Dominic's email address. My hand shakes as I click through and scan the words.

Ms. Cole,

I would prefer to discuss this in person; please come to the head office at 8 a.m. tomorrow.

Regards,
Dominic Odericco

The door clicks open to reveal Cecily with a fresh cup of coffee in hand.

"I think I'm being called to the principal's office," I say to her before turning to Oliver. "Is he going to murder me?"

Oliver scans the email over my shoulder. "I don't think so; he's a reasonable person when he wants to be. Do you want me to come with you?"

"We can both come," Cecily adds.

I run a hand through my hair, shutting down the screen. "No. Thank you, you're both doing enough. This is my mess. I need to fix this myself."

CHAPTER 31

Business Account (WYST) BALANCE: -£5,202.77
Personal Account BALANCE: -£2,055.57
Recent transactions:
Personal Account overdraft charge: £50.00

As much as it pained me, I sent Oliver home after a few hours. Our agreement is still the same until we know what is going on with Dominic. He could be pressing charges or filing a lawsuit. Only when I've washed my hands fully of this chapter in my life can I even dream about starting a new one.

My phone finally gave in under the weight of the notifications and crashed completely, but Cecily informed me over an early breakfast that the video has in fact gone viral. Hitting almost every social media platform overnight. The topics stretch into multiple industries beyond tech. Misrepresentation of your qualifications, with many leaders in business coming forward to talk about how they had to bullshit their way into their first jobs because every employer wants you to have the highest education and several years of experience in the field to gain access to an entry-level minimum wage job in your chosen industry. I chose not to mention Spencer by name to make sure the shrapnel didn't hit his career as well as mine, but I don't think his named involvement would have shifted the firestorm of cultural conversation. How women are not given the same amount of chances as men; men can continually fail upward, whereas women get one shot, and if they fail, the entire gender is marred with the same brush. The anti-feminist movement, using me as a shining example of how "women hate men because they secretly want to be them but can never achieve the same heights of success." How me "hiring an actor" shows that extroverts gain access to powerful roles in business, not because they are the smartest or the most qualified but because they know how to play the game. I'm being lauded for how I gamed the system but lambasted because I cheated my way to success. How I should be made Woman of the Year and stoned to death in the street. Malcolm set his article live overnight, seemingly as an attempt at retaliation. Rather than making the splash he intended, it was immediately drowned out by bigger publications reporting on the incident.

"We've had interview requests from *Forbes*, *FemTech Monthly*, *Fast Company*, *Business Insider*, and the BBC." Cecily shuts her notebook, lips pursed. "*The Cut* also wants you to write a personal essay."

"Shit," I say into my coffee, wiping my puffy eyes. I can already feel the weight of the digital eyes on me. Those publications are going to run something about me with or without my comment. But in the arena of social media, people have already cast their votes for or against me. Is a quote really going to change that?

"What do you want to do?" Cecily's hands are primed on her phone, ready to go to war if I ask her to.

I take a breath. "I don't want to make any more moves until we know what's happening with Odericco. For all I know, I might have a lawsuit on my hands." The one unfortunate thing about Oliver quitting is no longer having a man on the inside. I'm walking into a situation with no temperature gauge. Well, at least I know there's not a chance in hell I'm getting that prize money. Ironically, this is getting more press coverage than the winners of TechRumble. It's better this way; a company who didn't place at all will get to be third. And as long as I don't end up in jail by the end of the day, I'll be happy. Everybody wins.

I scroll through my inbox, now racking up to nearly four hundred new messages. I scroll down to one of the very first I received after the video went live. My gut twists as I skim the paragraphs of misogynistic lecturing, graphic insults, and death threats. I click through a few more with a similar tone until I hit something that contrasts so hard it almost gives me whiplash.

Hi Jess,

I've been following Wyst on Instagram for about six months, and I just wanted to say that I think what you did was really brave. Also kind of nuts, but as a small business owner myself, I know how hard it can be to be taken seriously.

Anyway, you probably won't read this, but I hope you're doing okay.

Best,
Charlotte

Dear Jess,

Good on you for exposing that creep. I had a stalker a few years ago and the police wouldn't do anything to help, so I know how it goes. I've started following Wyst and can't wait to see what you do next.

Karina

Jess,

My name is Sharon, and I represent the interests of Torrington Investors. Wyst is an incredibly exciting concept, and we'd love to arrange a sit-down with you to discuss a potential investment.

Kind regards,
Sharon Edgar
Torrington Investors

I scroll through several more emails, getting sentiment whiplash from people calling me a lying bitch to a feminist hero. People wanting me dead to people wanting to invest in Wyst. The mixed feelings gnaw at my edges, leaving me tender as I get dressed in a suit (black, just in case I'm stepping into my own funeral) and begin my first and last journey to Odericco Investments. I keep my head down on the Tube, wearing a baseball hat and sunglasses like a shitty disguise in a superhero movie. There's a numbing effect to knowing so many people have seen it, that the news is out of my control. The low rumbling as we zoom across to the financial district sets me into a meditative lull; I'm so tired but couldn't possibly sleep knowing what's coming.

After signing in with a pretty blond receptionist, I'm instructed to sit and wait at a cluster of white armchairs and sofas set out like a makeshift living room. I perch uncomfortably in the modern design chair, trying at once to both avoid eye contact with every person walking through the lobby while also making sure they aren't staring at me. After a few minutes, I realize I'm shaking. My mind starts to run at a hundred miles an hour. Am I having a panic attack? This doesn't feel like a panic attack. This feels like adrenaline surging through my veins until they pop. I try to self-soothe, repeating to myself that I've survived worse. At least people are talking about something I have control over. I controlled the narrative. I decided when and where to post it.

My mind glosses over Malcolm. I'm still fucking terrified he is going to do something beyond posting the article to retaliate, but for now, it seems like he's lying low. I've taken his story from him, his credibility, his reputation, his power over me.

I huff a laugh, a sick satisfaction in Malcolm being forced out of job because of me for the second time.

Eventually, a man in his late twenties comes to collect me, and we ride the elevator up to the thirty-seventh floor in silence. He's well-dressed in a custom suit but has an air of nervousness, like he's not fully settled in his environment. It quickly dawns on me that he's Oliver's replacement.

He leads me into a room tinged in a cool blue hue from the wall-to-wall glass. The colored film no doubt provides a level of privacy without compromising the view of London's skyline. Seeing all while never showing yourself, very on-brand for Dominic.

"Mr. Odericco will be in shortly," New Oliver says before shooting me a tight, knowing smile and closing the door shut.

I pad over to the window and stare at the crowds flowing over streets and filing in and out of public transport. Working in a place like this could give even the most grounded person issues with self-aggrandizement. Feeling huge compared to the thousands of indistinguishable masses forty feet below your shoes.

The door clicks open, and I flick my head around to see Dominic Odericco step into the room. He doesn't say anything, barely making eye contact with me. I remain silent too, my eyes flicking between him and the door. I'm waiting for the other people to file in behind him—legal representation, PR specialists, the crisis management team, the board of directors, anyone. After a pregnant pause, Dominic walks over to the coffee station and pours himself a cup.

"Don't you have someone to do that for you?" My voice is smooth and measured compared to my hands, which are shaking uncontrollably in my pockets. I grip the chair to steady them.

"I did, but the new guy doesn't get the milk ratio right." He takes a sip, steam still reaching out of the cup.

"Must be hard to find good help these days." Maybe it's a power play to suggest I know his cousin just quit, to throw him slightly before we do this. But I'm confused by the lack of bodies occupying the room, so I want to level the field a bit.

His sullen mouth softens, and he lets out a breath through

his nose. He looks through me with dark hazel eyes. "Take a seat, Miss Cole."

I pull the chair out from under the table and sit on the opposite side of the long table. "Are we waiting for anyone else?"

He raises an eyebrow. "No, unless you are?"

"No," I say, trying to keep my relief at bay from my tone.

We sit; the only sound is the running of chair legs against the soft gray carpet. He unbuttons his suit jacket as he lowers himself, so I do the same, leaning back in the seat to replicate every video I've ever watched about the art of negotiation. This isn't a negotiation, this is a sentencing, but I'd rather go down not clamoring against the table like a woman dying of thirst asking for a drop of water.

He leans back on his elbow, one leg crossed over the other as he examines me. "I thought Wyst was a great idea," he says, face completely void of emotion.

Trying not to read into him using the past tense, the only thing I can think to say is "Thank you."

"When your application was passed to me, I thought it was a no-brainer to include Wyst in TechRumble. We don't get many . . ." He thinks of the right word. "Alternatives to the banking, crypto, AI bunch in our application pools these days. Wyst really stood out."

My instinct is to say thank you again, but I swallow it, remaining both calm and tense, preparing my stomach muscles for the gut punch I know must be coming.

"It's a real shame you can't be a finalist after everything that's occurred." He begins to type on his phone, on to the next problem now that I've been dealt with.

"Mr. Odericco, I know what I did was misguided, but I would like the opportunity to explain my actions personally."

"Self-awareness does not supersede foolishness." He looks up from his phone, placing it face down on the table. "Besides, Mr. Cole has already told me everything."

My heart stops for a few beats as the latch clicks and a solemn-looking Spencer walks through the door, closing it behind him. My eyebrows raise off the top of my head as I watch my brother sheepishly take a seat next to Dominic Odericco.

My mouth falls open. "What are you doing here?" We haven't spoken since our fight, but I saw his name among the list of calls and messages barraging my phone before it went kaput this morning.

"Thanks for joining us." Dominic gives Spencer a genuine soft smile. My confusion rises. Why are they still so chummy? Spencer lied to him too.

"You didn't have to bring him in too; this was all me," I insist.

"I didn't invite him. I found him camped out in front of the building yesterday morning, claiming your entire plan was his idea and if anyone was going to be punished, it should be him.

"But while we were talking, you posted your video. And it quickly became obvious he was lying to cover for you."

Spencer shrugs. "I thought it was worth a shot."

My eyes fill with tears, stinging the edges of my eyelids as I blink them back. He stares at me, all warmth. An apology and a forgiveness all at once. Our bond goes beyond anything else. Even though we might piss each other off, we're still siblings. As annoying as Spencer can be, as much as our family favors him, he'll always be my brother. And I'm so glad he is here. I want to run and hug him, to squeeze his hand under the table, to tell him we're okay and we always will be. That I love him so much for what he tried to do for me.

"I appreciate that you have decided to step down as CEO. But as much as you two have fucked up, I still think Wyst has merit, and now . . . the whole world is looking at it." Dominic holds his hands up. "The last thing I want out of this situation is a loud public mess. TechRumble is something I'm very proud of, something that draws forth the newest innovations in technology. If this farcical series of events affects my one passion project, then there's going to be hell to pay."

I internally wince; seeing a glimpse of his wrath is terrifying. I glance at Spencer, who seems even more entranced by Dominic's shift in demeanor.

"But I still want to help fund Wyst. Odericco Investments' portfolio needs a bit of diversification. I've been attempting to spearhead this for several years now, but I haven't found a start-up that has the right . . ." He purses his lips. "Reputation."

I sit back. "Right . . . And by reputation, you mean what exactly?" Jesus, who am I right now? Three months ago, I would have burst into tears from just an invitation to the Odericco office. And now all of a sudden, I've become big balled enough to question his interest? "Because I don't want Wyst to be upheld as some shining example of FemTech just so you can use us as a stepping stone to a more diverse portfolio." I cross my arms for emphasis; even if I have stepped down as CEO, I'm still the sole owner and founder of the company.

Dominic takes a sip of his coffee, still boiling hot. "Can't it be both?"

I don't respond as he continues, "I assume you're now looking for alternative employment? I have a new role I think you might be interested in."

We stare at each other, and a shiver runs down my spine. This is the icy, determined robot stare everyone talks about; this is the legacy he has already written.

"I'll think about it," I say, taking a breath. "But only if you also pledge to implement blind applications. TechRumble should be putting its money where its mouth is."

Spencer covers his smile with a hand, squinting at me with gleaming eyes.

Dominic's mouth almost twitches into a smile before he decides against such a frivolous indulgence. He leans back, enjoying the delicious, stressed silence as he takes another slow sip of his coffee. "Done."

CHAPTER 32

Business Account (WYST) BALANCE: -£5,202.77
Personal Account BALANCE: -£2,055.57

Spencer and I step out of the Odericco Investments building with a renewed sense of bewilderment and vigor. Nine-to-fivers are pacing frantically to pick up a sandwich before heading back to their desks. They weave around us, barely leaving an inch of space. It's started to rain, but neither one of us has an umbrella. My body has just begun returning to normal after being in fight-or-flight mode for the past three hours. Dominic and I spent the last hour in his office discussing what a FemTech board would look like, how we would build it out, and who else we would bring in. All while Spencer entertained himself on a sofa in the corner, making the most of the break room's complimentary snack cupboard.

I slipped into the role quickly and efficiently in the meeting, which almost feels like a sign that I should take this position. I've blown up my only other option. This is the best-case scenario. It's marred by being backed into a corner, but in reality . . . how long would I have been able to play out the lie we built? How long would Spencer have to turn up and fake-run quarterly report meetings with Odericco Investments? How complicated would it have been to create a narrative in which Spencer steps down from his role of CEO as a TechRumble third-place finalist and puts his assistant in charge? Would I have had to change my legal name to Violet to stay on top of the lie? In a way, Malcolm's blackmail made me finally face the reality of the situation I had created out of panic, depression, and desperation.

A black cab speeding past pulls me back onto the pavement with Spencer. He's been staring at me as I've been zoning out, trying to analyze and process everything that has just happened this morning, not even the past few days. For now, I lock all that up to focus on the major decision. For the first time today, I study Spencer. He looks uncomfortable, more dressed up than usual, but his shirt and trousers are rumpled like he's thrown them on, whipping them from the chair known as the Clothes Horse in his flat at the very last minute.

Finally, he asks, "What are you going to do?"

What I *want* to do is sleep for one hundred days, being tucked up under full fluffy duvets in nice pajamas and kept alive by other people—namely, a certain amazing chef I know, who will feed me homemade meals and go down on me on request. Instead of saying that, I throw my bag over my shoulder, gripping the brown folder of documents I was going to throw at Odericco Investments lawyers when they were eventually brought forth by Dominic in the meeting. "I'm going to get a drink, and you're coming with me."

He nods, probably out of fear of doing anything else after going behind my back to Dominic. I'm wired, my brain running a thousand miles a minute with ideas. Possibilities. But I need to absorb what happened before I talk to anyone else.

That's one benefit of having a twin; they just get you because it would be impossible *not* to get you. It would be weirder if they couldn't predict your next words or how a single twitch is a window to your emotional state.

Ten minutes later, the smell of alcohol-soaked carpets, roasted nuts, and beer fills our nostrils as we sit down in a dark corner booth in the nearest pub, the Duke's Folly. Despite it only being midday, the room is almost full, circles of workers and people in business casual littering the floor; cheers and bursts of laughter, murmuring groups, and the occasional smashing glass soundtrack our entrance as Spencer runs to the only empty booth.

We get our drinks: me a Negroni, Spencer a straight glass of rye whiskey. My card bounces when I briefly forget that I'm still financially at rock bottom, but Spencer quietly taps his card to the machine over my shoulder.

Spencer's eyes are sorrowful but soft. The rain pounds against the stained glass window, purple, green, and red reflections trickling across the dark wood table as we people watch in silence and take the first few sips of our drinks. Easing into the inevitability of this conversation.

"I'm sorry for shouting at you," he says, running his fingers over the geometric pattern etched on the side of the crystal glass. He glances up, a sheepish smile appearing across his face. "And for not telling you about . . . him."

"Clearly, shouting and lying run in the family," I say, taking a breath. "And I'm sorry too."

We clink our glasses together, sealing the mutual apology like a contract. What else are we going to do? We're too far gone to let the past six weeks dictate the rest of our lives. We will be in each other's lives forever—that is the only constant either of us can rely upon; we have each other's DNA, and as much as we don't like to share, we shared a womb.

"So Dominic?" I arch a playful eyebrow.

Spencer's mouth twists into a reluctant smile. "Yeah, about that . . ." I don't see this kind of smile very often; it warms my heart to see my confident, no-holds-barred brother blush over someone.

"How long have you been seeing each other?" I ask point-blank.

Spencer blinks, as though I couldn't have possibly picked up on the ridiculous chemistry between the two of them. At first, I thought it was Spencer being on his best charming behavior and Dominic being the most watched person at the events, but some small piece of sunshine got through.

"We haven't . . ." he says, cheeks blushing the faintest shade of pink. "Today was the first day I asked him out."

I lift my eyebrows. "Really?" I wince internally over the assumption that he was being as reckless as me. I can't believe I've been the more daring of the two of us.

"I think we both knew there was something there from the start, but I didn't want to jeopardize the plan and he didn't want to be unprofessional." He gives me a look. A twitch of the eye that conveys multitudes. Telling me, yes, I should feel bad about getting involved with Oliver while Spencer was avoiding genuine feelings for Dominic, because I made it clear how bad it would be if he followed his heart.

"So, nothing happened at all?"

"I think we could both feel it; we'd catch each other looking in ways the others weren't. And then in Paris, I think Oliver had organized a private chat between the two of us and things got *very* close to happening, but we both knew we couldn't. Once the winners were announced it felt almost . . . inevitable." He goes somewhere for a few moments, smiling as he gazes into a fond memory.

"So you went there today to tell him the truth about your feelings?" I shift in my seat, imagining him going through that alone.

He takes a final swig. "I was there today to tell him about what happened at TechRumble *and* my feelings for him." Spencer huffs a laugh into his empty glass. "He saw right through me about Wyst, though. He knew I was lying about it being all my idea."

"Not as good an actor as you thought, hey?" I tease.

He snorts a shy laugh and throws a thin red straw at me. "Fuck off."

I laugh too. "And what did he think of the other stuff, the feelings?"

He purses his lips. "He was . . . reciprocal." His cheeks glow pink.

I prop my elbow on the slightly sticky wood table and rest my chin in my hand. "Can I just ask . . . Dominic is scary as fuck, and you are like a human bouncy ball. What drew you together?"

Spencer clears his throat. "He said he likes seeing the world through my eyes. Taking things seriously doesn't mean you have to lose every facet of your personality or that you can't relax and have a good time. I think somewhere down the line he'd forgotten that."

My chest warms; maybe it's the alcohol, but seeing my

brother look so at peace is a new experience. "And what's there for you?" I ask, taking another sip.

He sighs. "I'm surrounded by people whose goal in life is to be the center of attention. Sometimes it's to tell a story about something important, but most of the time it's to draw in a crowd for themselves. It was nice to talk to someone who had this ultimate goal, which is so much bigger than them as an individual. And there's this unbelievable pleasure in breaking a smile out of someone who is determined to be serious. When you see someone so rigid become elastic because of you." He looks down wistfully at the table. "Like when we used to pick stones from the beach and crack them open to find a geode hidden inside. That's what Dominic is."

My eyesight blurs as I blink away the fuzziness. Sure, he's had boyfriends and casual flings and even one very awkward girlfriend situation in secondary school, but I don't think I've ever heard him talk about someone like this.

My mind drifts to Oliver and why I was attracted to him in the first place. He at once could relate to the pain and grief but didn't hold it so close the poison would seep in. His willingness to adapt and mold into a new version of himself when the old one was getting to be too much. To ultimately prioritize his happiness because that was the only way he could give other people happiness. He couldn't not be his true self but still tried to honor his family any way he could.

We're lucky that our chemistry came first, then our feelings came second. The basis of attraction made us able to express ourselves to each other. If we'd gone the traditional route, or, god forbid, I'd matched with him on a dating app, taken him to a wine bar, and done everything the way it's "supposed" to be done, we wouldn't have stood a chance. We got lucky that we were both having a bad day and threw down our defenses.

Without thinking, I ask, "Do you love him?"

He looks at me with a twinkle of recognition in his eyes. "Do you?"

We curve the edges of our lips in unison, both too sheepish and British to say that sort of thing out loud. Maybe we do, but it's too soon to say it.

I roll my eyes cartoonishly, finishing off my glass and leaning back against the burgundy booth. "Imagine how awkward a double date would be." Smiling at the idea of us both being happy, the twins and the cousins. I wonder if Dominic and Oliver will have a conversation about everything soon; I guess if Dominic offered him a promotion when he tried to quit, there must still be a door that's open for a relationship outside of work.

Spencer laughs, rubbing his face. "Oh my god or at Christmas?! What a nightmare. The six of us and deaf Granddad Bob saying "Who's that?" every few minutes would be torture."

"Monthly newsletter–worthy for sure." I sit back in the booth seat, my hands in my lap. "Maybe even the end-of-year highlights."

I smile, thinking about us two little nobodies bringing home a gigantic American and an aristocratic billionaire. Our smiles dwindle as, in sync, our minds shift to our parents.

Spencer clears his throat, mulling on the question for a few seconds. "Have you spoken to Mum and Dad?"

Maybe I should respond to my parents; maybe now I've let go of the past, it's time to move forward with them too.

A sigh escapes me. "Not since her birthday. They've been calling me after I posted the video, but I've been sending them to voicemail. I'm not in the right headspace for a lecture." My phone also barely works right now with all the notifications blowing it up.

"They'll come around." He squeezes my hand.

I look down into my drink, watching the ice melt. "And if they don't?"

"You'll have me . . ." He bites his lip, considering something for a few seconds. ". . . And if they don't talk to you, their darling son won't give them any updates about his big new role with BBC America."

I blink and shake my head, stunned into silence. "I'm sorry, what?"

He laughs, wiggling his eyebrows. "I got the job."

I slam my hand onto his arm. "Why didn't you say something sooner?"

"I only found out yesterday!" He shrugs, a massive smile plastered across his face. "It felt mean rubbing it in when your life was falling apart."

I sigh, the guilt of being so vocal about my struggles over the past few weeks while choosing to ignore his makes me feel sick. It was a dick move. "You know you didn't have to do that. I will always be happy for you, even if I'm in the bloody gutter. I'm sorry if I made you feel like I wouldn't support you."

"Thanks," he says sheepishly as he fiddles with the collar of his shirt.

I lean in, knowing he probably can't tell many people about the news until it's officially announced. "What's the role?"

His mouth turns upward into a sly smile. "It's a period drama; my character is a plucky inventor trying to get his idea off the ground."

I scrunch my face and scoff a laugh. "Are you being serious?"

"They said my interpretation of the character felt very natural." He sucks in his cheeks.

We stare at each other, both in paused amusement, waiting for the other to break first. Of course Spencer would nail the audition; I didn't doubt that. I knew he was a talented actor, but having seen his improvisational skills up close and personal has reinforced my faith in his career choice. I used to think pursuing a career like that was an incredible risk, with the ultimate odds of success slim to none. But now I realize, the life I've chosen to pursue is no different.

"I wonder where you learned that from." I tap my finger against the table. "When does filming start?"

"In a couple of months, but it's in New York . . . so I won't be able to do those extra office hours now . . ." he says. "Do you think Wyst will survive without me?"

I smile at my brother; the never-ending well of pride just got a little bit deeper. "I think Wyst is going to be okay without either of us."

CHAPTER 33

FROM THE OFFICE OF DOMINIC ODERICCO:

After much deliberation over Ms. Cole's statement and her stepping down as CEO, we have decided to disqualify Wyst as a finalist from TechRumble. Wyst will not receive the allocated prize money, and Odericco Investments will choose another from our list of finalists to receive the third-place prize, to be awarded in the coming days.

However, we would hasten to admit that Ms. Cole's actions are a reflection and consequence of the current tech landscape. Only 11 percent of all applicants to TechRumble are female-founded or female-led companies. There is a major bias toward men within the tech industry. We cannot award Wyst a place in the final three of TechRumble. We will, however, include Wyst in a selection of female-owned businesses for our new venture, the FemTech Fund. Investment exclusively for companies prioritizing the improvements in the quality of life for women and women's issues. More to be announced soon.

Dominic Odericco

Oliver's chest rises and falls in deep movements as I read the statement out loud. We both scanned the draft Dominic's new assistant sent me last night but seeing it across the Odericco Investments website and social media felt like reading it in a different language. It's 7 a.m. The sun is barely ready to rise, and despite both of us waking up unemployed this morning (my new role working with Dominic starts in a month and Oliver's culinary course starts next week), our internal clocks are still set to wake up in a cold sweat of panic about whatever emails have landed while we were asleep.

Instead, we use the morning more wisely. My heartbeat spiking as he pulls the laptop out of my reach and lifts my T-shirt. He leaves slow warm kisses down my chest, my stomach muscles twitching at the contact.

"Do you remember what you told me your idea of a perfect morning was?"

My brain grapples to find the memory underneath the tingling sensation of his mouth. "I said I want someone to wake me up with coffee, feed me French toast, then go down on me."

From my waistline, he looks up through dark lashes, his fingers curling around the edges of my underwear. "Does it need to be in that specific order?"

I bite my lip and shake my head. "I could consider making an exception just this once. But I do need to talk to Cecily this morning before we release my counterstatement," I say.

"Mm-hmm," he says, his tongue running up the inside of my thigh.

My lips part on a gasping inhale. "And I need to meet with Lana about coming on board in three hours," I say to the ceiling.

He laughs, his breath tickling against the soft cotton of my underwear. "Does that brain of yours have an off switch?"

I sink deeper into the mattress. "Yes, try and find it." My voice is hoarse as my fingers dig into the sheets.

He climbs back up my body, sinking his lips into my collarbone, my hands running down his bare taut back. "Is that a challenge, *Miss Cole*?" The friction of his thick thigh sliding between mine runs straight to my center.

"That depends on how competitive you are. And if your French toast is as good as you say it is."

My palm circles the back of his neck, pulling his soft lips to mine. My tongue slides against his, the taste of minty toothpaste waking me up even more. He wraps an arm around me and shifts us farther up the bed, placing my hands on the headboard.

"Oh, it's as good as I say it is." He takes my wrists in his palms and slides them under the pillows. "These stay here, all right? No checking your emails," he instructs onto my lips.

I nod silently, blood rushing to my cheeks.

He drags my underwear down my legs, leaving them hanging off one ankle, before licking his way back up to my center. My body jolts with pleasure, riding the feeling of his tongue pressing into me. My blood pulses through my head, the need building and building until I'm clawing the edges of the pillows. My throat is dry from gasping inhales and whispering his name, "oh god," and "don't stop" into the morning air.

His hands follow the sloping path of my breasts, squeezing and pinching my nipples in rhythm to his tongue's thrusts. He adds a finger, then another, priming me for him.

"Fuck, you taste amazing," he says, his lips glistening. The sight takes me over the edge, keening and moaning so loud I thank god the only other being in the apartment is Warren Buffett.

AN HOUR LATER I'm gulping down my first sip of freshly ground coffee at the kitchen counter when Oliver's phone vibrates against the countertop.

He answers, nodding a few times with a serious expression shadowing his face before holding the phone out to me. "It's for you. Maybe you should ask Dom if you can hire an assistant."

I raise my eyebrow at him. "Looking for a job?"

He rolls his eyes and kisses me on the cheek before shoving the phone into my hand. "I'll *assist* you anytime you need."

Cecily's voice rings through the speaker. "Hey, I know you're meant to be lying low right now, but you're going to want to take this. Can I merge the call?"

"I'm going to take this in your room," I say to Oliver, who nods in return and goes back to the saucepan sizzling on the stovetop.

"Hello, this is Jess Cole." I tuck my hair behind my ears.

"Hello, Jess. This is Bernadette Reid."

My body freezes, alarm bells going off all around me. "Oh my god! Hi!" I immediately cringe at my overexcited tone, clearing my throat. "How are you doing?"

"I'm good. I imagine I'm doing better than you this morning." Her accent makes it hard to understand if she is being sarcastic.

To be safe, I laugh nervously. "You're probably right."

"I watched your video. What you did was . . ." She mulls her words on a hum. "Inadvisable."

My feet begin to stalk back and forth around Oliver's bed as though they are trying to run away from this conversation. "Yes, I know. And I just want you to know that when we had our meeting I was complet—"

"Inadvisable but admirable," she clarifies.

I stop pacing. "Oh. Thank you?"

"I have had many emails and messages from my audience to interview you."

My heart begins to pound. "Right, well, I am technically still the owner of the company but I'm no longer the CEO, so I'm not really doing any press at the moment. But maybe in the future we coul—"

"I do not want to interview you," she says matter-of-factly.

"Okay," I say, finally matching the flow of her speech.

"I'd rather meet to discuss prospective investment options."

My eyebrows hit the ceiling. "Excuse me?"

"Do you have a portfolio you could send to my business manager? Some of my network is also very interested in hearing more."

I scramble to the floor, pulling my laptop onto my lap. "Umm, yes, of course. I will send it over right away!"

"Thank you. I'll have my team contact you to discuss next steps."

"Great, thank you so much!" My voice wobbles as I try to get the words out.

"I am hosting a women in business event in London next month. You should come."

"Ummm, okay. I'll discuss it with Dominic and get back to you." As amazing as that sounds, I don't know if I'm quite ready for it yet.

With every neuron in my brain firing at five times speed, I tentatively step out of Oliver's bedroom and into the kitchen.

Oliver is clanging pots and plates around, dipping his finger into some sort of jammy sauce and tasting it. "What was that about?"

I blink furiously, trying to decide whether the call was real, before looking over to him. "I think I just got an investor for Wyst."

He drops his pan of eggs into the sink. He scoops me up, arms linked under my backside, and spins me around. "Are you serious?"

Droplets of liquid appear on his T-shirt, and I realize I'm crying. The relief, the stress, the pain, the excitement. Everything swirls in my head and comes out of me in a teary fit of laughter.

EPILOGUE

One year later

Personal Account BALANCE: £27,340
Recent transactions:
The Withering Vine New York: $150.00

Thoughts?" Dominic asks.

I examine my glass of Château Batailley 2005. "Mmmm, it's a lot nicer when you're not swigging it from the bottle."

Dominic crosses the wide carpeted expanse overlooking Queens and sits in an office chair next to me, "I meant the location," he clarifies. "It's not Manhattan."

I give him a look, my face reflecting against the floor-to-ceiling windows framing the city skyline. We're not quite on bestie terms yet, but we sit comfortably somewhere between "my boss" and "my brother's boyfriend." This means most of the time we can skip the polite pleasantries neither of us is interested in. Also, I'm in love with his cousin. It's messy, but luckily, I don't see any of it going south anytime soon. Spencer and Dominic are so sickeningly in love. It always hits me like whiplash when Dominic's demeanor shifts from an immovable stoic businessman to a malleable lovable boyfriend around my brother. Over the past year, I've had the good fortune to meet him somewhere in the middle.

"I think if you squint hard enough you can see Spencer from here," I say with an impish grin.

Dominic rolls his eyes, pouring his own glass from the bottle I brought to celebrate signing the lease. I think he is secretly using our trip to find an office space for the new FemTech Fund headquarters as an excuse to go see his boyfriend, but he's refusing to admit it. Spencer has been back in New York for four months now, filming on and off for the second season of his show with BBC America. Weirdly, I think many couples would have struggled to make long-distance work so soon into a relationship, but dating an international businessman with offices in London and New York helps considerably.

Oliver is flying in later today, a few days after the first semester of his advanced course finishes, and then we're traveling to see his mum. It's the first time I'll be meeting her in person, but Oliver's weekly FaceTime calls quickly turned into mine and his mum's FaceTime calls. She says she gets more information out of me than him, and when his course days run long or the time difference gets in the way, I'm more than happy to step in. It's nice to feel that undivided love from a mother figure. I think she secretly always wanted Oliver to pursue his dreams, but just like Oliver, she didn't want to betray her husband's wishes. After some coaxing from his therapist, including a session in which his mother joined in to talk about his dad, they began to open up their dialogue surrounding his career more and more. From what he's shown me, his mum's house is nestled in the countryside, between forests of redwood trees. She says no wonder Oliver grew up to be so tall; surrounded by woods reaching up to the sky, it would be impossible not to.

Cecily and Pacha were more than happy to hold down the fort back home with Lana, our new head of legal. She officially started a few weeks after helping me through the process of taking action against Malcolm. Ensuring the blocked number he threatened me from was traced back to his IP address and the CCTV footage of him approaching me on the street outside the Wyst office was taken into account. After his computer was seized, it was found that he was doing even more than blackmail. Dodgy accounts, wire fraud, and a variety of other activities mean he is potentially looking at jail time, but Lana has warned me that with his family money he'll likely just get probation. Just to be safe, she gained a restraining order against him for me, Spencer, and any employee of Wyst.

WHEN OLIVER JOINS us in New York, we share a table at a crawfish seafood restaurant that he has been desperate to go to ever since we put this trip on the books. He manages to wangle his way into the kitchen and is chatting to the chef behind the counter.

Dominic furrows his brow but retains a small smile. "That boy has never met a door he couldn't finesse his way through."

"Be nice," Spencer says, squeezing his broad arm.

"It was a compliment," Dominic assures him, his hard surface cracking just enough for some unspoken communication to slip through.

"We could go with the smaller place uptown?" I ask, continuing our office space debate.

"I know what I want," Dominic says, "and luckily I'm good for it."

"When are you seeing the period app people?" Spencer asks.

"Tomorrow," I say as Oliver slides into the booth beside me. "Have fun?"

"They let me feed the lobsters," he says, his eyes wide and joyous.

"And during your adventure to the zoo, did you happen to find out if we can eat one of them soon?" Dominic's eyebrow lifts.

"Dodo, I don't work for you anymore, remember?" Oliver quips, using the nickname we all know Dominic publicly hates but secretly loves ever since Spencer also started using it.

Oliver and Dominic both get up to use the bathroom before our food arrives, leaving Spencer and me alone at the table.

We smile at each other before Spencer breaks the silence. "I think Dom is going to propose."

I almost choke on my spiked lemonade, sputtering, "What?"

"He's booked a very fancy hotel for this weekend while you guys are in Montana and apparently has some sort of surprise, but he's been acting less naturally grumpy than usual. I even saw him smile at a crying child yesterday."

"Whoa, if you're correct that's amazing news, right?" I hold my straw in anticipation.

"Oh my god, yes. If he doesn't do it soon, I will. I nearly did the other night with a Krispy Kreme doughnut as the ring."

"Oh, Spence, I'm so happy for you." I place my hand on his across the table.

He eyes me suspiciously. "So you don't know anything about this weekend?"

"No." I shrug nonchalantly. "I wish I did."

I'm lying of course. Well, bending the truth. Choosing my words carefully because I know for a fact that Dominic is going to propose *very* soon. I'm pretty sure Oliver and Dominic are conspiring in the bathroom right now, but I won't press Oliver for the details. Dominic showed me the ring on our flight over and then asked the flight attendant if he could be moved to another seat when I started loudly sobbing in business class. Blaming the altitude pressure instead of when he said he "wants the most important person in Spencer's life" to know beforehand. My legitimate surprise comes from Spencer having suspicions and actually being correct. I thought he would have no idea as he's been too busy rehearsing, learning lines, and shooting his show.

Oliver and I have our apartment together in London, but we're a few years away from even thinking about marriage. We've been taking things slow, using the past year to work on ourselves and become actual human beings rather than the crazed emotional messes we'd both been living as. Decorating our new space has been cathartic. Both building and creating our home, our safe space to be our true selves. When flat hunting, we obviously had to prioritize the kitchen for Oliver and a second bedroom turned office space for me. One of Cecily's family's many ventures includes an estate agent firm, so she helped us get the first application in on a perfect flat overlooking a lush green park in Stoke Newington before it had even hit the market. Oliver spends most of his downtime experimenting with new recipes, all of which I am more than happy to consume and review for educational purposes. Our favorite part is the living room with a giant crockery cupboard, which folds down into a huge dining table. London flats being low on dedicated functional space is just a fact of life at this point, so having those small details built into our space means monthly dinner parties at ours. I choose the wine, and Oliver sorts the menu. Dominic reluctantly joins us even when Spencer is away filming, but I think he secretly loves our weird little supper club.

"You two have that look," Oliver says, shifting his gaze between us as he and Dominic return to the booth. "The twin telepathy thing."

"Just plotting," I say.

"And scheming," Spencer adds, clinking our glasses together.

"Because that went so well last time," Dominic deadpans.

"I think I got a pretty good deal out of it," Spencer says, sipping his drink.

"Me too," Oliver whispers into my ear.

CREDITS

I'm a big believer in giving credit where it's due. The creation of a novel does not just include the obvious author, agent, and editor. A plethora of talented individuals have touched this book, a lot of them without me even knowing. I want to thank every single person who has aided in the production of *Risky Business*.

Everyone who wanted to be included is listed below:

Editorial
Shannon Plackis
Sally Williamson

Copy Editor
Kathleen Scheiner

Proofreaders
Amanda Irle

Marketing
Deanna Bailey
DJ DeSmyter

Audio
Abigail Marks
Dom Francisco

Cover
Yeon Kim
Mallory Heyer

Publicity
Danielle Bartlett
Jessica Cozzi

Production
Brittani DiMare
Robin Barletta

Managing Editorial
Hope Ellis

Contracts
Tanya Seamans

ACKNOWLEDGMENTS

This story is ultimately a love letter to scrappy women. Women who are willing to do whatever it takes to achieve greatness, in whatever shape they deem it, however they define it.

Thank you to the readers who loved and championed *The Launch Date* and took another chance on *Risky Business*. You have changed my life for the better and in every way imaginable. I hope Grace's and Jess's stories help you as much you have helped me. I am eternally grateful.

A special thanks to Penelope Gazin, Kate Dwyer, and Keith Mann, who will probably never read this, but who inspired the inception of this book.

Writing is a very isolating experience, and without the following people, I would become even more unhinged:

My parents, Karen and Albert, who have taken on the additional role of chief author cheerleaders. Thank you for being an amazing sounding board and supporting me in achieving my dreams.

Alex, it constantly amazes me how happy you are to listen to my bullshit. Your willingness to groove and change with me over the past few years of evolution from former creative writer to aspiring novelist to published author constantly exceeds my (admittedly very high) expectations.

This book wouldn't exist without the ongoing and outrageous support of my incredible agent, Silé Edwards. This story started as a one-line Notes app pitch, and she immediately said, "That's your second book." She was right, as usual. If I take big swings, she makes sure they are home runs.

To my number one bookseller, Karen McHale, who has likely sold more copies of *The Launch Date* than all the bookstores in all of England. Thank you once again for being the best mother-in-law an author could ask for!

My beta reader team: Annabel Faulkner, Charlotte Hay, Kat Grant, Emma Burgoyne, Christina and Sophie Hilton, Georgie Arnold, Hannah Worth, Charlotte McHale, and Karen McHale. It's incredibly heartwarming to discover your willingness and enthusiasm to read ANOTHER one of my books. Thank you for once again correcting my mistakes, questioning my bizarre turns of phrases, and laughing at my many many inconsistencies.

My incredible editors, Sally Williamson and Shannon Plackis, continue to surprise me with how much they enjoy my first drafts. I appreciate your patience with this one. It's such a privilege to work with talented people I admire and respect. Let's do it again sometime?

Alice Rodgers and Asanté Simons, who both used their final months in the publishing industry to push my agenda for some reason. I hope I've lived up to the advance you spent on me. I'll always be in your debt for granting me my first book deal.

To Leanna and Ceylin, who, for reasons I can't say publicly, shocked me to my core by expanding my worldview for Grace and Jess.

And finally, to the author and writer community who have become genuine friends, confidantes, and support systems over the past three years. I didn't anticipate how sitting alone in a room talking to a page could result in so many amazing mates.

ABOUT THE AUTHOR

Annabelle Slator grew up writing stories in the depths of the British countryside. After achieving a degree in creative writing, she spent most of her late teens and early twenties writing social media and blog posts for start-ups and tech companies in London. Nowadays, if she isn't spending time writing, you can almost always find her obsessing over niche internet drama, practicing her fencing parry, or mooching around vintage fairs and flea markets with her husband and two mini dachshunds, Gruffalo and Gryffin.

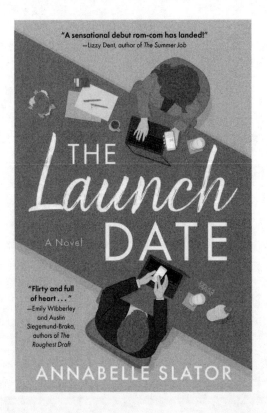